A CARLETON CONTEMPORARY

THE
CANADIAN
GENERAL
ELECTION
OF
1 9 8 8

BY
ALAN FRIZZELL
JON H. PAMMETT
ANTHONY WESTELL

Carleton University Press
Ottawa, Canada
1990

©Carleton University Press Inc. 1989

ISBN 0-88629-089-9 paperback

Printed and bound in Canada

Reprinted January 1990

A Carleton Contemporary

C
C

Canadian Cataloguing in Publication Data

Frizzell, Alan, 1947-
    The Canadian general election of 1988

ISBN 0-88629-089-9

    1. Canada. Parliament—Elections, 1988. 2. Canada—
Politics and government—1984-   . 3. Mass media—
Political aspects—Canada. I. Pammett, Jon H.
1944-   . II. Westell, Anthony, 1926-   .
III. Title.

FC630.F74 1989   324.971'0647   C89-090164-3
F1034.2.F74 1989

Distributed by: Oxford University Press Canada,
                  70 Wynford Drive,
                  Don Mills, Ontario,
                  Canada M3C 1J9

                  (416) 441-2941

Cover design: Aerographics Ottawa

Acknowledgements

Carleton University Press gratefully acknowledges the support extended to its publishing
programme by the Canada Council and the Ontario Arts Council.

355152

Contents

Preface   vii

Chapter 1   Setting The Stage   1

Chapter 2   The Parties and the Campaign   15

The Progressive Conservatives: Mission Accomplished   15
Robert Krause

The Liberals: Disoriented in Defeat   27
Stephen Clarkson

The New Democrats: Dashed Hopes   43
Alan Whitehorn

Chapter 3   On the Hustings   55
Peter Maser

Chapter 4   The Media and the Campaign   75

Chapter 5   The Perils of Polling   91

Chapter 6   The Changeable Canadian Voter   103
Lawrence LeDuc

Chapter 7   The 1988 Vote   115

Conclusion   131

Appendix   The Results:

Nationally   133

By Province   134

By Region   135

By Province 1974-88   137

By Constituency   139

By Proportional Representation   170

Contributors   171

Preface

This is the second in a series of Canadian election studies, and it is planned to publish a volume after each federal election. The goal is to provide a concise, readable and yet analytical account of the election, and the method is to blend journalism and social science.

For this study, the two original authors, Alan Frizzell and Anthony Westell, both from the School of Journalism at Carleton University, are joined by Prof. Jon H. Pammett from the Department of Political Science. Prof. Pammett has enlisted three other political scientists to write on the parties and their campaign organizations and strategies. They are Stephen Clarkson, Robert Krause and Alan Whitehorn. In addition, Prof. Lawrence LeDuc who has worked with Prof. Pammett on previous National Election Studies here provides a chapter on Canadian voting patterns as a background to analysis of the 1988 vote. On the journalistic side, Peter Maser, Quebec correspondent for the Southam News Service, writes a lively account of what it was like on the hustings in 1988.

A number of students at Carleton worked on research for the chapter on media coverage, completing what is probably the largest content analysis ever undertaken in Canada, and they are acknowledged in the Endnotes to that chapter. We wish to express special thanks to those people who managed research projects, helped with data management, or made other important contributions: Steven Ainslie, Ilona Kauremszky, Robert Roth, Wendy Watkins, and Michael Way.

Ottawa
March, 1989

Alan Frizzell
Jon H. Pammett
Anthony Westell

CHAPTER 1

Setting the Stage

By Anthony Westell

The Progressive Conservative party won the election of 1984 with an extraordinary 50 percent of the vote and 211 out of 282 seats in the House of Commons. The Liberal party was devastated and the New Democrats were happy merely to have avoided the disaster which had threatened at the outset of the campaign. The new government took office with the goodwill of much of the country and seemed to have a firm grasp on power. For the first year, it enjoyed a honeymoon with public opinion, if not with the news media, but in the second year its popularity began to slip. By September, 1986, it was down to 35 percent in the popularity polls and, according to Gallup, was in second place to the resurgent Liberals. The decline accelerated, and by February of 1987, it had slumped to third place, behind the NDP and with only about half the support enjoyed by the leading Liberals. At that point, it seemed as if the Conservatives under Prime Minister Brian Mulroney were doomed to repeat the fiasco they had suffered 20 years earlier under Prime Minister John Diefenbaker when they went from the largest victory in Canadian history in 1958 to defeat in 1963. Perhaps they could hope to be only a second party holding power for brief periods during which the natural rulers, the Liberals, would rest and prepare again to take charge in Ottawa.

In 1988 as the election approached the outlook began to change, and on the eve of the campaign the Conservatives stood at 40 percent, the NDP at 31 percent, and the Liberals were third with 26 percent. As the polling figures make clear, it had been a period of remarkable volatility in which all three parties had months in which they led and others in which they were in third place. Was it that the electorate had become more fickle in the age of television, had the nature of politics changed in some way as yet undefined, or was there some simpler explanation?

In seeking answers, the first major fact to consider is that in the 21 years 1963-84 the Conservative party had enjoyed only 259 days in power — the life of the Clark minority government in 1979-80. It was therefore unavoidable that the Cabinet sworn in on Sept. 17, 1984 would be made up largely of ministers with little or no experience. Indeed, the Prime Minister had become Leader of the party and a Member of Parliament only in the previous year. Almost all the 58 Conservatives elected in Quebec were new to Ottawa and to government, and many were new to the party. Yet the province had been central to the Conservative victory, was key in Mulroney's strategy for the future, and had to be strongly represented in the Cabinet. In the circumstances, the learning curve for the new government was bound to be long and bumpy, and ministers made things more difficult than they might have been by viewing with suspicion the Liberally-appointed senior civil servants on whom they had to rely for guidance.

In this respect, Mulroney set a poor example by surrounding himself with cronies and by encouraging his colleagues to appoint chiefs of staff who were better known for their Conservative loyalties than their experience in government. It was not surprising in the circumstances that the government soon ran into difficulties. As Michel Gratton, a rakish French Canadian journalist who was Mulroney's somewhat curious choice as second press secretary, put it in his insider's account of the Prime Minister's Office in its first months: "As winter approached, the formidable Conservative machine, so smooth-running during the election campaign, began to show signs of being under the control of a gaggle of amateurs."[1] These were not the scandals, real and imagined, which came later, but accidents, naiveties, and blunders on which the waiting media were able to pounce in their role of unofficial opposition to a government with a huge majority.

During the election campaign, Mulroney had scored powerfully — some said decisively — by attacking the Liberal record on patronage and, in particular, the wholesale appointments of party faithful made by the new leader, John Turner, on behalf of his predecessor, Pierre Trudeau. Mulroney promised on the platform to end such practices, although in private he was ready to jest about all he would do for Conservatives if elected. Since patronage had always played an important part in the normal course of Canadian politics by rewarding work for a party, the jests were more realistic than the promises. Mulroney proceeded to clear out Liberal appointees as soon as possible and replace them with Conservatives on hundreds of boards and commissions and in other federal positions. But that contradicted the expectations he had created by his public piety. Again the media pounced, expressing shock and dismay at what every experienced observer knew to be within the bounds of Canadian political practice.

The period of scandals leading to resignations began in early 1985 when the *Ottawa Citizen* reported that Defence Minister Robert Coates, one of the few Tory veterans and a former President of the party, and two aides, while on a visit to Canadian forces in Germany, had visited a dubious bar which featured pornographic films and obliging ladies. There was a suggestion that the indiscretion might have endangered security, although this was later discounted. Coates chose to resign rather than fight an embarrassing battle in the Commons and the media. In the fall, just a year after the election, Eric Malling, an investigative reporter on CBC-TV's *fifth estate*, revealed that Fisheries Minister John Fraser, another Tory veteran, had overruled two of his department's inspectors and authorized the distribution to supermarkets of almost a million cans of tuna which the experts had said was rancid and unfit for the market. The opposition and the media were soon alleging that public health was the issue, but Malling had made no such allegation: It was, in his report, a matter of judgement and integrity. As he later described his interview with Fraser: "I didn't accuse him of anything. I just asked him his opinion, his honest opinion, whether this was a story about fish or a story about integrity. And after I mentioned the word integrity, for some reason, he chased himself around the room smashing himself with his own 2 by 4. I didn't have to interview at all. . . He asked himself some real good questions too. It's the answers that got him into trouble."[2] Indeed, Fraser had to resign despite his explanation that he had merely given the benefit of the doubt to a company important to the Maritime economy — an explanation which raised in some minds the question of whether the Conservatives were ruling in the interests of the public or of business. (Fraser later became the first Speaker of the Commons to be elected by his fellow MPs instead of appointed in effect by the Prime Minister, testimony to the respect in which he was held despite his misadventures.) These two affairs created sensational news, but they arose from political error rather than dishonesty.

Treading on Fraser's heels came Communications Minister Marcel Masse, the leading Quebec minister, who took the honorable course of resigning when he learned that the RCMP were investigating his election spending to see if the law had been broken. He was subsequently cleared and returned to the Cabinet, but he never fulfilled his early promise. More serious were resignations which involved charges of conflict of interest and outright corruption, and by the end of the first term, seven ministers had left the Cabinet under some form of cloud. All this kept alive, perhaps unfairly, the suspicion which had attached to Mulroney since his entry into federal politics in 1976, that there was something not quite straight about him and his politics. He tried to offset the damage of the scandals by introducing tougher guidelines to govern the behavior of ministers and of MPs, but it is reasonable to say that blunders, patronage and scandals dominated the public perception of the Conservative government in its first few years. It was almost certainly this record which, more than any other factor and for reasons not at all mysterious, led to the rapid decline in popular favour. However, there was also a more serious agenda of public business on which the government was working and the question was whether this in the longer-term would prove successful enough to restore its standing. This agenda was summarized in the first Throne Speech as "national reconciliation, economic renewal and social justice," and it is convenient to examine the record briefly under those headings.

National Reconciliation

The 1970s and the early '80s were turbulent years in Canada, both economically and politically. The federal government was often at loggerheads with the provinces as Prime Minister Trudeau sought to establish national authority, for example, in the area of energy policy, and in the process gained a reputation for favouring confrontation over co-operation. It was this to which Mulroney was referring when he spoke, frequently, about national reconciliation, and it was an attractive idea to Canadians wearied by years of struggle and crisis. He was promising not so much a new policy as a return to what in the 1960s had been called co-operative federalism, an attitude to which Trudeau had objected when it seemed to surrender federal power and to encourage provincialism, even separatism. Trudeau's great achievement had been to persuade nine provinces to agree on patriation of the constitution with the addition of a popular Charter of Rights and Liberties. But Quebec, under Premier Rene Levesque and the separatist Parti Québécois, had refused to sign, and the priority for any prime minister taking office in 1984 had to be to bring Quebec into the agreement. This was the task facing Mulroney, and it could be achieved only by winning the goodwill of all the provinces so that they would agree to re-open the constitution and make yet another deal.

Mulroney convened a First Ministers' Conference in 1985 to discuss the economy and it was widely described as a "love-in". It was agreed to hold a similar conference on the economy at least once a year for five years, and that was only the beginning of the new era. Meetings of first ministers, lesser ministers, and officials multiplied. The goal seemed to be to bring the provinces into national decision-making as full partners with Ottawa. The Conservative government also dismantled Liberal programmes which had been offensive to the provinces, notably the National Energy Policy which had outraged the West, and negotiated an Atlantic Accord to give to Newfoundland control of off-shore energy resources in much the same way as mainland provinces controlled resources within their borders. The opportunity to build on all this goodwill came in December, 1985 when Robert Bourassa and his Liberals defeated the Parti Québécois to become the government of Quebec. With the PQ in power, no constitutional settlement had been likely; with Bourassa, a deal could be made, although he would certainly demand a high price. In fact, the new Quebec government set out five conditions: constitutional recognition of Quebec as a distinct society; increased powers over immigration; limits on the federal spending power in areas of provincial jurisdiction; a veto for Quebec over major constitutional change in future; and participation in the appointment of Senators and Judges of the Supreme Court of Canada. These proposals became the basis for negotiation with all the provinces, and for what came to be called the Meech Lake Accord.

Mulroney and the premiers met at the Meech Lake conference centre outside Ottawa on April 30, 1987 and reached an agreement in principle — an accommodation among elites because the public knew very little of what was being negotiated. With some changes, the deal was finally approved at an extraordinary, all-day-and-long-night session at the Langevin Block in Ottawa in June. The triumph was that Quebec had agreed to a new constitution for Canada, and this was hailed as the proof positive of the effectiveness of Mulroney's sunny and co-operative ways. The critics, on the other hand, charged that Mulroney had merely given to Quebec all it wanted, and bought the consent of the other provinces by giving them most of the same powers. This is not the place for a detailed examination of the Accord, but in essence there were, and remain at the time of writing, three main concerns:

— Would the recognition of Quebec as a "distinct society" take precedence over the Charter, allowing the provincial government to put measures for the preservation of the society ahead of, for example, the rights of women or of minority language groups?

— By recognizing the "distinct society", would the accord grant to Quebec a special status and special powers unavailable to other provinces, pointing the way eventually to separation?

— By making it easier for all provinces to opt out of national programmes initiated by the federal government, and by giving the provinces control over appointments to the national Senate and the national Supreme Court, would the accord weaken the federal government to the point at which national purpose and identity would be threatened?

While there was considerable comment on these issues, political debate was limited because the Accord was supported in Parliament by both Liberal and New Democratic party leaders who tried also to suppress dissenting voices in their parties for fear of offending Quebec voters. Eight of 10 provinces quickly ratified the Accord, leaving new governments hesitant in Manitoba and opposed in New Brunswick. The overriding question remained a matter of some public controversy which could be settled eventually only by Supreme Court interpretation: would the Accord, as Mulroney claimed, achieve a new level of national unity, or would it, as Trudeau and other intellectual leaders of opinion argued in articles and evidence before Parliament, weaken the national spirit of Canada, encourage provincialism and lead eventually to the break-up of Confederation? Because the agreement was between governments with little public participation, and because it did not become a major subject for partisan debate, it seems not to have attracted wide popular interest, and possibly for that reason did not win for Mulroney the national acclaim for which he hoped. But it did of course win him all-important support in Quebec.

One of the country's foremost students of federal-provincial relations, Richard Simeon, summed up the record in this way:

> The Mulroney conduct of federalism is not the only cause of reduced competition, greater harmony and improved collaboration, but it has played a significant role. These — especially the reconciliation with Quebec — are not achievements to be gainsaid. On the other hand, nor has the Mulroney government recast federalism in a mould which cannot be changed. Levels of interregional and intergovernmental conflict, co-operation or competition, are not primarily a matter of constitutions or of intergovernmental machinery. They are a function of the underlying political economy, the issues that arise, the mobilization of interests, and the ambitions of federal and provincial leaders.[3]

It was Mulroney's good fortune that the political economy underlying his policies of national reconciliation was strongly favourable, as we shall see in the following section. But it is worth noting one curious episode in which the new government sought to overlap national reconciliation with economic policymaking. A national conference in March, 1985 was supposed to bring together government, business, labor and various interest groups to agree upon an economic strategy. It was a total failure because there was no agreement on what was wrong with the economy. The Finance Minister and business community were interested in controlling the deficit, while labour and social reform groups wanted action to reduce unemployment. Thereafter the government made policy by more conventional means, issuing discussion papers to test its intentions, consulting usually in private with interest groups, relying on official advice, and obtaining Cabinet consensus.

Economic Renewal

In company with other leading industrial countries, and indeed with much of the world, Canada suffered in 1981-2 the worst economic recession in half a century. A strong recovery began in 1983, and when the Conservative government took office in 1984, its happy task was to manage and sustain growth. The principal problem appeared to be the budget deficit (much larger in relative terms than the much-publicized U.S. deficit) and the consequential growth in the national debt — partly the result of the fiscal measures the previous government had taken to counter the recession. The cost of servicing the debt had become a major cause of the annual deficits, and so the problem was not merely to balance the books, but to reduce the debt as a proportion of national income.

During the 1984 election campaign, Turner, as the new Liberal leader, had paid more attention to the deficit than had Mulroney who preferred optimistic themes. But the first Conservative Throne Speech declared, "That we must deal urgently with the deficit is beyond dispute," and in *An Agenda for Economic Renewal* the government set out its strategy: putting its fiscal house in order; fostering entrepreneurship, risktaking and innovation; making the Canadian economy more dynamic, more flexible and more competitive in world markets; and providing an improved framework for sustained, non-inflationary economic growth and job creation. It was one thing, however, for the Finance Minister to make controlling the budget deficit his first goal and quite another to achieve it when the Prime Minister's priority seemed to be to avoid any hard decisions that might cost political points. In fact, Edward A.Carmichael, of the C.D. Howe Institute, has argued that it took the new government 18 months to come to grips with the problem and devise a strategy, and even then it lacked resolution in its follow-through.[4] Spending continued to rise more or less in step with revenue, so that in dollar terms the deficit in the 1987-8 fiscal year was almost exactly the same as it had been in 1983-4 under the Liberals. But as the economy had grown strongly, the deficit had fallen as a proportion of the Gross Domestic Product. Assessing the government's record in its first term, Carmichael wrote:

> The conventional wisdom is correct in asserting that Canada still has a serious federal deficit problem. Few people recognize, however, that as a percentage of GDP, the deficit is already lower than it was during the eight years preceding the Mulroney government's election.The point is that deficits have been too high since the mid-70s and further steps need to be taken in the years ahead to bring the deficit down further. . . Looking ahead, a major challenge facing the

next government of Canada will be how to cope with the continuing vulnerability to fiscal crisis posed by a federal debt that is almost 60 percent of Canada's annual national income.[5]

If the government had a decidedly mixed record in dealing with the deficit and the debt, it did enjoy four years of vigorous economic growth, with relative stability in prices. In fact, in 1986 and again in 1987 Canada led the Big Seven industrial countries in growth of output and employment. Over the four year term, more than a million new jobs were created — 486,000 in 1987 alone — and unemployment fell steadily. The strongest growth was in Ontario, where Toronto in particular became a boom city, and in Quebec, on which the government lavished attention to secure its new political base. Times were much less good for the Atlantic and Western regions until 1987 when commodity prices and business investment spread the prosperity.

Mulroney had campaigned in 1984 with the promise of Jobs, Jobs, Jobs, and he delivered. Critics argued that the good times were mostly the result of buoyant demand in the United States fuelled by the Reagan Administration's expansonist policies. The government, on the other hand, claimed that growth was the result of its own policies. Whichever was right, it is undeniable that the government did embark on new economic strategies and make far-reaching changes in the economy. While lacking, or at least not proclaiming, the missionary zeal of the neo-conservative governments in the United Kingdom and the United States, it did share with them — and in fact with many others around the world — the goal of encouraging market forces by reducing state intervention and encouraging entrepreneurship. The Foreign Investment Review Agency which had been established by the Liberals to assess proposals by foreigners to invest in Canada and allow only those that were deemed to benefit Canada, was replaced with Investment Canada with a mandate to welcome foreign capital. A number of Crown Corporations were sold to private investors, continuing a trend started by the Liberals. The energy industry was substantially deregulated, and a start was made on transportation. Financial markets were opened to increasing competition. And then there was the free trade initiative to be discussed shortly. In terms of immediate results — jobs, growth, the public perception that the economic tide was rising — the record might have been expected to bring its reward in the popularity polls. But it seems to be a rule in politics that while voters punish governments for bad times, they take good times for granted — at least until their attention is concentrated by an election.

Free Trade
Free trade with the United States, or at least freer trade, has been a recurring idea in Canadian politics, sometimes debated privately within a government, sometimes a burning public policy issue dividing a party, sometimes boiling over into a general election. In recent times, Joe Clark, during his brief prime ministership, suggested cautiously that maybe there should be a national debate on the idea. In the 1983 race to succeed Clark as Conservative leader, one

candidate, John Crosbie, campaigned for free trade and another, Brian Mulroney, opposed it. The review of trade policy initiated by the Trudeau government in its last years led, over the objections of nationalists in the Cabinet, to a proposal for free trade in some sectors of the economy, but preliminary talks with the United States were not encouraging. In the 1984 Liberal leadership race to succeed Trudeau, Donald Johnston, a minister, made free trade a major plank in his campaign. The Royal Commission on the Economic Union and Development Prospects for Canada, appointed by Trudeau in 1982 under the chairmanship of a former Liberal minister and nationalist, Donald S. Macdonald, was known to be working toward recommending free trade — a "leap of faith," as Macdonald described it to a journalist in 1983. Thus, while it had not been an issue in the election, the idea of freer trade was very much alive in politics and the bureaucracy when the Mulroney government came to office in 1984. Given the new government's enthusiasm for free markets, it was natural that some ministers would champion free trade, and they found allies waiting in the public service where some of the preparatory work had been done. It remained to persuade Mulroney to change his mind on the subject, and it seems probable that two types of argument were effective. He had made clear during the election his determination to form a strong personal relationship with U.S. President Ronald Reagan, repairing what he saw to be the damage to Canada-U.S. relations caused by the nationalist policies of the Trudeau Liberals. And one way to be co-operative with Reagan was to respond to his long proclaimed interest in negotiating a new economic accord for North America. On the economic front, there was much concern in Canada about the trend in the United States toward more protectionist policies and the catastrophic consequences they could have for a Canadian economy heavily dependent on exporting into the U.S. market. A trade treaty would give Canada at least a measure of security. When Mulroney met Reagan at the so-called Shamrock Summit in Quebec City in March, 1985 to sing "When Irish Eyes are Smiling" and to discuss mutual problems, they found it easy to agree on a Declaration on Trade in Goods and Services setting the goal of a more secure climate for bilateral trade. In September, the Macdonald Commission published its report recommending free trade, indicating that there was at least some bipartisan support for the idea, and later that month Mulroney announced to Parliament that his government would seek a trade agreement which would "secure, expand and enhance" access to U.S. markets. On Oct. 1 he wrote to Reagan proposing "the broadest possible package of mutually beneficial reductions in barriers to trade in goods and services," and the President at once welcomed the Canadian initiative. Negotiations began in May, 1986.

Free trade had now become a major thrust in the government's economic strategy, promising both a way around U.S. protectionism if it should develop and a way of forcing Canadian business to become more competitive. It fitted well, also, with the government's theme that Canadians, under wise and courageous leadership, were casting off their old inferiority complex, demonstrating new confidence and maturity, and making ready to take on the world. The initiative was well received by business, by most of the provinces, and generally in the media. But it was bound to be in the longer run highly controversial, a departure from tradition without a mandate from the electorate — a contradiction in fact of what had been known of the Prime Minister's views on the subject — and an idea capable of arousing widespread concerns about loss of national identity and sovereignty. Initially, however, the public appeared to be more confused than divided, and there was no dramatic impact on political opinion. It was not until Oct., 1987, when an agreement was reached and became public, that opposition was organized effectively. Criticism focussed not on the agreement to eliminate tariffs over 10 years — indeed, many opponents insisted that they favoured free trade as such — but on:

— What was seen as the creation of a continental energy market in which Canada would not be able to pursue national advantage;
— The lowering of barriers against U.S. investment which it was feared would invite U.S. take-overs of Canadian business;
— The measures for resolving trade disputes which did not preclude the continued use of U.S. and Canadian countervail taxes against each other's exports, and did not therefore guarantee access to the national markets; and
— The plan to continue negotiations in search of a definition of subsidies which might distort trade, raising the possibility that social services and regional development programmes might in future be disallowed.

In general, critics claimed that economic integration would require harmonization of tax, social and environmental policies, leading to political integration and the loss of Canadian culture and identity. The government, business and much of the media comment dismissed such fears as groundless, and argued that the treaty would strengthen Canada by encouraging investment and creating jobs — 250,000 over 10 years by the estimate of the Economic Council of Canada.

The two governments agreed that the treaty should take effect on Jan. 1, 1989 and Mulroney hoped to have it approved by Parliament before a fall election. With his majority, he was able to secure the consent of the Commons, but Turner requested the Liberal majority in the Senate to hold its hand until the people had had a chance to speak in an election. This was a startling move, raising the question of whether the appointed Senators of a party out of power would be seen to be frustrating the democratic will of the Commons, but it worked for the Liberals in two ways. First, Turner had seized from the New Democrats the initiative in opposing free trade. Second, it forced Mulroney into an election in which the explosive and unpredictable debate on free trade, rather than the record of the government and its promises for the future, was certain to be the dominant issue.

Social Justice

It has been part of Canadian mythology that Conservative governments are opposed to the Welfare State and anxious to slash social programmes. In order to protect himself against such charges in the 1984 election, Mulroney announced that he would regard the universal availability of such programmes as "a sacred trust," a typical rhetorical flourish which went farther than was necessary and against which his every action in future would be measured. The measuring began immediately after Wilson's first budget, in May, 1985 in which he proposed partially to de-index old age pensions — that is to say, they would not rise as rapidly as the cost of living. It was not a major change in social policy, but it was seen as a breach of the sacred trust and provoked a severe political storm. Old age pensioners organized protests, the opposition parties pounded the government, and inside the Cabinet there was a battle between ministers who wanted to back down and Wilson who feared for the credibility of his strategy for containing spending and reducing the deficit. Mulroney first sided with Wilson and then, as the credibility of his own commitment to social justice became doubtful, changed his mind, admitted a mistake had been made, and withdrew the plan. The episode persuaded the government that it would be dangerous to attempt any major overhaul of the social security system, although the country had probably been ready for a serious review of the principle of universality which insisted that social benefits had to be available to all regardless of need.

But if one good test of social policy is the degree of poverty in the society, the government could claim a modest success. Poverty had declined during the 1960s and 1970s, but then economic recession and unemployment had driven it back up again. With the return of growth and employment, the rate began to fall, from 15.6 percent of the population in 1985 to 14.5 percent in 1986 and 14.1 percent in 1987. It was hard for many observers to reconcile these statistics with what appeared to be an increase in the number of beggars on the streets and an increasing demand on food banks. But there was obviously some truth in Mulroney's boast that the best form of social security was a good job.

This is not the place for an account of all the minor changes in social policy introduced by the government over four years and, as might be expected, they received mixed reviews from the activists and advocates who monitor policy and seek to represent the disadvantaged. For example, the Social Policy Reform Group, a coalition of six major organizations, published in 1988 a review of government performance in areas ranging from tax reform to refugee policy, giving it a passing a mark in 27 areas, and a fail in 37, with 10 still to be evaluated.[6] Others would no doubt enter very different judgements, but the truth seems to be that apart from the blunder of de-indexing, social policy was not highly controversial in the minds of the public during years of rising prosperity. If the government lost support over the pension issue, it was because competence and integrity were called into question, more than social policy as such. Certainly the government did not attempt to make up lost ground with new social programmes: the only major new programme proposed was to create 200,000 daycare spaces over seven years at a cost exceeding $6 billion. It was questioned because it set no national standards, relying instead on cost-sharing with the provinces to provide public spaces and on tax deductions for parents to help them pay for private care. While in keeping with conservative ideology, it was not recognizably a "national" programme. The legislation had not passed Parliament when the election was called, but it remained a subject of controversy and it probably earned the Conservatives more criticism than congratulation.

The Liberals

For the Liberal party, the 1984 election was a disaster rather than a simple defeat. Their number of MPs was cut from 147 to 40 and their share of the vote fell from 44 to 28 percent. Worse, the Liberals' Quebec fortress was stormed and captured by the Conservatives, while the Liberals failed to make much ground in the West. The new Leader, Turner, had proved to be a poor campaigner with ideas more conservative than those of Mulroney, and after 20 years in power the party itself had run out of steam. The party organization, where it existed at all, was a wreck. There was a clear danger that the Conservatives would become the centre party and the New Democrats would become the opposition on the Left, leaving the Liberals with no natural constituency. The question was whether the Liberals would be true to their frequent boast of loyalty through thick and thin, close ranks around Turner and begin rethinking and reorganizing, or whether they would follow the pattern of the Conservatives in opposition — the so-called Tory Syndrome[7] — and fall to bickering, recrimination and plots against the leader. Complicating the future was the fact that Jean Chrétien, who had lost the leadership race to Turner but won the hearts of most Liberals, held his own seat in the Commons and a place therefore on the national political stage. It was natural that many in the Liberal party and beyond would think that the party had made the wrong choice of leader and that the sooner Turner retired and Chrétien took over the better the chance of recapturing Quebec and the affections of the rest of the country.

At best the years after 1984 would be difficult for Turner and for the Liberals, but they turned out to be almost for the worst. Turner seemed seldom to be in control of the fractious remains of his party in the Commons and, in the headlines at least, much of the opposition was carried on by a small gang of noisy backbenchers who earned the descriptive title of Ratpack. Turner wanted to reverse the style of the later Trudeau years when the party was run from the leader's office and, as he said, to give it back to the members. But this goal of democratization was perhaps too idealistic for Liberals trained in a different school of politics, and little progress was made. In his own office, his style, it was said, was autocratic, and there were frequent changes of staff. While the party was riding reasonably well in the popularity polls, the public ranked Turner as a leader well below both Mulroney and Ed Broadbent of the New Democratic Party. As the Liberals approached a convention in 1986 at which delegates would vote on whether they wished to hold a leadership contest, it was clear that discontent with Turner was widespread. Chretien retired from Parliament, distancing himself from Turner and possibly preparing to challenge his leadership. Keith Davey, who had been chief party organizer under both Lester Pearson and Trudeau, published a book in which he politely but pointedly drew attention to Turner's failings. Marc Lalonde, who had been Trudeau's first lieutenant and a leader in Quebec but who had supported Turner as the successor, now published an open letter in which he called for a review of the leadership, in part because the party was millions of dollars in debt. But there were also of course forces organizing to support Turner, and reports of all sorts of skulduggery in the struggle to elect and control delegates. When the vote was held at the Ottawa convention, on Nov. 30, 76 percent of delegates voted against a review of leadership, thus giving Turner a second chance to estabish his position. Less clear were the resolutions on policy which showed that the party remained deeply divided on key issues.

Part of the problem here was Turner's habit of suddenly announcing policy positions. For example, he responded to Mulroney's free trade agreement by declaring that if returned to office, he would tear it up. This alienated a variety of interests which supported free trade and on which the Liberal party might have relied for money and votes. Those in opposition included Premier Bourassa and the Quebec government, public opinion in Quebec, traditional Liberals in the West for whom free trade had always been a party cause, and most of the business community. By endorsing the Meech Lake Accord, Turner outraged the Trudeau Liberals who saw it as a reversal of the policies for which they had stood and fought, "One Canada" with a strong central government and two official languages. Much of intellectual opinion and the *Toronto Star*, the country's largest and most liberal newspaper, also opposed the Accord.

It is hard to quarrel with the judgement of political journalist Greg Weston when he called his book on Turner's leadership *Reign of Error*.[8] A different but more speculative criticism was offered by Tom Axworthy, formerly Trudeau's chief of-staff, and Marvin Goldfarb, the party's long-time pollster. In their book, *A Different Drummer*,[9] they argued that at heart the Liberal party was social democratic and had made a mistake in choosing a conservative Liberal as Leader. Turner's difficulties during the 1984 election and in the following years, they wrote, arose from the fact that he was out-of-step with his party and with the natural Liberal constituency of women, youth and the lower income groups. Whatever the accuracy of this analysis, there was no doubt that Turner's leadership failed to impress the public, the media and significant sections of the party. Although the public seemed at times to be looking for an alternative to Mulroney and the Conservatives, Turner was not able to establish his claim that he was the man, and so the government's weaknesses were not effectively exploited.

The New Democratic Party

The NDP went into the 1984 election facing a disaster: it had dropped to 11 percent in the polls, down from 20 percent in the previous election, and it was in danger of losing half its 32 seats. By dint of its own campaigning, and helped mightily by the collapse of the Liberals, it survived on polling day with 18 percent of the vote and 30 seats. It was by no means a victory, but the future looked brighter. Its principal rival, the Liberal party, had been reduced to a squabbling rump with only 10 more seats than the NDP; outside Quebec, the Liberals had 17 seats, the NDP 30. As a leader, Ed Broadbent was a veteran compared with Mulroney and Turner, and the longer he served the more Canadians liked and respected him. There seemed to be a real chance that the perennial third party could at last replace the Liberals as the alternative to the Conservatives. To make the most of the opportunity, the party needed to convince Canadians that it was responsibly reformist and not revolutionary, and to establish itself in Quebec where it had never had a viable organization or won a single seat.

Broadbent had begun before 1984 to edge the party toward the centre of the spectrum, seeking to gain economic credibility the lack of which was a weakspot revealed by the party's polls. He expressed concern about the budget deficit and the level of spending and made thoughtful speeches about industrial strategy, and that presumably was helpful in the 1984 battle for votes. Now he continued the effort, explaining that he was a social democrat who recognized the importance of the private sector, and not a socialist who wanted wholesale nationalization. Public ownership was not disowned as a tool that might be used on occasions, but neither was it emphasized. Little was heard about the plan to nationalize one of the major banks, and in fact the party embraced small business which it saw as the main provider of jobs. The problem of the deficit was recognized, and reform of the tax system to take more from corporations and the wealthy was offered as a solution. On the other front, the decline of the Parti Québécois left social democrats without a strong party in the province, and seemed to offer an opportunity for the NDP. Broadbent made himself adequate if not fluent in French, and overrode opposition in his ranks to endorse the Meech Lake Accord with its recognition of Quebec as a distinct society. A new provincial NDP party was launched in Quebec, and in 1987 the party held its national convention in Montreal and again endorsed the province's constitutional ambitions. Polls showed its share of the vote in Quebec to be soaring, promising a breakthrough in the coming election.

The party was quick to reject the goal of free trade with the United States, arguing that economic integration would undermine political sovereignty and the social democratic attitudes which distinguished Canadian from U.S. society — for example, comprehensive social security, a mixed economy in which public ownership had a role, and interventionist government. In this area, it stole an early march on the divided Liberals and made a bid for the support of all the lobbies and interests which opposed free trade, such as cultural nationalists and women's groups which had previously tended to support the Liberals. To correct as far as possible any lingering suspicion that NDPers might be soft on Communism or wooly on defence, the party managed after much internal manouevring to qualify its policy calling for withdrawal from the North Atlantic Treaty Organization by saying that, well, it wouldn't happen in the first term of NDP government. And while rejecting the government's plan to buy a fleet of nuclear submarines, it offered instead a programme for reequipment with conventional arms that would cost about as much.

In the Commons, the NDP was usually a better opposition than the Liberals, and the worse Turner and Mulroney looked as leaders, the better looked Broadbent. The NDP's strategy seemed to be working wonderfully, and by the summer of 1987 it had climbed to the top of the national polls. The gathering hope now was not merely to replace the Liberals as the second party, but to defeat the Conservatives and form a government.

On the Eve

From this brief review of events between the election of 1984 and the calling of the 1988 election, it will be seen that there were many contradictory currents to sway and confuse the public. If opinions were more fluid than ever before, there were good reasons. The Conservative government was, on the one hand, initially incompetent in administration, uncertain in direction, and more prone to scandal than was normal; but on the other hand, it was managing prosperity, and national harmony had been restored. Free trade was exciting to some, frightening to others, but at least a bold new initiative for a country feeling more confident about its future than it had since the euphoric 1960s. So the record was, to say the least, mixed. The government was vulnerable, but so also were the opposition parties. There was a residue of confidence in the Liberal party as an alternative, but not in its leader who seemed able to get nothing right. Indeed, had the party labels been reversed, it would have been a familiar situation with the voters unhappy with a Liberal government, but lacking confidence in the Conservative alternative. As for the NDP, it faced two crucial questions: was its popularity based on its own appeal or on the temporary unpopularity of its two rivals, and in the test, would voters entrust it with power? It would take an election to find out if anything fundamental had changed.

Endnotes

In preparing to write this chapter, I had the valuable assistance over two years of a researcher, Steven Ainslie, then a graduate student in the History department at Carleton University. While I am indebted to him he is in no way responsible for the use I have made of the material he provided.
1. Michel Gratton, *So What are the Boys Saying?*. (Toronto: PaperJacks Edition, 1988).
2. Eric Malling, unpublished speech to English teachers, Saskatoon, 1988.
3. Richard Simeon, "National Reconciliation: The Mulroney Government", in Andrew B. Gollner and Daniel Salee, eds., *Canada Under Mulroney. An End of Term Report*. (Montreal: Vehicule Press, 1988).
4. Edward A. Carmichael, "The Mulroney Government and the Deficit", in *Canada Under Mulroney. An End of Term Report*.
5. ibid.
6. Social Policy Reform Group, *Federal Report Card, 1984-1988*. (Ottawa, 1988).
7. George Perlin, *The Tory Syndrome*. (Montreal: McGill University Press, 1980).
8. Greg Weston, *Reign of Error*. (Scarborough, Ont: McGraw-Hill Ryerson, 1988).
9. Martin Goldfarb and Thomas Axworthy, *Marching to a Different Drummer*. (Don Mills, Ont.: Stoddart Publications, 1988).

CHAPTER 2

The Parties and the Campaign

The Progressive Conservative Campaign: Mission Accomplished

By Robert Krause

The Progressive Conservative party began to prepare for the campaign almost a year prior to the calling of the election. Organizationally, the key operatives for the forthcoming campaign were brought together in February at the National Meeting, or conference, of the party. With the key players in place, the fleshing out of the provincial campaign organizations began with follow-up provincial organizational meetings across the country, where the responsibilities for the campaign within each province were allocated.[1]

During this period the 1988 budget of the party was established. Of the $24.8 million, $8.1 million was set aside for the election campaign. The remaining revenue was to be utilized for the operating expenses of the party and pre-writ campaign disbursements. Once the general figures had been determined the provincial campaign chairmen were asked to submit proposed operating budgets for their provincial campaigns. In total $2.4 million was to be utilized for provincial campaigns while the rest of the $8.1 million was to be set aside for anticipated national election expenses in areas such as advertising, tour and operations.

Politically, preparations for the election had also begun. By February, the party logo which was to be employed on all party communications had been re-designed. Focus groups of voters had been asked a series of questions designed to probe how they viewed the party at present and, more crucially, how ideally they would like to visualize the party in the future.[2] From the responses to the questions a series of prospective logos had been constructed, and after testing by focus groups a new forward-looking party logo was created. Additionally, between May and the end of September over 70 federal projects which were to be implemented by the government had been announced across the nation by the Prime Minister or his cabinet colleagues.[3] These announcements were designed to increase favourable media attention for the government, and to send out a message to the general public: "These guys have a plan, a plan for the future."[4] This message would be more carefully crafted and repeated in the months ahead.

The Campaign Theme

While the pre-election planning and preparation was underway the crucial question of a campaign theme was addressed. The theme would set the campaign agenda and ideally structure the issues voters would think about.[5] As the precise

15

date of the election call was in doubt, planning for the campaign theme was to some degree a matter of timing. Initially, party polls which tested various scenarios concerning parties, leaders and issues, suggested a campaign theme which emphasized "hard work."[6] The basic premise of this theme was that just as Canadians were hard working and had to make tough choices on how they would lead their lives, so too had the government. It is was felt by its proponents that such a message would personalize and link the party's campaign with voters and allow the party to concentrate during the election on its perceived strengths of a strong economy and sound fiscal management, as well as deflect opposition criticisms of alleged shortcomings in the government's record. However, when the "hard work" theme was introduced to members of the parliamentary caucus for their information and approval it encountered little enthusiasm. Members from Quebec and particularly the Maritimes were quick to point out its shortcomings. Many felt it was too defensive in orientation and was less than inspiring in directing attention to the period after the election. Consequently, in spite of the research and planning which had gone into its development, the theme was dropped. Finally, after considerably more re-examination the eventual campaign theme which was to give direction to the campaign emerged. The theme would be, "The party and leader capable of managing change."

The "managing change" theme had several attributes in its favour. First, it focussed the electorate's attention on the past accomplishments of the party in government: the reduction in the budget deficit, the strengthened economy, and improved federal-provincial relations could all be emphasized as 1984 election campaign commitments made and kept. Second, the theme directed public awareness to the future beyond 1988. Here, Meech Lake, the Free Trade Agreement, and the national day care programme could be pointed to as proof that the party had the vision, a leader and a team capable of meeting domestic and international challenges.

The theme for Quebec would be, "Continuer dans le bons sens," or "Keep following your good instincts."[7] This theme had the virtues of permitting the party to utilize the same basic arguments used in support of its overall national campaign theme as well as re-emphasising the Quebec roots of the party's leader and Prime Minister.

Party Polls

The party's electoral themes were primarily a product of its own internal polling research. Polling was a key method for acquiring information upon which campaign strategy, both prior to the dropping of the election writ and during the actual campaign, was based. Four national polls were used — three during the campaign and one just before it began — to probe voting preferences, issue concerns, and leaders' images. The early national polls were instrumental in defining and shaping both the overall strategic dimension of the campaign and the operational strategy. Polling results identified target groups of voters in the electorate and constituencies and regions across the nation where the party's electoral fortunes were in need of attention. Information from the polls assisted the party in setting the broad outline of the advertising, tour and issue agenda for the campaign. Supplementing the national polls were the party's "tracking" polls used in 25 selected ridings across Canada. The tracking polls, conducted by telephone with approximately 200 voters in each riding, were each done at three different times during the election when national polling was not being done.[8]

The polling results gave information about three principal areas of concern: the nature and composition of party support; assessments of party, leader and candidates; and voters' issue concerns. Party support was divided into core voters (voters who always supported the party) and swing voters (voters who changed their votes between elections). These were categorized by the degree of intended vote commitment (hard or soft) and by the demographic characteristics of age, sex, and income. Leadership evaluations were determined from a series of questions pertaining to such attributes as:
— Believes most deeply in the things he has said;
— Can best represent Canada in the world;
— Is the most competent; and
— Has the most new ideas on how to make Canadians prosperous.

Party and leader evaluations were further analysed from a series of closed-end questions which asked voters to assess which party they felt could best deal with 10 to 12 issues found through the national polls to be important concerns for the voting public, such as:
— Which party and leader has the position closest to your own on free trade?
— Which party and/or leader can best manage governmental finances?

Finally, issue concerns of individual voters were probed by asking open-end questions like:
In your view, what is the most important issue in the election?[9]

The tracking polls gave the local constituency organizations advice on local strategy. However, when the information from each riding was combined with the results of the findings from the other ridings being surveyed and with national polling results, the party had a daily "rolling poll" from which electoral trends could be deduced and from which the national election strategy could be fine tuned.

The Campaign Organization

The structure of the campaign organization closely resembled the model used in previous national campaigns.[10] It consisted of two tiers, provincial organizations and a national organization given responsibility for the leader's tour, media and advertising, press releases and candidate services. However, more than in previous campaigns, the Quebec provincial organization was given discretionary power in planning and implementing its own unique campaign. While it operated in concert with the national campaign structure, the Quebec organization had considerable freedom in planning its own advertising within the province, conducting its own polling operations and scheduling tour events within the province.[11] The national committee, based in Ottawa under the supervision of Senators Norm Atkins and Michel Cogger, consisted of a strategy team of approximately nine members supported by an additional 38 directors and co-directors.[12]

While the overall direction of the campaign was the responsibility of the national campaign team it would be erroneous to assume only members of the strategy committee and the national office staff were responsible for campaign strategy. Rather, four distinct groups were consulted and utilized in planning, developing and implementing the party's electoral strategy.

First, there were those members of the National Campaign Committee who had responsibilities for operations which lent themselves to strategic considerations: public opinion research and polling (Allan Gregg), and the leaders's national tour (George Stratton, John Tory). Second, there were the chairmen of the 10 provincial campaign organizations.[13] Each of these individuals had the right to "consult and liaise" with the national campaign. Third, there were those who, while not formally members of a specific campaign organization, were persons whose advice and counsel had proven valuable in past campaigns and/or whose counsel the Prime Minister considered sound: individuals such as Dalton Camp, Finlay McDonald, and Peter White. Finally, there were the political ministers from each of the 10 provinces.

The second tier of the campaign organization consisted of the provincial campaign organizations which were responsible for "carrying out the national campaign as it affected their particular area and to oversee the proper functioning of the local constituency campaigns."[14] While the provincial organizations were designed to mirror the National Campaign structure they were modified when necessary to fit provincial needs or to more realistically reflect the electoral size of the province within which they functioned.[15] For example, in the case of Ontario (See Figure One) the organization was directed by the campaign chairman with assistance from the deputy campaign chairman and the directors of administration and operations. The director of administration's role was to ensure that administrative services, offices, telephone, photocopying etc., were in place for the proper functioning of the provincial campaign. The director of operation's task was more complex and multi-functional, but was in essence a role which entailed the co-ordination of all provincial campaign activities. The deputy campaign chairman's responsibilities were directed towards facilitating riding campaigns within the province.[16]

While the provincial chairmen bore the ultimate responsibility for the proper functioning of the campaign organization within their respective provinces, eight of them also had electoral responsibilities which required them to "liaise" with their national campaign counterparts, the deputy campaign chairman, comptroller, tour director, communication director, group communication director, women's director, director of youth, and director of legal services.

The major purpose of the provincial campaigns was the direction and co-ordination of the constituency campaigns. In larger provinces the ridings were grouped in regions. The regional groups were guided by a regional chairman and a locally-based resource team. This allowed the party to conduct regionally sensitive and specific campaigns assisted by local volunteer activists. The

Figure One
Ontario Campaign Organization

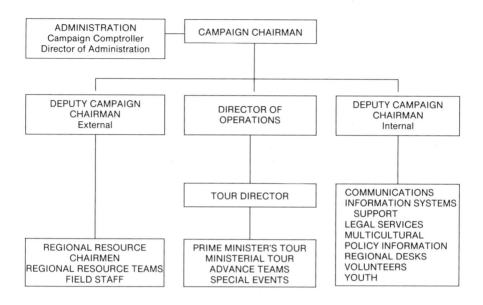

regional organizations were linked to the provincial campaign through the deputy campaign chairman and this was facilitated by the use of regional desks. Each of the regional desks located in the province's central campaign headquarters was used to answer queries on matters of policy or campaign questions which emanated from individual ridings within a particular region. The provincial regional desks were in turn linked to regional desks in the national campaign office. Thus, campaign information and instructions could flow upwards from the regions of the province to the national campaign or could flow downwards from the national office to the regional provincial desks and from there to the individual riding campaign organization.[17]

The Leader's Tour

The Prime Minister's tour put into operation the party's campaign strategy. During the first weeks it was structured to highlight the theme of "managed change" and to emphasize that the Prime Minister and the party were leading in the national opinion polls and were competent to govern. Nothing was left to chance as the "advance men" sought to maximize favourable media coverage of the daily scheduled tour events. Each day's tour was constructed around three events. First, there was a morning event "to give the cameras some pictures to illustrate the day's theme".[18] Second, a luncheon speech gave thematic substance to the morning event. Finally, there was the evening rally, held most often with local

Conservative partisans and designed to illustrate local party enthusiasm and support for the leader and the local candidate.

The tour venues while nationally dispersed were not randomly selected. The national tour office, together with the provincial chairmen, first reached agreement on overall time allotments for each region of the country. Next, the specific constituency locales within the province were selected because they gave local meaning to the day's theme and/or because the local party's election fortunes were considered particularly important in attaining the objective of a majority government. The second week's tour format was a repetition of the first with an emphasis on correcting or alleviating mistakes or problems. One of those problems was the media's assertion that the Prime Minister's tour was too tightly controlled and that consequently they were not being given adequate access to him. In response, access to the Prime Minister was improved and even more attention was given to the national media assigned to cover the tour.

While the Prime Minister's tour was the focal point of the campaign, it was not the only tour organized by the party. Ministerial tours by prominent cabinet ministers across the nation also were organized. These were designed to complement the leader's tour, and to reinforce the campaign theme as well as give the party increased local media coverage in electorally sensitive constituencies. Through the ministerial tours, regionally specific issues were addressed and more efficient use was made of the provincial tour offices in the periods in which the Prime Minister was not in the province. Together, the tours by the leader and ministers gave the party increased media visibility and subsequent public awareness while keeping the campaign agenda to the forefront. However, the party's tour strategy and agenda-setting role were dramatically changed as a result of the television debates.

The Debates

The importance of the television debates is due to the fact that they constitute the only time in the election campaign when the leaders of the major parties meet head to head. For the Conservative party the debates offered much to lose and little to gain. As the party was leading in the polls, public expectations about the performance of the Prime Minister were high, while those for his opponents, particularly John Turner, the Liberal leader, were very low. With high expectations there was much room to drop in popular esteem and much less room to grow. Recognizing the problem, planning for the debates involved three phases of preparation; the predebate, or metadebating period, the debate, and the post debate stages.

The metadebate stage "is a psychological game played by candidates and their surrogates through the media to influence the public. The essence of metadebating is to clothe decisions made on the basis of self interest with the mantle of public interest and to shift to the opponent the blame for any delay or complication in the debate planning process."[19] In this stage of debate preparation six questions were significant for strategists: (a) Will there be a debate? (b) Who will participate? (c) What will be the format? (d) How many debates will there be? (e) When will the debates occur? (f) Where will the debates be held?[20]

Four of the questions were particularly salient. The most important was the primary question of whether there would be a debate. In the 1980 national election the Liberal party had been successful in avoiding one and this obviously would have been the preferred option for the Conservative party in 1988. However, it was soon recognized that this option was not viable, and consequently three other questions became paramount in setting the stage for the debates. The question of how many debates there would be was a matter of considerable strategic importance for the campaign. The opposition parties favoured a minimum of three debates to achieve greater visibility and to set the agenda in light of their own campaign strategy. For the Conservatives the objective was to hold only two debates, one in French and one in English, denying opportunities to the opposition parties to focus on any one issue where they might be vulnerable.

Closely related to this objective was the matter of the ideal format for the debates. Here, two subsidiary considerations were paramount. What should be discussed and how? The subjects to be discussed had partially been settled by the decision to hold only two debates, meaning all issues would be covered in either or both the French and English debates. For the Conservatives this was the preferred option for it allowed them to concentrate on the debates in terms of their own theme and political agenda. The second consideration revolved around the actual debate format itself. Here, it was felt it would be desirable to have the Prime Minister debate each leader "one on one." This format had several advantages. First, it allowed for more exchanges on more issues, and second, it avoided the "double negative" thrust which would naturally emanate from a debate which pitted the Prime Minister in a series of single-issue exchanges between himself and two opponents at the same time.[21]

Finally, there was the matter of when the debates would occur, and on this there was considerable division among party strategists. For optimists, debates occuring late in the campaign would allow the party to maintain its momentum, solidify support, and cap it all with an impressive debating victory by the Prime Minister in the closing days. For others, a late debate meant the campaign would leave little room to manoeuver if the debates turned out to be less than satisfactory. While both these positions had strategic merit it was decided, with the Prime Minister's intervention, a debate early in the campaign was the correct option.

In planning for the actual debates, both relational and substance tactics were considered.[22] Relational debate tactics are personality and perception-oriented and deal more with the image to be presented. While significant in the preparation, they took second place to tactics based on substance.[23] Substance involves issue positions and the manner of couching them for maximum strategic advantage.[24]

To prepare for both the English and French debates the Prime Minister used a specially constructed briefing book. The French debate, which preceded the English one, was handled by strategists and a group of consultants from Quebec. This debate was felt to be less crucial than the English debate in that the Prime Minister's command of French and his "native son" image would give him a natural advantage over his opponents. The English debate preparation involved close examination of opposition positions on important issues like free trade, and possible responses. Advisors like Finlay MacDonald, trade lawyer Jim McIlroy, and Chief of Staff Derek Burney drilled Mulroney on the details of the issues.[25]

The post-debate reaction was in the hands of designated "spin doctors" whose role was to give a positive evaluation of the leader's performance. But it was quickly realized that while the party strategists were initially pleased with the Prime Minister's performance, the media and subsequently the public were not. The media and the polls declared Turner and the Liberal party the winner and the campaign entered a new stage in which a new strategy had to be devised and implemented. A major element in orchestrating a recovery had to be advertising.

Advertising

The Election Campaign Expense Act stipulates that paid party advertising can begin only half-way through the campaign. The commencement of advertising by all parties thus happened only days prior to the debates. The Liberal party's television spots were particularly effective in casting doubts on the government's free trade initiative. One ad in particular, which showed the government removing the boundary between Canada and the United States as a result of the free trade policy, tugged on the nationalist heartstrings of Canadians. The emotional appeal to the electorate to reject free trade cast doubts among the elecorate about the Conservative party.

On the other hand, the Conservatives' early advertising efforts lacked the emotional appeal found in Liberal advertising. The initial strategy was to rely primarily on endorsements. By utilizing non-party spokespersons, it was hoped to show that the party had an agenda, good leadership and broad based support. To ensure the message could be targetted to the appropriate audience, polling research first revealed specific groups which were soft in their support of the party — women and low-to-middle income earners. To reach this audience, more radio time than usual was purchased. Further, rather than purchasing advertising time around "elite" programmes, the television and radio buys were directed to a great extent to the "soaps" and mass orientated programmes. The net effect of the advertising campaign was to produce a series of election advertisements which tended to be more re-assuring to voters than hard-hitting or emotional, stressing the government's record and the general competence of the Prime Minister and his party team.

After the debate, this approach to party advertising had to change, and change quickly. The party was able to respond promptly because the advertising strategists located in their Toronto and Montreal offices had prepared three different types of advertising messages in anticipation of this eventuality. The strategists had determined, through the use of "focus" groups and polling results, which opposition ads had been particularly effective among voters. These results showed that while the electorate was turning to the Liberal party, voters still had considerable doubts in their minds about the personal credibility of the Liberal leader, and many felt he would do and say virtually anything to get elected. In addition, criticism of the free trade initiative had become an emotional matter focussed around issues such as national sovereignty and the potential loss of social and regional development programmes for Canadians. For these reasons, Conservative advertising became more aggressive and partisan. To counter-attack the Liberal advertising, television spots showed the Conservative party drawing the line between Canada and the United States. Other spots cast doubts on the credibility of the Liberal leader and his party.

Broadcast advertising was not the only area which underwent revision. Prior to the election it had been decided there would not be a party-produced piece of literature to be used in the ridings across Canada. This decision was reversed and the party rushed out, within 10 days following the debates, a "Ten Big Lies" pamphlet, printed in tabloid format, and listing and answering the 10 major criticisms of the free trade bill. The effectiveness of the post-debate advertising was such that by Nov. 10 a tracking report could state:

> Our latest wave of tracking . . . reveals that our post-debate slump has been arrested and we're on the way back up. Liberal support has peaked and the N.D.P. are heading for a distant third place showing . . . P.C. support has not only bounced back from its post debate slump, but it is the hardest of the three parties.[26]

With the recovery in the polls, the advertising thrust began gradually to shift back to the original campaign theme. Particularly effective was an ad which showed that it took only "four seconds" to cast a ballot but the voter had to live with the results for four years. This message not only allowed the party to get back to its basic theme of who was most capable of managing change in the future, but also reminded the voters that a vote for the Liberal party was a vote for Turner.

In the last week of the campaign the recovery in the party's electoral fortunes was stimulated by the use of almost saturation television advertising. The onslaught accomplished two objectives. First, it avoided the "double negative" of two opposition party ads running against one P.C. ad and put the party on equal or better footing with the other parties. Secondly, the messages were designed to be particularly salient for "switch" voters who were vacillating between support for the Conservatives and the Liberals. The impact of the heavy media concentration was particularly evident in the province of Ontario where within the last four days of the campaign an Ontario loss was turned into a province-wide electoral plurality.

Post-Debate Fine Tuning

Fine tuning of advertising did not take place in isolation; it was part and parcel of all the changes which were being made in the campaign strategy. Supplementing and reinforcing the advertising were changes in the tour strategy in the last few weeks. The ministerial tours became much more "free trade focussed" immediately after the debates. Ministers, such as Finance Minister Wilson, who possessed considerable credibility, went out on the stump to attack Turner and the Liberal party directly on the "lies" they were disseminating concerning free trade.

The Prime Minister's tour also changed focus. As he headed into Western Canada he began his "myth a day" format which had been suggested to the strategy team by the "tracking" experts, David Crapper and Michael Coates. In each

Western locale, he addressed a specific "myth": in Edmonton it was the question of free trade and its impact on pensions, while in Winnipeg he addressed the concerns of Canadians on the environment and free trade. The tour strategy reinforced the advertising message of the party, answered opposition criticisms and tied directly into the new aggressive image which was being fostered.

During the last week of the campaign, the tour began to criss-cross Canada from West to East. The evening rallies became the central events of the daily tour, with the Prime Minister appearing on stage with some of his prominent cabinet "team" giving visual substance to the campaign's original theme. During the day, the ministers who were accompanying the Prime Minister fanned out across the targetted province, visiting every possible media centre where they reiterated the party's message and lent support to the campaigns of local candidates. The campaign now emphasized the record of the government and set out positive reasons for the electorate to support the Progressive Conservative party on election day.

Important to the P.C.s in this period was the support given by the business community. Whereas, prior to the debates, for all practical purposes, the business community had given only muted verbal support, it was now energized into mounting a vocal and far-reaching campaign in support of free trade. Lethargic support became proactive support, with the business community spending considerable sums of money in the print media in support of the government's free trade initiative. Numerous targeted letters bearing the same message were delivered to employees within their companies.

Conclusion

The Progressive Conservative party met its campaign objective of forming another majority government. It has been found in past campaigns that "with regards to the timing of the vote decision . . . almost one-half of all Canadians made their choices during the campaign period."[27] In the 1988 campaign one survey indicated the percentage was even higher with "three out of five" voters making their decision during the campaign.[28] While one may point to the organization, polls, tour and advertising as being instrumental in the victory, two other elements, often overlooked in analysing election campaigns, were significant in binding together the disparate elements which made up a successful campaign. First, the organization consisted of individuals who knew each other through working together in past national and provincial campaigns. The effect of the familiarity among key campaign organizers was that they were able to work together more effectively than those in other party campaigns. Second, there was the role of the leader. Election analysis too frequently views the leader as a mere "marionette" who blindly follows the instructions of his handlers. In this campaign the Prime Minister was not an idle bystander; Mulroney made several key decisions, and knew when to follow and when to lead.

Endnotes

1. For example, the first Ontario Campaign meeting was held on Mar. 5, 1988. Generally, the provincial campaign meetings dealt with organization and operations, regional teams, headquarters services, budget, communications, campaign training, tour, multicultural programme, women and youth organizations.

2. For a discussion of "focus groups" see, David C. Walker, "Pollsters, Consultants and Party Politics in Canada" in A.G. Cagnon and B. Tanguay (eds.) *Canadian Parties in Transition*. (Scarborough: Nelson, 1989) p. 393-394.

3. Mary Janigan, Hilary Mackenzie et al, "Anatomy of An Election, The View From the Trenches", *Maclean's*, Toronto, December 5, 1988 p. 21.

4. *Ibid*, p. 21.

5. For a discussion on the procedures and methods used in selecting a campaign theme see, S.A. Salmore and B. Salmore, *Candidates, Parties and Campaigns* (Washington: Congressional Quarterly Inc. 1985) pp. 115-143.

6. The original idea for the campaign theme was also introduced at the provincial campaign meetings.

7. Theresa Tedesco et. al., "The French Facts: In Quebec Tories Bank on the P.M.'s Appeal", *Maclean's*, Toronto, November 21, 1988, p. N2.

8. The polls were conducted around Oct. 3 to 13, Oct. 19 to 27, Nov. 2 to 10.

9. For a discussion of "tracking polls" see, S.A. Salmore and B. Salmore, *Candidates, Parties and Campaigns* p. 119. Information on the nature of tracking polls used by the Progressive Conservative Party was derived from an examination of the results of several of the tracking polls employed in the campaign.

10. See, John C. Courtney, "Campaign Strategy and Electoral Victory: The Progressive Conservatives and the 1979 Election" in Howard R. Penniman (ed), *Canada at the Polls, 1979 and 1980: A Study of the General Elections* (Washington: American Enterprise Institute, 1981) p. 129.

11. Personal interview with Progressive Conservative campaign participant.

12. Progressive Conservative Party of Canada, *National Campaign Directory*.

13. Progressive Conservative Party of Canada, *Ontario Campaign Organization Description*, p. 1. The functional responsibilities of a provincial campaign chairman were for all aspects and operational elements of the provincial campaign. As Chairman of the Provincial Committee he was a member of the National Campaign Committee and was responsible for appointment of all provincial senior campaign personnel. He would consult and liaise with the national campaign on a regular basis, oversee preparation of the provincial campaign budget, and consult and liaise with members of caucus and members of the national executive from the province.

14. John C. Courtney, "Campaign Strategy and Electoral Victory: The Progressive Conservatives and the 1979 Election", pp. 129-130.

15. The smaller provinces with few seats, not unexpectedly, had smaller organizational structures. In Alberta there were two provincial headquarters, one in Edmonton and one in Calgary. Additionally, Saskatchewan, Manitoba and Newfoundland found it necessary to have a director in charge of telephone banks while the other provinces did not.

16. In Ontario responsibility was divided between two deputy campaign chairmen. The DCM, internal, was responsible for disseminating services "from the national campaign including policy information, materials distribution" while the DCM, external, was responsible for ongoing electoral activities of riding constituencies.

17. Personal interviews wih William J. McAleer, Ontario Campaign Chairman, and Fred Clark, Director of Operations, Ontario and other national campaign personnel.

18. Val Sears, "P.M.'s Shepherds Guide Media Flock," *Toronto Star*, Oct. 23, 1988, p. A1.

19. For a discussion of the concept of metadebating see, Chapter Six, "Metadebating", in Myles Martel, *Political Campaign Debates: Images, Strategies and Tactics*, (New York, Longman, 1983) pp. 150-1/2.

20. *Ibid*, p. 151.

21. While several of the fringe parties contesting the election sought to participate in the debate, the P.Cs recognized that the three parties with seats in the House of Commons would be the participants. Also, the question of where the debates would occur was a matter for the television networks.

22. See, M. Martel, op. cit., p. 71-115.

23. *Ibid*. p. 77.

24. *Ibid*.

25. Hugh Winsor, "The Battle of the Potential Network Stars," *The Globe and Mail*, Oct. 22, 1988 p. D2.

26. Progressive Conservative Party of Canada, Riding Report Memorandum, Decima Research, Nov. 13, 1988.

27. Barry J. Kay et al, "Some Aspects of Electoral Change in 1984" in Paul Fox (ed.) *Politics: Canada (6th ed.)* (Toronto, McGraw-Hill Ryerson, 1986) p. 431.

28. "The Voters Reflect, Conflicts in a Post Election Poll," *Maclean's*, Toronto, Dec. 5, 1988, p. 19.

The Liberals: Disoriented in Defeat

By Stephen Clarkson

It is a curiosity of contemporary Canadian politics that John Turner, formerly the most conventional of politicians, has turned out to be the least conventional of political leaders. In the two elections he has fought as leader of the Liberal Party of Canada (LPC) he has managed to do what was completely unexpected:

— In June 1984, with all the advantages of incumbency and an 11 percent lead in the opinion polls, Turner seemed poised to win the election he had called for Sept. 4. But the newly minted prime minister managed to sabotage his own campaign by a series of misguided decisions that produced his party's worst defeat in memory.[1]

— In October 1988, with all the disadvantages of being the least respected of the three party leaders — this time the figure of 11 percent represented that tiny proportion of the public who felt he would make the best prime minister — Turner seemed poised for annihilation. But the man who had been written off as a political 'loser' managed single-handedly to execute such a reversal of his standing by mid-campaign that, for a few heady days, a Liberal victory seemed possible.

That he went down to defeat for a second time despite his Herculean effort showed the extent to which he had failed to accomplish the primary goal he had articulated in 1984: rebuild his own party. At the end of the 1988 campaign, the Liberal Party was bereft of direction, depleted in its organization, and devastated in its former stronghold of Quebec.

Turner's Electoral Challenge

When the election writ was issued on October 1, 1988, John Turner faced three near-impossible tasks.

First he had to prove that the decentralization he had brought to the Liberal Party could be electorally effective. To achieve this he needed to win the active political support of the two most powerful Liberal politicians in the country, the provincial premiers, Robert Bourassa in Quebec and David Peterson in Ontario.

Next he had to remind voters of their earlier scorn for a Progressive Conservative government that had wallowed in scandal and incompetence for its first two-and-a-half years in office but had then managed largely to redeem itself and seize control of the public agenda through increasingly capable management in its final 19 months.

Finally he had to convince the Canadian public that he was a politician who could lead Canada back from the historical brink at which it stood as the country considered whether to ratify a free-trade agreement with the United States. For this he had to establish his leadership of the opposition by neutralizing the campaign on his left flank of a New Democratic Party that had been riding high in the polls.

This was a formidable set of campaign assignments for a man whose performance as Leader of Her Majesty's Official Opposition for the four years since he had lost the previous election had been notable for its almost uninterrupted record of pratfalls.

Opposition party leaders typically control few of the factors affecting their fate. But even in the one domain where Turner was supreme and to which he brought firm convictions — the principles guiding the Liberal party's internal organization — it was by no means certain when the writs were issued that what he had wrought since 1984 would stand the test of electoral fire.

The Organizational Conundrum

Because of the overwhelming impact that leaders still have in Canada on the parties they command,* the key to understanding the state of any political party in this country is the nature of its leadership. Understanding John Turner's notion of what the Liberal Party should be helps explain what the party became under his tutelage. In his political exile from 1975 to 1984, Turner had criticized Pierre Trudeau's centralized pan-Canadian way of operating the party and favoured a return to the regionally-based system used in the party's golden age under Mackenzie King and Louis St. Laurent.[2]

From the time he resigned as Trudeau's Minister of Finance in 1975, Turner positioned himself within the extra-parliamentary ranks of the Liberal Party as the man around whom all those who were hostile to Trudeauism could rally. At the Liberal convention in November 1982, Turner had supported the undercurrent of discontent within the party that focussed on the perceived disdain for the party organization of Trudeau's camarilla, the men and women grouped around James Coutts, the prime minister's principal secretary from 1975 to 1981, and Senator Keith Davey, the prime minister's apparently permanent campaign chairman. Eighteen months later when Turner declared his candidacy for the succession, he had explicitly attacked this party oligarchy in the Prime Minister's Office (PMO) claiming that, under his leadership, there would be no "backroom boys" and signalling that the party's provincial cadres would regain their place in the sun. In June 1984 when he entered the PMO in triumph, he threw out the plans for re-election that had been prepared for him by

---

*Despite the substantial institutional development of Canadian political parties in the last half century, H.McD. Clokie's classic statement made in 1944 still rings true: "In Canada more than anywhere else it is possible to define a party as being a body of supporters following a given leader." *Canadian Government and Politics* (Toronto: Longmans, Green. Rev. ed.,1950) p. 97.

the departing Trudeauites, despatching their files to the public archives as if they belonged to a discredited government whose tarnished remains needed to be swept away before the new regime could function. The problem was that he turned out to have nothing of his own to substitute for these plans and, following his electoral defeat on September 4, Turner moved into the Office of the Leader of the Opposition humiliated personally and very nearly wiped out politically.

For a defeated prime minister to turn for help to the extra-parliamentary party was not unusual. Wilfrid Laurier and Mackenzie King had done the same thing before him in 1911 and 1930. But for Turner to hark back to a formula that was 50 years out of date was something else again. During the decade from 1958 to 1968 when Lester B. Pearson was leader, the Liberal party had been rebuilt according to the centralized management principles of Walter Gordon, the successful business consultant whom Pearson had recruited to modernize the party's organization and redirect its policies. This was a time when Quebec and the anglophone provinces went through an impressive "province building" process that saw their economic and administrative powers develop at the expense of Ottawa's. With the provincial Liberal parties taking regionalist stands that increasingly challenged the federal party's positions, Walter Gordon and Keith Davey, the party's national director, had moved to become independent of their provincial cousins' organizations.[3]

This process of federal-provincial differentiation continued during the Trudeau regime. Even if he had wanted to build his federal party on regional foundations, Pierre Trudeau would have found few powerful, provincially based chieftains to aid this cause. During his term in office, the Liberals gradually lost power in the six provinces whose governments they held when Trudeau became prime minister: New Brunswick in 1970, Newfoundland in 1971, Saskatchewan in 1971, Quebec in 1976, Nova Scotia in 1978, and Prince Edward Island in 1979. With Ottawa as the sole source for partisan patronage, the federal party naturally had become the dominant force in Liberal circles at the end of the Trudeau years.

The strong ideological component in Trudeau's federalism had a particular impact on the Liberals' fortunes in Quebec. His dogmatic anti-nationalism made him the committed foe not just of separatism in Quebec but of the neo-federalism embraced by the *Parti Liberal du Québec* (PLQ). As polemicist and rookie M.P. in the early and mid-1960s, he had fought the special status proclivities of the Lesage government. As prime minister in the 1970s he had mocked Premier Robert Bourassa's ambivalent federalism. As constitution-maker in the early 1980s he had repudiated the neo-federalism of the defeated PLQ's austere new leader, Claude Ryan, thereby fracturing the tenuous solidarity between the federal and provincial Liberals that had been cobbled together during the No campaign against the referendum over sovereignty-association in 1980. Despite their defeat of separatism, the federal and provincial Liberal parties in Quebec had emerged from the Trudeau era deeply alienated from one another.

This same period had also radically changed the federal party's organizational structure. Far-reaching reform of the system's election expense legislation created a new legal context for federal parties. Although they remained private associations operating by their own rules in such areas as candidate nominations, parties now became publicly accountable bodies whose legislative research activities, constituency offices and riding campaigns were largely financed by the federal state. What was initiated at the federal level soon spread throughout the provincial political systems so that, by the early 1980s, provincial parties had also been transformed from private clubs of partisan activists into legally bound institutions financed in large part by the same taxpayers whose votes they courted at election time. As a result, the Canadian party system was firmly institutionalized and Canadian parties were clearly differentiated between their federal and provincial levels in a way they had never been before.

So when John Turner promised Alberta Liberals on January 18, 1985 that he would rebuild the federal party on the basis of strong provincial party foundations,[4] he was operating in a context fundamentally different from the situation in which Mackenzie King had found himself when, in 1932, he had created the National Liberal Federation.

Nevertheless, one of Turner's prime organizational preoccupations as opposition leader was to invest what resources he could muster to support his Liberal counterparts in their provincial election campaigns. He believed that the route back to federal power led through recapturing power in the provincial capitals. For instance, he designated the young M.P., Sheila Copps, who had previously been a member of the Ontario legislature, to liaise with Queen's Park and establish closer co-operation between the two opposition caucuses. By mid-1985 he could exult in renewed provincial Liberal strength throughout anglophone Canada: from gains in Newfoundland (15 seats from 8), to the election of two Liberals to the territorial legislature in the Yukon, to encouraging provincial by-election performances in British Columbia, Saskatchewan and New Brunswick, and, most tellingly, the swearing in of David Peterson's minority Liberal government in Ontario in June.[5]

The provincial co-operation strategy served a second, if less overtly expressed, goal: Turner's own struggle to secure his confirmation as leader by the federal party's convention. As none of the provincial leaders to whom he offered electoral support had ambitions for his job, identifying himself with their causes could do him little harm, particularly when their fortunes were on the rise. When the LPC convention was held in November 1986 this strategy proved to have been astute. Having control of the party machinery, Turner's loyalists managed to engineer a far higher level of vote for the leader than continuing dismay with Turner's generally poor political performance had led observers to expect: 76.3 percent of the delegates voted No on their mandatory secret ballot about holding a leadership convention. The covert campaign to oust Turner by the faction supporting Jean Chrétien, his chief rival for the leadership in 1984, had been warded off.

The party's euphoria induced by this apparently definitive resolution of Turner's position was short-lived. In concrete terms of financial and organizational restructuring, Turner had little to show for the two years that had passed.

The party was still deep in debt. Although large amounts of money were being raised, the expenses of the national organization were rising faster than its income. The process of party reform inherited from the Trudeau period had produced few substantial results.[6] The leader's own office was in a state of continual turmoil. Turner never found a principal secretary strong and experienced enough to bring order to his affairs. Members of his staff kept resigning and emerging from his office to recount to an avidly listening press new horror stories about what was to be christened John Turner's "reign of error."[7]

More important to many Canadians, both in the Liberal party and the mass media, was Turner's continuing failure to resolve the ideological uncertainties he had created when he rejected Trudeau's federalist legacy in 1984. Though his caucus had been reduced to the manageable size of forty, he had been unable to discipline the various factions still stirring within it and to meld them into a coherent team united behind his leadership. It was wracked with dissension over such fundamental and divisive issues as the testing of cruise missiles and the negotiation of free trade with the United States. In June, 1987 he exacerbated the dismay of the party's Trudeau loyalists by endorsing the Mulroney Conservatives' Meech Lake Accord on constitutional decentralization.

Battered by these problems of leadership, organization and policy, the chances of the Liberals getting their electoral machine onto a campaign footing appeared dim as the federal election loomed in early 1988. As late as April 1988 over half his MPs took part in an abortive mutiny, drafting letters urging Turner to step down and make way for a more effective leader.

The LPC had done well in the public opinion polls because of the Tories' failing, but Turner's third-place standing among the party leaders was a strong disincentive to possible recruits. Though a search for substantial candidates had been entrusted to Paul Martin, Jr., a Montreal business executive and a candidate of star quality himself, few strong figures emerged to contest and win constituency nominations. Candidates were given to understand they could not expect significant help in their efforts either from the Leader or from party headquarters. Displaying a stance strikingly similar to that of his predecessor, whose attitudes to party matters he had so noisily repudiated, Turner adopted a hands-off attitude to recruiting.

What made contesting a Liberal nomination even less attractive to established public figures was the prospect of having to spend well over $30,000 with little assurance of success against possible single-issue or "ethnic" rivals who could capture ridings by enlisting hundreds from their organization or their particular ethnic community's members.** With Turner adopting a hands-off, this-is-democracy-at-play attitude towards the nomination process, the party seemed

---

**Patrick Johnston, a social-policy expert and the co-chair of the Liberals' platform committee, worked for 10 months recruiting members to support his candidacy for the nomination in Scarborough West. He lost to an anti-abortion candidate sponsored by Campaign Life, a militant organization which mobilized all the Catholic churches in the riding and pumped in large amounts of money to finance a virulent campaign in this one of the four constituencies it had targeted.

unable to resolve the tension between its old Anglo- and French-Canadian base and the new multicultural forces that were demanding admission into the ranks of the party's elite.

By the summer of 1988 the Liberals' situation looked disaster bound. Although the party was still wallowing in what was reported to be a $5 million debt, Turner had to fire his Quebec fundraiser, Senator Pietro Rizzuto, for leading the caucus mutiny against him. With the national campaign preparation still embryonic, Turner acted as though Mackenzie King's decentralized party federation were alive and well and would come to his rescue. He turned to his provincial counterparts and asked them for organizational help. Since Turner's own leadership was a factor dragging the Liberal cause down, the success of his risky gamble hung largely on whether his policy positions could galvanize the various provincial Liberal organizations into action.

Policy without Presence

The image of policy confusion had been a continuing problem for Turner ever since he had returned to politics in 1984 and shown his grasp of current issues to be rusty. Whenever caucus members squabbled over a question, the media reinforced the impression that the Liberals were hopelessly divided on the major issues. Even active and experienced party loyalists could be heard bewailing their party's intellectual void. The reality was somewhat more complex.

True to his own promise to hand the party back to its members, Turner had stood back while its activists designed their own process and brought in their own ideas. As those who were active on policy issues tended to the nationalist Left of the party's ideological spectrum, Turner in effect let his policy agenda be rewritten by those who theoretically should have been most alienated from his pro-business stance in 1984. They consulted policy experts. They organized three regional thinkers' conferences. They established a platform committee to draft position papers that dealt with the broad spectrum of public policy concerns. Working with Brooke Jeffrey, the director of the Liberal caucus's research bureau and her dozen staff people, they prepared 40 separate policy positions for the campaign. Each policy was supported by an extensive background paper that analyzed the government's record and the NDP's position, explained the principle on which the Liberals stood and outlined what action a Liberal government would take. An outside expert, the political scientist Robert Jackson, was hired to liaise with the leader's office and monitor this policy work. David Husband, an economist with Finance department experience, was engaged to cost each proposal professionally and prepare a careful document to describe how the party would pay for all its campaign promises. In brief, Turner had learned from his 1984 trauma, when he had started his campaign with no policy weaponry, by methodically equipping himself with more than enough ammunition. What went wrong was both the strategy of how to use policy in the campaign and its tactical execution.

In an action that indicated how rooted Turner was in the politics of the King/ St.Laurent period, the Liberals unveiled their 40 policies as an election manifesto on September 28, just before the writs were issued. Admittedly there were advantages to this pre-emptive strike. Turner could make the point that he did have a comprehensive set of policies ready for the campaign. He was able to give his candidates solid material with which to prepare their campaign appeals. But the electronic media, which have trouble transmitting more than a single idea in a 30-second clip, could not cope with such a cornucopia of ideas that had not been pre-digested into a simple theme wrapped around a few easily grasped issues.

The strategic decision to release frequent and detailed policy statements but to withhold until late in the campaign the explanation of how the Liberals would pay for their promises went off track from the very beginning. Bad tactics and poor staff work between the leader's office and Lucie Pépin, the caucus member responsible for the issue, led to a damaging debacle for the leader in front of the press when the child-care policy was released in Montreal on the first Wednesday of the campaign. Although a comprehensive housing policy was successfully presented, the collective journalistic mind had clearly decided that the Liberals had no policies and could not do anything right. Though Turner continued to release policy positions in his daily speeches — half of the 40 planks were formally announced in this way — the media seemed interested only in his flag-waving attacks on the Conservatives' free trade agreement. By mid-campaign Turner's handlers decided to give the media what they apparently wanted. The leader would no longer try to remedy the party's perceived weakness in policy; for the duration of the campaign Turner would lead to his strength as champion of the anti-free trade cause.

Presence without Policy

Taking a nationalist position was not an obvious stance for a politician whose absence from politics had been spent in the private sector serving the continental interests of Toronto's business community. His former business allies and present political enemies could never quite bring themselves to believe that the John Turner they thought they knew had defected to the nationalist camp out of conviction. After all: Turner had always been close to his American counterparts both in politics and in business; he had been well known as a strong critic of Trudeau's interventionist actions from the Foreign Investment Review Agency of 1973 to the National Energy Program of 1980; he had been invited by George Shultz, who later became the American Secretary of State, to join the board of the giant U.S. engineering firm, Bechtel; for many years one of his closest advisers had been Simon Reisman, the man Prime Minister Mulroney had appointed to be Canada's chief free-trade negotiator.

But something had indeed happened to change Turner's mind on the question of free trade with the United States. Unlike many politicians who took positions on the issue, he had grasped the broader implications of the Canada-United States Free Trade Agreement (FTA). Immediately following the publication, early in October 1987, of the FTA's main outlines, he read it and came to the firm conclusion that it was, in itself, a bad deal: Canada's negotiators had given up too much and got too little in return. More seriously, it would imperil the country's survival as the autonomous state he thought it had become in the golden age of Turner's political heroes, Mackenzie King and Louis St. Laurent.

From the time the text was made public John Turner and his trade critic, Lloyd Axworthy, established a confident leadership of the anti-free-trade position thereby making the NDP leader, Ed Broadbent, and his trade critic, Steven Langdon, appear to be less clear-headed and decisive. Whereas the NDP talked about abrogating the deal should they come to power after it was implemented — an action that could involve serious retaliation by the United States — the Liberals insisted an election be held on the issue and vowed to "tear up" the document if they won. Representatives of the Pro-Canada Network, the coalition of church, union, women's, cultural, environmental, ethnic, elderly and native groups who were against the FTA found the Liberal caucus to be more responsive than the NDP to their briefings.[8] John Turner, the nervous achiever who had always tried to do what the elites with whom he associated expected of him, had turned into a champion of the people. He was defying the business establishment that had produced him with a calm self assurance he had never achieved at any other time in his life.[9]

Although Turner spoke consistently and strongly against free trade throughout the early months of 1988 and although he had presented an integrated alternative to bilateralism in his response to the FTA's implementation legislation, his low ratings in the public opinion polls had prevented the Liberals from causing the Conservatives much grief on the issue.

Faced in the summer of 1988 by the muffling of the one issue that had explosive potential with the public, the Liberals decided to use the majority they commanded in the Canadian Senate to block the FTA's implementation. As party leader, John Turner announced in August that he had instructed the Liberal Senators not to consider the implementation legislation until the Canadian people had been given a chance to vote on the issue.

With one brilliant stroke he used the politically discredited Senate to make two politically credible points: the FTA put Canada at risk and the public must pass judgement on it before the agreement became law. With the public favouring a let-the-people-decide position by a 2:1 margin, Turner breathed life into a moribund issue, dramatized its importance to the country and forced the government's hand. At the same time Turner was able to revive his appeal to one of the two branches of the traditional Liberal vote, that coalition of working people, women, disadvantaged, elderly and ethnic voters who looked to government for security. Having already lost the support of the other branch — the high income earners who made up the business and professional class and populated the suburbs of the large metropolises — Turner was at least making a bid to wrest the anti-business, social democratic centre and Left away from the NDP. This was the broad mainstream of middle and working class voters who had prudential concerns about the maintenance of the country's social programmes, who appreciated the quality of Canadian life and felt it threatened by further Americanization, and who had moral concerns about Canada's role on the world stage as mediator of conflicts and provider of aid to the third world.

For a week or so in late summer, as the nation's hot-line radio shows debated the pros and cons of the Senate action (denounced haplessly by Ed Broadbent as undemocratic), Turner caught the public's attention. But the government put off the election campaign in the expectation that the issue could not be sustained. As the days passed, the Tories' successfully regained control over the public agenda. Premier Robert Bourassa's endorsement of the Tories' FTA offset Turner's impact on Quebec opinion. Guided by expensive polling data, the Conservatives tried to distract lingering public concerns about free trade by launching new initiatives in environmental protection and housing and so rework their image as a government willing to intervene on the public's behalf.[10] When Prime Minister Mulroney finally called on Governor General Jeanne Sauvé to precipitate the election campaign on October 1, it seemed that the free-trade genie had been safely coaxed back into its bottle and that John Turner's political chances were still bleak.

The Campaign Organization

Not only was Turner low on the leader-popularity scale as the election campaign began but his organization was generally third compared to the well-financed professionalism of the Conservatives and the experienced discipline of the New Democrats. Not that the Liberals presented the same chaotic face as they had shown under Turner in 1984. The men and women around Turner who staffed the central campaign were certainly conscious of what errors they needed to avoid, though how much they could achieve without a substantial organization of their own in each province remained to be seen.

In Ottawa the co-chairmen of the overall campaign structure, Senator Alasdair Graham and André Ouellet, kept tempers and turf-fighting, natural to any fractious party's campaign, within bounds. John Webster, a novice, had proved an effective campaign director. Peter Connolly, Turner's controversial principal secretary, continued as chief of staff on the tour, acting as gatekeeper to the Leader's mind. The equally controversial Senator Michael Kirby headed the national strategy committee and controlled the flow of speech ideas to the Leader's tour. He applied the opinion data received from Martin Goldfarb to determine the political impact of the party's proposed policies and, along with policy consultant George Radwanski, worked to translate them into one-liners for the leader. (To the Wall Street Journal's jeremiad against Canadian free-trade opponents who were described as wanting to become the Argentina of the North, they had Turner quip "Don't cry for me, Wall Street Journal!")

The caucus research bureau staffed a policy hotline to provide candidates with answers to voters' questions and devised replies to the myriad questionnaires with which special interest groups inundated riding offices. Fax machines kept the riding campaigns in touch with the Leader's daily positions.

In Toronto a prominent Liberal business executive, Gerald Schwartz, took charge of fund raising, persuading business that, while it might not like Turner's position on free trade, it should shell out generously to the Liberals lest the socialist NDP sneak up the middle and control a minority government situation.

David Morton, vice-president of Quaker Oats of Canada, headed Red Leaf, the party's advertising consortium, which created strong but subtle commercials bringing to a wide audience the Liberal message about free trade's threats and Turner's commitment to Canadian sovereignty. (The French language commercials produced in Montreal carefully ignored Turner and free trade.)

The normal tensions that plague the crisis-management climate of campaign structures broke into open view in mid-October when a CBC broadcast elevated an apparently deliberate leak from the Leader's tour group into a devastating story alleging that yet another coup against John Turner was being hatched by none other than his campaign strategists. Based on two real facts — Michael Kirby had brought gloom to party headquarters in the shape of Martin Goldfarb's latest disheartening poll data, and the strategy committee had debated what to do should Turner's acute back pain cause him to step down — the highly embroidered story devastated the party's morale for a precious week.[11] Whatever the media might suggest, the party was stuck with its leader, for better or for worse.

The Leader in the Campaign

That anything involving John Turner could be for the better seemed close to impossible as the two, three-hour televised debates approached in late October. Having made the mistake of agreeing to debate in French with the bilingual Brian Mulroney in 1984, an encounter that put him on the defensive and precipitated his electoral downfall, Turner was stuck with the precedent and could hardly back out of a repeat engagement. It looked as though the French debate on October 24 would prove an unpropitious prelude to the following day's debate in English. But Turner surprised first French Canada and then the rest of the country by outperforming Mulroney on both occasions. In the French debate he was both more at ease with himself and his material and in better humour than Mulroney whose mellifluous verbosity appeared evasive and defensive. To their own astonishment Quebec editorialists declared Turner the debate's winner, spurring him on for the next day's rematch in English.

When the three party leaders convened for their encounter in English, Turner managed to accomplish two objectives. First he effectively branded Ed Broadbent a pacifist by linking him to the NDP's unpopular defence policy which promised withdrawal from NORAD and NATO. This reminded Atlantic Canada, where military bases form a crucial element of the federal income-support system, that it was the Liberals, not the NDP, who understood their employment needs. Then, as the political scientist, Robert Young, described it:

> With less than 15 minutes left in their last head-to-head encounter, Chick Turner started to jab desperately on the trade issue. Mr. Mulroney, doubtless to the dismay of his corner-men, neither clinched nor danced away, and the two heavy-weights stood toe-to-toe, punching and counter-punching, slugging it out in a sheer test of power and commitment which enormously enhanced Turner's stature, punctured the prime ministerial balloon of inviolability, and

left Ed Broadbent looking like the kid peeking over the fence at the big guys.[12]

In the context of the low esteem in which the Liberal leader was widely held, the fact that John Turner proved in these exchanges to be both coherent and persuasive had a powerful impact on the millions of Canadians who watched part or all of the six hours of debates. When the polls judged him winner of the second debate, his standing increased with the millions of other voters who heard about the debates or saw short clips from them repeated in news reports. Suddenly the inevitable Tory majority was in doubt. Turner had made Liberals feel good again about being Liberal and those who had been sitting out this campaign because they couldn't stomach the Leader or the organization or the platform turned out to canvass. Jean Chretién re-entered the fray and started making pro-Turner speeches. Public opinion polls recorded precipitous gains for the Liberals and equivalent losses for the Conservatives. Environics, the polling organization used by *The Globe and Mail*, quickly proclaimed the Liberals to be in first place with the prospect of winning a majority.[13] In Quebec the tribal voting question was raised: if the country appeared to be going back to the Grits, would Quebec swing behind Turner in order to remain on the winning side?

In his exchange with Mulroney, Turner did more than just reverse the standing in the polls. He succeeded in transforming a normal election campaign into a referendum in which the dominant issue became free trade. The public had been sensitized by three years of consciousness raising by the various elements of the Pro-Canada Network. The millions of upbeat pamphlets distributed by the government in praise of free trade had not satisfied the public, 70 percent of whom wanted more concrete information about the deal. Turner had finally managed to wrest control of the public agenda from the Conservatives and turn it to the one issue on which he was the most credible leader. The question now became whether he could maintain the referendum quality of the campaign for the four weeks remaining.

Advertising as the Ultimate Weapon

When the Gallup organization announced on November 7 that the Liberals had leaped to 43 percent in the polls while the Conservatives had fallen to 31 percent and the NDP to 22 percent, Liberal insiders knew that their chances of pulling off a political victory had diminished. Not only were these figures out of line with what their own pollster, Martin Goldfarb, was reporting — the Liberals and Conservatives were running neck and neck — they set the Liberals up to appear to be losing rather than gaining momentum as soon as more accurate polls were published, as they were on Nov. 10 when Environics showed the Liberals and Conservatives at 37 and 35 percent.

Worse still for the Liberals, Turner's triumph in the debates and the apparent Liberal leap in the polls shocked both the Conservatives and their business allies out of their complacency. The Conservative strategists decided they had to go for broke. They unleashed their leader, Brian Mulroney, his trade negotiator,

Ambassador Simon Reisman, and his senior ministers, John Crosbie and Michael Wilson, in a campaign of political attacks that branded Turner a liar and even a traitor. The Tories cancelled their bland and ineffectual commercials in favour of a counterattack that took a leaf from the George Bush campaign for the U.S. presidency. South of the border the Republicans were proving that vicious commercials could persuade the public if they were repeated frequently enough. Since the TV advertising time allocated to the governing party was far greater than the quotas of the other parties and since the Tories had plenty of money in their campaign war chest, they were able quickly to order a television commercial onslaught aimed at destroying John Turner's reputation and credibility.

At the same time their allies in the business community swung into action. Taking advantage of a successful 1984 court challenge to legislation which originally prevented special interest groups from intervening in elections, corporate Canada poured millions of dollars into advertising to defend free trade.[14]

Faced with this sustained barrage by superior fire power, John Turner proved unable to play David to the free-trade Goliath. Rejecting advice that he should supplement his flag-waving attacks on free trade by explaining his alternative solution, he kept to his one dimensional line that Canada's survival was at risk. Turner carried on his single-issue campaign in an emotional bubble while infighting broke out among his staff. He strongly rejected the idea of retaliating with a "negative" response to the commercials that the Tories unleashed and he disallowed a plan for a mass rally in Toronto's Maple Leaf Gardens but was indecisive in proposing alternatives. As the last two weeks of the campaign wore on, he failed to broaden his attack beyond its narrow, one-note range, to turn back the charge of liar against Mulroney or to present the Liberals' positive alternative to the FTA. With the Leader's national campaign faltering and the party's standing sinking at the rate of one percent per day, Liberal riding campaigns reaped the whirlwind Turner had sown during the previous four years when he had failed to restructure his party.

Assessment

When the first results came in from Atlantic Canada on election night, Liberals could hardly contain their joy. A breakthrough in the Maritimes where the Liberals almost tripled their seats from 7 to 20 seemed momentarily to prove the wisdom of Turner's return to the King/St.Laurent model of the decentralized party. In Newfoundland and Nova Scotia healthy federal organizations had been able to capitalize on Turner's articulation of the region's concerns about the impact of free trade in Atlantic Canada. But in New Brunswick where the Liberals had recently won all the provincial seats, Premier Frank McKenna went one step further. His organization had responded to Turner's call for help by taking over the federal Liberal campaign lock, stock and barrel. Camille Theriault, a member of the provincial legislature, was made chairman of a campaign committee that consisted of exactly the same people who had run and won the provincial campaign the previous autumn. With McKenna personally making the major campaign decisions, this group had raised money, recruited candidates and activated riding organizations, all to telling effect. In Prince Edward Island the federal Liberals were overwhelmed by Premier Joe Ghiz's troops. However, the positive results in the Atlantic provinces were the exception, as the results from central and western Canada soon showed.

The Liberal premier of Quebec had also participated in the federal election, and with telling effect, but in his case the outcome was to defeat, not elect, federal Liberal candidates. Bourassa had several motivations. Partly it was to repay Prime Minister Mulroney for securing the Meech Lake Accord on the constitution which accepted Quebec's demands for recognition as a distinct society. Partly it was gratitude for the massive amounts of federal money that had poured into Quebec since 1984. Partly it was to defend the free trade agreement, which was strongly supported by Quebec's business community, opinion leaders, and political elite as a godsend for the provincial economy.[15]

While Bourassa could take much of the credit for the federal Liberals' worst Quebec defeat in their history, Turner deserved much of the blame for letting his fortunes in Quebec depend on its premier's whims.*** Back in 1984 Turner had deliberately repudiated Trudeau's federalist legacy of resisting both separatism and neo-federalism. Though forced to make some "clarifications" vis à vis the Quebec situation to try to mollify the Trudeauites, Turner had remained a consistent supporter of provincialism. In 1987 he had believed assurances by Raymond Garneau, his Quebec lieutenant and finance critic, that Bourassa would reward Turner's present political support for the Meech Lake accord with future electoral support. Having failed to rebuild a federal party apparatus in Quebec even though his party president, Michel Robert, was a Quebecker, Turner left himself with no option should his strategy fail. Without an effective organization of their own, the federal Liberals in Quebec went down like nine pins, with even Raymond Garneau and Lucie Pépin falling victim to the Tory sweep.

It was understandable that Turner's anti-free-trade position harmed the federal Liberals in Quebec where all but the major trade and farmers' unions favoured the FTA. It was less clear why the Liberal Party in Ontario proved incapable of delivering even half of Ontario's seats to Turner. Certainly Premier David Peterson offered considerable moral support to the federal leader during the campaign. He cut short a trade-promotion trip to Asia to campaign for a number of federal candidates, in particular his own brother, James Peterson, who was running in a Metro Toronto riding. He invited John Turner to a well-publicized meeting with his caucus whose members campaigned actively for their federal counterparts. But the Queen's Park Liberals did not make up for

---

***The Liberals' previous low was in 1887 when they won 13 of Quebec's 65 seats.

the inadequacies of the federal party's weak organization even though many of them were seconded to bolster its staff.

While various factors such as the nomination imbroglios, which gave the electorate the impression of a party riven with conflict, can be cited in explaining the Liberals' poor showing in Central Canada, it can also be argued that no organization could have withstood the sustained punishment the Liberal leader had to take from the NDP on the Left and the business-Conservative alliance on the Right in the closing weeks of the campaign. In an age of TV politics, it would have taken a brilliant political performance by the leader as well as impeccable organization for the Liberals to withstand the combination of negative news reports (Ed Broadbent attacking John Turner's credibility) and negative commercials (Conservative ads impugning Turner's integrity). In the end the Liberal campaign of 1988 had neither. The leader's campaign, after a weak beginning and an astonishingly strong middle period, faltered. The organization needed to squeeze the extra few hundred votes needed in every riding had never been there.

Liberal gains in Manitoba did show that a strong regional figure in the person of Lloyd Axworthy could successfully affect a local federal campaign. The federal party also profited from the provincial Liberals' electoral success earlier that year: the five seats the Grits won on November 21 were all in the city of Winnipeg where the provincial Liberals had made an electoral breakthrough. Further west, the pathetically weak provincial Liberal organizations could hardly have done much to bolster the federal Liberals: Western alienation from the Liberal party which began in the 1950s was so entrenched in the 1980s that it was hard to imagine what strategy could reap an electoral harvest from such barren political soil.

As the Liberals shifted in early 1989 from electoral post mortems to active consideration of the next leadership campaign, two somewhat contradictory conclusions were drawn about John Turner's stewardship. On the one hand it was thought that Turner could retire with honour, ennobled by having fought free trade with tenacity in what he himself called the cause of his life. On the other hand, he was seen as likely to go down in Liberal annals as the man who single-handedly jeopardized the future of the federal party. It was still too early to tell whether internal factionalism would become linked with provincial regionalism in a syndrome that would perpetuate the federal Liberals' new loser-party status. It was already too late to point out the danger of trying to return to the formulae of the golden age of Liberalism now that permanently changed conditions made the past impossible to replicate. The tragedy of John Turner lay in his inability to comprehend the nature of the political change that had engulfed him.

While losing the Liberal party's century-long hold on Quebec, Turner had failed to rebuild its base in the West. He had continued his party's alienation from the business community that had begun under Lester Pearson and worsened dramatically under Pierre Trudeau. He had not been able to convince broad sections of his own party that free trade was lethal for Canada. Having achieved a personal redemption — the courage he showed in the campaign was everywhere admired — he left his party disoriented in defeat.

Endnotes

This chapter has benefited from interviews with Lloyd Axworthy, Tom Axworthy, Duncan Cameron, Tex Enemrk, Mel Hurtig, Lorna Marsden, William Macdonald, Richard O'Hagan and Robert Jackson and from seminar presentations by Michael Adams, Norman Atkins, Hershell Ezrin and Robin Sears. On the coalition against free trade I leaned on work by André Blais, Marjorie Griffin Cohen and David Laycock. I am indebted to research by Dominic LeBlanc on the Liberal party's electoral organization in the Maritimes and to comments on an earlier draft of this manuscript by Michael Adams, Stefan Dupré, Dale Godsoe. Lorna Marsden, Patrick Johnston, Richard O'Hagan, John Roberts, David Trick and Nelson Wiseman. The text gained most from the editorial rigour and ideas of Christina McCall.

1. These errors are documented in Steven Clarkson, "The Dauphin and the Doomed: John Turner and the Liberal Party's debacle," *Canada at the Polls*. 1984 (Raleigh N.C.: Duke University Press, 1988).
2. For a thoughtful analysis of the distinction between the "accommodative" and "pan-Canadian" models of party organization see David E. Smith, "Party Government. Representation and National Integration in Canada," in Peter Aucoin, ed., *Party Government and Regional Representation in Canada*. Royal Commission on the Economic Union and Development Prospects for Canada, Vol. 36 (Toronto: University of Toronto Press, 1986).
3. Joseph Wearing, *The L-Shaped Party: The Liberal Party of Canada, 1958-1980*. (Toronto: McGraw-Hill, 1981) p. 22 ff.
4. Bob Bragg, "Turner Pledges Western Base." *Calgary Herald*. January 19, 1985.
5. Rt. Hon. John Turner, Speech to the Liberal Party of Canada (Ontario) Annual Meeting. Toronto. June 22, 1985.
6. Joseph Wearing, "Can an Old Dog Teach Itself New Tricks? The Liberal Party Attempts Reform." In Alain Gagnon and Brian Tanguay, Eds., *Canadian Parties in Transition: Discourse, Organization and Representation*, (Toronto: Nelson Canada, 1988) Ch. 11.
7. Greg Weston, *Reign of Error*, (Toronto: McGraw-Hill, 1988).
8. Interviews with Duncan Cameron: assessment confirmed by Majorie Griffin Cohen.
9. Christina McCall-Newman, *Grits: An Intimate Portrait of the Liberal Party*, (Toronto: Macmillan of Canada, 1982) Part V.
10. The $90,000 Angus Reid poll was paid for by the Department of Finance. "PCs Tipped on Pollution by Survey; Public Paid," *The Globe and Mail*. December 30, 1988. A1.
11. For Michael Kirby's account of this debacle see Geral Kaplan, Michael Kirby and Hugh Segal, *Election; The Issues, The Strategies, The Aftermath*, (Toronto: Prentice-Hall, 1989) pp. 131-143.
12. R.A. Young, "The End of the Political Centre." University of Western Ontario, November 11, 1988. Mimeo. p. 6.
13. Michael Adams, Donna Dasko and James Matsui, "Liberals Move Ahead of PCs in Wake of Leaders' Debates." *The Globe and Mail*. November 1, 1988. A1.
14. David Laycock, "Organized Interests in Canada and the Free Trade Election of 1988." Paper presented at Centre For International Affairs, Harvard University. December 9, 1988. p. 10.
15. Sheilagh M. Dunn, "The Free Trade Initiative and Regional Strategies," in Peter M. Leslie and Ronald Watts, eds., *Canada: The State of the Federation 1987-1988*, (Queen's University, Kingston: Institute for Intergovernmental Relations, 1988) pp. 69-71.

The NDP Election Campaign: Dashed Hopes

By Alan Whitehorn

From the perspective of left-wing reform movements and parties, there have been several key elections in federal politics. That of 1988 seemed to present a potential for an historic breakthrough. The New Democratic Party, like its precursor, the CCF, in 1945, found itself leading in public opinion polls in the year prior to a federal election and many party members and strategists felt that at long last a social democratic party would displace one of the two older parties.

Following the 1984 election in which the Liberal party received its lowest ever percentage vote (28 percent) and number of seats (40), the NDP with 18.8 percent of the vote and 30 seats (32 with the results of three by-election victories in 1987) was the closest it had ever been to overtaking the Liberal party. The reasons for the growing belief that the NDP might finally displace the Liberals included the following:

— Liberal leader John Turner was held in very low esteem by much of the Canadian public. Even members of his own party and caucus did not seem enthusiastic about his leadership. In contrast, for two straight years from September 1986 to August 1988, Ed Broadbent topped the polls as the leader the public would most prefer to have as Prime Minister. In September 1987 Broadbent's level of support even surpassed the combined total of Turner and Mulroney.

— The Liberal party was seen as divided and fractured. The NDP, in contrast, was portrayed as a disciplined yet democratic organization in which its leader was firmly at the helm of both party affairs and the caucus.

— The federal Liberal party appeared to be undergoing a long term decline in membership and income. While the NDP's finances had never been its strength, NDP membership, public support and income had been on the rise in recent years.

— The Liberal party, often perceived as Canada's governing party for much of the twentieth century, was unaccustomed to the role of performing as a small opposition party. In contrast the CCF-NDP had a 55 year-long tradition in this regard and was expected to outperform the Liberals in the role.

In addition to the perceived weaknesses of the federal Liberal party, senior NDP strategists had believed that an historic opportunity existed for the party in Quebec in light of the decline in support for the provincially-based Parti Québécois. The existence of the pro-separatist PQ as a rival social democratic party had in the past created an obstacle to an electoral breakthrough for the

NDP in Quebec. However, the defeat of the PQ provincial government in 1985 had seen the virtual disintegration of its organization. The 1987 federal convention in Montreal was the first ever by the NDP in the province and its success offered yet another reason to believe that hopes might be justified. Quebec membership had skyrocketed from less than 500 persons in 1983 to 10,000 on the eve of the 1988 election.

However, there were also important reasons for scepticism and caution which were for the most part ignored or downplayed by political pundits, key party strategists and the public at large. These would become more apparent as the 1988 campaign unfolded.

NDP Election Organization and Committee Structure

At the outset of the 1988 campaign the NDP organizationally looked solid. Normally, between conventions, the federal executive and federal council are the principal decision-making bodies of the party. Technically, the Strategy and Election Planning Committee (SEPC) is a committee of the federal executive. However, immediately prior to an election campaign, the SEPC becomes the pre-eminent organ of the party. Working closely with its steering and platform committees, the SEPC designs the strategic election plan. Day to day administration and execution of the plan are left to the federal secretary, operating as the campaign manager, and his staff. In 1988, the SEPC was composed of the chairman; the party leader; the federal president; the federal treasurer; the federal secretary; the principal advisor to the leader; one representative from each of the parliamentary caucus, the participation of women (POW) committee, and the Canadian Labour Congress; plus one to two persons from each of the provincial sections, for a total of 21.

Several party strategists have suggested that the SEPC has become too unwieldy in size in its quest for greater regional representation. Instead of a small semi-professional advisory group, it has become a more open and democratic body but also less efficient.[1] Given the size of the full SEPC and its diverse regional compositon, it is not surprising that a smaller body was created. The SEPC Steering Committee was composed of 13 persons, half of whom were members of the SEPC proper, while four of the others were key personnel from the federal office. Given that seven members overall were based in Ottawa, this clearly was intended to be a committee that could meet more frequently and quickly than the full SEPC.

The 13 person Election Platform Committee, a sub-committee of the SEPC, culled the hundreds of resolutions passed at previous party conventions, and strove to draft a coherent policy platform to maximize the party's electoral appeal. Amongst the publications emanating from the committee was a 14 page pamphlet entitled "A Fair Deal For Canadians: New Democrats Speaking for Average Canadians."[2] The title of the document conveyed the main campaign message.

During the actual campaign itself two key groups supervised and, where necessary, modified the application of the election strategy. At the pinnacle of the decision-making hierarchy was a very small inner circle of advisors to Broadbent. George Nakitsas, travelling daily with Broadbent, was the tour director and the closest to Broadbent's ear. Bill Knight, the federal secretary and former principal advisor to Broadbent, was campaign director. Robin Sears, a former federal secretary, was deputy campaign director. Arlene Wortsman, the lone female, was caucus research director. Each Saturday night, they discussed the past week's events and endeavoured to anticipate the next. Each Sunday, following the meeting of this inner circle, the SEPC steering committee met for three to four hours to go into the details of the campaign.

NDP Election Finances and Party Income

In previous federal elections, the NDP's campaign expenditures had been lower than those of the Liberals and the Conservatives. Early NDP projections for the 1988 federal campaign aimed at $4.7 million, virtually the same as in 1984. However, as the NDP began its rise in the opinion polls in 1987, many in the party believed that to tap effectively the new support in Quebec, the past practice of spending very little in that province would have to be reversed.[3] Accordingly, Terry Grier, the chairman of the SEPC, recommended to the 1987 federal convention that the campaign budget be raised by 50 percent, to the $7 million range.[4]

The NDP advertising budget for 1988 was set at $3 million. The leader's tour, the second largest portion of the campaign budget, was projected to cost over $1.5 million. The remainder of the campaign expenditures were primarily for organization ($500,000), direct mail and fund-raising ($500,000), riding support materials ($330,000), opinion research ($330,000), and the pre-election campaign ($500,000).[5] Funds for the campaign were to be raised in the following manner: almost half (46.8 percent) coming from the various provincial sections, notably Ontario, British Columbia and Saskatchewan, the provinces with the largest memberships; 16 percent from the affiliated member unions of the Canadian Labour Congress, the largest proportion of which were based in Ontario; 8.5 percent from the growing funds derived from direct mail; an estimated 26.6 percent from the anticipated government election rebate; and 2 percent in interest from bank accounts.

Polling

In the 1984 election, NDP federal surveys had been confined to 40 or 50 key ridings, with the focus on the seats where the party had incumbents. This meant effectively that the NDP polled no ridings east of the Ottawa River and the polling also lacked depth in coverage over time and continuity in pollsters. By contrast, the 1988 campaign drew upon a solid four years of surveys covering the entire country. Quebec was not only included in the national sample, it was even the target of special surveys. Over $200,000 was allocated for survey research during the election and just over $100,000 in the immediate pre-election period. The architect of NDP polling strategy was Washington-based Vic Fingerhut. The bulk of NDP polling data was gathered by Access Survey Research, a

Winnipeg-based company linked to pollster Angus Reid. However, the NDP opted to do its own Ottawa in-house analysis of the data under the supervision of Brian McKee. Thus a computerized electronic triangle emerged with data gathered from Winnipeg, detailed analysis occurring in Ottawa, while under the supervision of a polling specialist in Washington. In addition to conducting mass surveys, the NDP made greater use of small focus groups in selected cities. About a dozen persons were drawn into group discussion about party ads, and arguments for and against voting NDP were tested.

NDP Strategy

Whereas the 1984 campaign strategy evolved with the party a distant third at 11 percent in the polls, the 1988 NDP campaign was inspired by a party soaring to 41 percent in 1987. Believing that an historic opportunity existed, a decision was made to expand the scale of the campaign. It was to be fully bilingual and national in scope.

The 1984 campaign was defensive, trying to protect the crumbling fortress by focusing on 40 to 50 ridings west of the Ottawa River. By 1987 party strategists believed that they could win an election and form Canada's first socialist federal goverment. Accordingly, 144 ridings were targeted for attention, 59 in the West, where the party had always been strong, 39 in Quebec, based on the party's lead in public opinion polls in the province, 35 in Ontario, where the largest section of the affiliated trade union movement was located, and 11 in Atlantic Canada.[6] What was most striking was the number deemed winnable in Quebec. Strategists recognized the danger of being overextended, with too few funds and experienced personnel for the large number of ridings selected.[7] However, they assumed that for the party to stay above the 30 percent level in the national polls it must continue to be a strong new presence in Quebec.

Given the high levels of support for both Broadbent and the party in the 1987 polls, strategists expected that the party would undergo unprecedented scrutiny and attack. To lessen the potential negative impact of greater media and public attention, it was decided to defuse the effects of some of the party's more controversial policies in the pre-election period. Accordingly, in April the International Affairs Commmittee and the Policy Review Committee issued a report entitled "Canada's Stake in Common Security." This report effectively postponed for at least one term of office the NDP's past commitment to pull out of NATO. Also, in an effort to retain support in Quebec, party leaders endeavoured to silence critics of the Meech Lake Accord, such as Manitoba leader Gary Doer. In the case of British Columbia, the NDP provincial caucus voted for the Accord despite rank and file membership opposition at the provincial convention.

During the campaign itself, party spokespersons were advised to minimize references to controversial matters such as withdrawal from NATO, nationalization of private corporations or abortion. Most notably, neither the terms socialism nor social democracy were present in the 24 page election policy statement. In an effort to minimize adverse media coverage, the Broadbent itinerary stressed partisan NDP meetings or scripted photo opportunity sessions, and scheduled few unstructured settings such as talk shows. Instructions were also given that fewer persons were to talk to the press.

In candidate selection, the NDP had two major aims. The first was to attract as many high profile personalities as possible and thereby to enhance the party's image of being ready to govern. Such highly visible individuals would also partially compensate for organizational weaknesses in areas such as Quebec. Broadbent and his staff endeavoured to recruit the so-called NDP dream team of four ex-premiers (Dave Barrett, Allan Blakeney, Ed Schreyer and Howard Pawley) and the eloquent former UN ambassador Stephen Lewis. In the end, Barrett and Pawley accepted nomination, but only Barrett was elected.

Endeavouring to meet the official party policy of commitment to gender parity, a greater number of women candidates were sought. The party nominated far more women than any other party (84), but this was still well short of parity.

Those planning the campaign were confronted with at least three interrelated image problems. The first was that sustained polling revealed that too few persons identified themselves as NDPers. In fact, even in targeted and incumbent ridings, identification with the NDP often ranked second or even third among the parties.

The second problem was that socialism was the least appealing of the three party ideologies in Canada. This had been a major factor in stalling the federal CCF. Lastly, while both the Conservatives and the Liberals relied on significant financial contributions from private corporations, the NDP in contrast, drew upon the support of the trade union movement. Unfortunately for the NDP, the labour movement was regarded less favourably than the business community.[8]

With these significant handicaps, the NDP had to make extensive use of the one major asset it possessed — its leader Ed Broadbent. With a very likeable leader, the strategy team decided to run on a populist programme. Instead of references to socialist doctrine about nationalization and public ownership, the stress would be upon "fairness" for "average Canadians" and the "average family." Broadbent would tell his listeners that only the NDP would protect the interests of average Canadians in the fields of taxation, pensions and child care. The themes of honesty and integrity were considered a strong suit for Broadbent. Perceiving the Conservatives as the main target, the NDP chose to attack the Mulroney record of scandals and patronage, while the Liberals were in organizational disarray and saddled with a vacillating and unpopular leader. The public, as a result, would be receptive to a change. Accordingly, the strategy was to stress the party's positive election prospects in a close "three way race." Certainly, many party members enthusiastically embraced this belief.

A $3 million ad campaign ($2 million for English ads and $1 million for French ones) was designed. In both sets of ads Broadbent's name was stressed. In contrast to past years, when few ads were made in French or had often been poor literal translations of English scripts, this time the French ads were prepared with great care and designed with a French audience in mind. Not wishing to appear too strident or ideological, the NDP opted for relatively soft ads which sought to remind the audience about the erosion of the health care system and the environment.[9]

The party approached the topic of free trade, the dominant issue of the campaign, with some ambivalence. The NDP had a solid and clear record of nationalist concern about increased corporate integration into the U.S. economic sphere. The NDP had consistently called for greater controls on the extent of foreign ownership in Canada. Thus it was no surprise that the party was highly critical of the Mulroney-Reagan trade agreement. Nevertheless, there was widespread concern amongst NDP election strategists that free trade was not a particularly good issue.[10]

There were several reasons for this perception. The first was that the party pre-election polling suggested that the public saw free trade as a "managing the economy" issue. The NDP generally does poorly on such issues. Secondly, it was felt too much attention on free trade would deflect the public away from areas such as integrity, where the party would score much higher. Lastly, the anti-free trade vote was divided between two parties. If the public was roughly balanced for and against free trade, the two parties opposing free trade would each end up with a smaller percentage of the vote than the solitary major party supporting free trade. This latter fear proved to be remarkably accurate.

In order to overcome these problems, the NDP decided that when it addressed concerns about free trade, it would link it to areas on which the party was seen as strong (e.g. protection of health care services and the environment). The irony about the NDP's initial efforts to downplay the free trade issue was that its trade union affiliates in the CLC both before and during the election campaign spent considerable effort and money in criticizing the deal.[11] Inevitably, some tension arose over the different emphases of these two groups.

The importance of free trade grew as the campaign unfolded. Given the combination of the NDP's efforts initially to downplay the issue (e.g. it was not even mentioned in the leader's opening campaign speech) and Turner's success in the television debates, it was not surprising that the party continued to place third in the polls on the issue. To halt this hemorrhaging in support, strategists endeavoured to find a new campaign theme that would put the party back on track. While it never found a fully satisfactory replacement theme, the closing weeks of the campaign did see the use of the phrase "reject the values of Mulroney's Wall St. and Turner's Bay St. and instead support the NDP's values of Main St." Unfortunately for the NDP, it was too little, too late and a bit dated.

Several overall weaknesses in the campaign strategy existed. The assumption that the party's main asset was its leader, Ed Broadbent, was a claim with which few would disagree. The problem, however, was how extensively an NDP campaign could be built around the leader. The strategy assumed that he would remain extremely popular and that the high evaluation would cover a wide enough range of areas. In fact, Broadbent's popularity, along with the NDP's, plummeted during the campaign. In June, Broadbent was rated first (34 percent) among party leaders on the question of which leader would make the best Prime Minister. By November 10 he had slipped to third (17 percent). In the span of four and half months his popularity had been halved and the party's election strategy of tying so much to his rating meant that as he faltered, so did the NDP.

Leader's Tour and Campaign

Given the importance of Broadbent in the NDP campaign, it was not surprising that the leader's tour was perceived as the main vehicle for communicating the party's election message. In any federal election the party leader endeavours to travel to as many regions as possible to give the party the greatest media profile in each locale. Since the NDP's goal in the 1988 federal election was to make significant inroads in previously barren electoral regions such as Quebec and Alberta, the 1988 tour was more ambitious in scope than ever before.

The 51 day campaign saw the leader jetting each week in a zig-zag fashion from one region of the country to the next. The ideal was to be in each region at least once a week and thereby maintain media coverage. Broadbent appeared in Ontario and Quebec weekly, travelled to the West in five of the seven weeks of the campaign, and in Atlantic Canada in three weeks. He spent by far the most time in Ontario (54 percent). Toronto was the hub of his cross-Canada itinerary and Ontario, with 99 seats, offered the greatest prize in terms of number of parliamentary seats. Given the successful electoral history of the party in the West, Broadbent chose to spend the next largest amount of time there (23 percent). The remainder was allocated to Quebec (15 percent) and the Maritimes (8 percent). There was a weekly cycle to the campaign that would see the leader's tour return to either Toronto or Ottawa on each Saturday. This allowed his four or five most senior strategy advisors to meet each Saturday night, and on Sunday with key staff.

The tour was coordinated by two groups. Travelling with Broadbent in his cross Canada odyssey was a band of 15 party personnel and three policemen. George Nakitsas, Broadbent's principal advisor, acted as the tour director, while Anne Carrol, his executive secretary, supervised the on-site details of the itinerary arrangements. Providing long-distance logistical support was the tour office staff based in Ottawa with Wayne Harding as coordinator.

The leader's campaign can be divided into three segments. The pre-debate period, the debates and the post-debate phase. Week One of the campaign saw the NDP in third place in the polls with an average standing of 25.5 percent,[12] a far cry from the lofty levels of the summer of 1987. The historic endorsement of the NDP by Louis Laberge of the 450,000 member Quebec Federation of Labour, combined with favourable press coverage, however, lulled many into thinking that NDP fortunes were perhaps on the upswing again. Week Two saw a rise to 27.7 percent support for the NDP but also a somewhat controversial statement. In reply to a question about the Liberal party's ongoing woes, Broadbent indicated his hope that Canada someday would see a two party system and the demise of the Liberals. While the statement's impact would not be immediately felt, Broadbent's comments had the effect of alarming many life-long Liberals and causing them to rally behind the party, whatever their misgivings about the current Liberal leader. NDP support during the campaign peaked in Week Three at 29.5 percent, enough for second place ahead of the Liberals. Dramatic reports of alleged attempts by senior Liberal strategists to dump Turner in the midst of the campaign tantalized NDPers with the hope that the Liberal campaign would continue to disintegrate. All seemed well and the NDP ship on course. Then came the television debates.

Historically, the NDP, as a smaller third party, has been delighted to be able to participate equally in a forum with the Liberals and Conservatives. On the eve of the two three-hour television debates, virtually all NDP strategists expected Broadbent to perform well overall. In years of tenure, he was the most experienced of the party leaders and he had the most practice in television debates. While his French was the weakest of that of the three party leaders, Broadbent had been a pleasant surprise in the shorter 1984 French debate. Most assumed that on October 24 Broadbent would somehow again cope in French and not lose too much ground. The next night in English, they assumed, he would excel.

The French debate was a fairly restrained and moderate affair. Broadbent did not blunder while speaking in his second language, but the longer debate painfully revealed his lack of fluency. The fully bilingual Turner and Mulroney easily outperformed him. This debate burst the bubble of hopes for a dramatic breakthrough in Quebec. The NDP through its leader was seen to be a distant third. Unfortunately, the French debate, even if not seen by many in the rest of the country, set the mood for the next debate.

The English language debate of October 25 was polemical and heated. NDP strategists generally expected that Turner would not perform very well given his performance in 1984, Mulroney would be handicapped with a government record to defend, and Ed Broadbent would do well. Instead Broadbent was fatigued from the marathon session in French the night before. His eyes looked haggard. His performance, while passable, contained little spark. He erred in using an eight year old quotation. More importantly, his efforts were eclipsed by the electrifying exchange of patriotic fervour between Turner and Mulroney over the issue of free trade. The impression was that Broadbent had lost, and the NDP had become marginalized in the crucial debate. Four years as an effective opposition, it seemed, had been displaced by a one minute television excerpt.

As a consequence of the debate performances the NDP fell dramatically in the polls. The post debate period saw even more unpleasant news. Retired Supreme Court justice Emmett Hall, considered by many as the architect of Canada's national medicare system, categorically rejected NDP and Liberal assertions that free trade would jeopardize medicare. Also, in an effort to make gains in Quebec, the NDP had flirted with Quebec nationalists. Accordingly, seven leading figures in the Quebec wing of the party indicated their support for provincial legislation stressing the use of French in the province, and suggested that the Quebec English-speaking minority was already overprivileged. These two events damaged the NDP's credibility in a number of important policy areas. The post-debate period also saw another blow against the NDP — the massive intervention into the campaign by large corporations. These private interest groups spent millions of dollars on political ads criticizing the opponents of free trade. In so doing, they overwhelmed the NDP's much smaller ad campaign.

Week Six saw the Quebec French language controversy continue to dog Broadbent. Not wishing to alienate his Quebec lieutenants or potential Quebec voters, Broadbent, when asked to comment on the statement of the Gang of Seven, pleaded that as a non-Quebecer, it would be out of place for him to comment. To many Canadians who had admired Broadbent's past principled statements, this seemed a particularly opportunistic stance. It would win him no seats in Quebec and no laurels elsewhere. In the last week of the campaign the party inched upwards in the polls by stressing Main Street's values instead of Wall Street's or Bay Street's and ended the campaign with an actual vote of just over 20 percent and yet another third place finish. It was not one of Broadbent's best campaigns. Instead of a giant leap forward for socialism, the NDP had lurched ahead by mere inches.

NDP expectations declined throughout the campaign. At the issuing of the writs there was confidence that an NDP government might be formed. A few weeks later hope was for a second place finish and the status of the official opposition. With the slide to third place after the debate, NDPers speculated about a role in a minority government and hoped at least to achieve a toehold in Quebec. None of these hopes was to be realized. Still, results from the West helped to propel the NDP to a record high 20.4 percent of the national vote. With 43 MPs in the enlarged House of Commons, the party has more seats than ever before and the largest percentage of seats (14.5 percent). The NDP has 19 MPs from British Columbia, 10 from Saskatchewan, 10 from Ontario, 2 from Manitoba and one each from Alberta and the Yukon. The party, however, has no elected members East of Oshawa, Ontario. The obvious consequences of this pattern is that the NDP is perceived by many to be more a Western based party, making it more difficult for the party to adequately represent and make gains in the other regions of Canada.

Post-Election Reaction: The Labour Backlash

The focal point of the early post-election criticisms were two lengthy and stinging letters from the head of two of the largest unions affiliated with the NDP. Canadian Autoworkers president Bob White's analysis was in a seven-page letter dated Nov. 28, and Steelworkers Director Gerard Docquier's in a 12-page, Dec. 5 letter. White described the 1988 election as "disastrous." He expressed dismay that labour's "financial and people support is accepted gratefully, but its ideas and leadership are completely ignored." He condemned the inadequate attention to free trade and questioned the wisdom of the "small group running the campaign", particularly the party's American pollster who had labelled free trade as merely an economic management issue. White concluded with the declaration, "This party doesn't belong to a handful of people who ultimately think they have all the answers . . .", and although he stopped short of criticizing Broadbent directly or asking for the leader's resignation, he did call for a thorough post-mortem on the campaign.

Gerard Docquier's letter addressed what he termed the "most important Canadian election in a generation" and perhaps the "most important of this century." He suggested that the "serious problems" of the campaign were rooted in a "highly suspect plan" filled with "fundamental errors in tactics and strategy." Characterizing the central operations as too dominated by paid "employees of the party", Docquier condemned the party planners' for a "betrayal" of principles and for allowing polls to "dominate our strategy." He chastized the incapacity of the planners to adjust the strategy as events warranted and cited examples of "ineptitude" that contributed to Broadbent being "unprepared" for the free trade debate. His overall conclusion was that the "link between the trade union movement and the party at the strategic level failed completely."

Several tense post-election meetings were held, including a joint CLC-NDP gathering, a session of the federal executive and a meeting of the parliamentary caucus. The post election period saw a proliferation of formal internal reviews by special committees including one by the caucus.

Several major issues lie ahead for the NDP. One is whether it will ever be able to build a successful organizational structure in Quebec. A second involves the leadership and who will follow Ed Broadbent and guide the NDP into the next federal election.[13] The third issue, like that facing so many social democratic parties, is what policy direction to take into the 1990s. In the 1988 election the party drifted to the Right to woo the electoral centre. This strategy of trying to outperform the Liberal party in the political centre has largely failed, as New Left critics had suggested it would. A number of party members believe the party should now redirect its efforts back to the Left and return to being the conscience of the nation.

Endnotes

This article is a revised and expanded version of a paper presented to the Centre of Canadian Studies at the School of Advanced International Studies at Johns Hopkins University on Nov. 18, 1988. I am grateful for the forum provided by Professor Charles Doran and his colleagues at the Centre.

1. Since the completion of the 1988 campaign and the vocal criticism from key figures of the Canadian Autoworkers and Steelworkers unions, questions have arisen over whether there was sufficient labour representation on the SEPC. Given the growth in number of provincial representatives, labour probably should been granted greater representation . This certainly would have helped convey labour's concern about the greater emphasis on free trade in the campaign strategy.

2. Believing that socialism had little appeal to the ordinary Canadian, the campaign team made conscious effort to downplay an ideological programme and stressed instead the personality of the leader. The pamphlet itself contains no mention of the words socialism or social democracy. The party's stands on public ownership, nationalization, withdrawal from NATO and NORAD and its favouring of the right to an abortion are ignored.

3. For some time the number of individuals donating to the NDP had exceeded those contributing to the Liberal party.

4. The Chief Electoral Officer set the NDP's 1988 spending limit at $8,005,799, the same as that for

the Conservative party.

5. At the time of writing, final accounting by the NDP was not complete. Thus the numbers represent only preliminary estimates.

6. Subsequent success rates of targeted seats were as follows: 54 percent for the West, 29 percent for Ontario, and 0 percent for Quebec and Atlantic Canada.

7. This is doubly so given the bias in Canada's electoral system which does not reward a party for close second-place finishes.

8. In Jan. 1988 Gallup reported that 32 percent of all Canadians saw big labour as the greatest threat as opposed to 17 percent selecting big business. See also Alan Whitehorn, "The CCF-NDP: Fifty Years After", in Hugh Thorburn, ed., *Party Politics in Canada* (Toronto: Prentice-Hall, 1985).

9. A Nov. 15 Gallup Poll found that Canadians rated NDP ads as the least informative. See also Gerry Caplan, Michael Kirby, and Hugh Segal, *Election; The Issues, The Strategy, The Aftermath.* (Toronto: Prentice-Hall, 1989) p. 224. In 1988 television time allocations were a whopping 195 minutes for the Conservatives, 84 minutes for the Liberals and 67 minutes for the NDP (only 16 percent of the available time). As in 1984, the NDP was in third place in access to the powerful medium of television. *The Globe and Mail*, Oct. 12, 1988.

10. Many saw an uneasy parallel to the polarized wage and price controls debate in the election of 1974, an election in which the party lost substantial ground.

11. The CLC NPAC had spent the two years prior to the campaign in opposing the Mulroney government over free trade, privatization and deregulation, and had donated funds to the party to publicize the problems of free trade.

12. Rather than take only one poll of the more than 25 national public polls conducted during the campaign, a weekly average of all the polls is calculated for this and subsequent weeks. Compiled from a larger sample, such an average provides a more stable base to compare developments from week to week.

13. The December Gallup reported that 58 percent of Canadians believed Broadbent should stay on as leader, while 25 percent felt he should resign and 17 percent had no opinion.

CHAPTER 3

On The Hustings

By Peter Maser

When Governor-General Jeanne Sauvé dissolved Parliament on the foggy Ottawa morning of Oct. 1, 1988, there were few who believed the ensuing election — the 34th in Canadian history — would generate anything beyond the modest levels of interest usually produced by such exercises. With the Conservatives running well ahead in the polls and seemingly poised for a second majority government, the only serious question seemed to be whether the Liberals or the New Democrats would form the official Opposition. Fifty-one days later, on Nov. 21, the Tories emerged with their majority, followed by the Liberals and then the NDP. But in between Canadians had been treated to a rollicking, roller coaster of an election the likes of which will not soon be seen again.

What caused this was the Canada-United States Free Trade Agreement, a 1,407-page plan to eliminate tariffs over 10 years, liberalize the rules on agriculture and direct investment, grant the right of establishment and national treatment to service industries, create a common market in energy and establish a dispute settlement mechanism. It was a document few Canadians had read and fewer still understood, although that did not prevent it from becoming the emotional centrepiece of the election. In retrospect, that may not seem surprising since various forms of freer trade with the U.S had been proposed — and rejected — several times since Confederation, often amid an outpouring of passion and anger. There would be an abundance of that in 1988 as well, but it was not evident on Oct. 1 as a smiling but reserved Prime Minister Mulroney emerged from his meeting with Sauvé to announce that the election was under way.

Smiling, but reserved — it was something Canadians had been getting used to as Mulroney worked to erase the so-called sleaze factor that had dogged him and his government. Gone or sharply toned down were the looks of wounded indignation, the excesses of rhetoric, the withering partisan attacks. In their place and to the delight of his advisers, Mulroney was looking sober, dignified and prime ministerial. Sometimes he spoke so softly he could barely be heard, even with the aid of a microphone. For months his office had been functioning efficiently, the excesses of patronage had been curbed and for the most part the government had been setting its own agenda. Along with free trade, there were major commitments on day care, nuclear-powered submarines, the Meech Lake Accord and the second phase of tax reform. Together these formed the backbone of the Tory platform, although they weren't the only initiatives with vote-getting appeal. A strong economy was throwing off jobs galore, and in the run-up to the campaign, Mulroney and his ministers had announced plans for spending some $8 billion on projects ranging from an oil upgrader at Lloyd-minister, on the Alberta/Saskatchewan border, to a native land agreement in the Northwest Territories.

By making them before the election writ was dropped, the Tories could avoid these announcements during the campaign and, more important, the inevitable opposition charges that they were trying to buy the election. Harry Near, Operations Director for the Conservative campaign, would later explain that the spending was also intended to project the image of a government in control. "We wanted people to say, 'These guys have a plan'," he explained. Whether it was seen that way or not, by the time the election was called, the Conservatives had a comfortable lead in the polls and had designed a low-key, positive, campaign pitch that stressed prosperity, past and future, and sound economic management. "This election is about challenge and change and vision for the future," Mulroney said, as he set about extolling the benefits of free trade for forestry one day, agriculture the next and so on across the country, "Continue working with me for a united, prosperous and generous Canada."

If there were grumblings about the early days of the Mulroney tour they came not from the Tories but from critics who complained that the Prime Minister was running a tightly-scripted American-style campaign. In fact, Mulroney was running a tightly-scripted campaign, although it was hardly fair to call it American. In 1980, an equally inaccessible Pierre Trudeau conducted what became known as the "peek-a-boo" campaign, and the whole process of keeping a leader under wraps had been dubbed "low-bridging." In practice it required a controlled agenda that left little room for spontaneity or error. In Trudeau's case, it helped carry him and the Liberals back to power. In Mulroney's case, there was plenty of squawking from the press corps and the opposition parties. According to Conservative polls, however, the public were so pleased that three weeks into the campaign they were ready to elect him and some 200 of his fellow candidates, a remarkable turnaround from the unpopularity that hounded them through much of their mandate.

Although they could never say so publicly — it would look like gloating — a good part of the Tories' success lay in the disintegration of Turner and the Liberals. As they entered the campaign, it was possible to believe the Liberals were still capable of adequacy if not competence. In the week before the election, they had released a coherent and generally progressive policy platform that, among other things, called for tough new environmental laws, the scrapping of phase two of the tax reform package and a new national housing policy that included tax breaks on mortgage interest payments. The problem was that the Liberals were wracked by internal problems and lacked money, morale, and leadership. What frustrated many ex-loyalists was Turner's poor people skills and, more important, his chronic inability to make a decision and then stick to it. Why this was so became a subject of considerable speculation among political junkies. Did it result from a lack of firm, personal convictions? Was it a case of mental flabbiness after too many years on Bay Street? Whatever the cause, the man who had once been trumpeted as a saviour came to be widely seen as a monumental flop, a leader unable to impose a sense of direction on a caucus and party that badly needed it.

The result was anger, disappointment, confusion, inconsistency and some highly-embarassing splits on issues like trade, cruise missile tests and the Meech Lake Accord. All too frequently the frustration would produce a challenge to Turner's leadership, but ironically, these revolts seemed to invigorate him, and he often gave his best performances when somebody was calling for his resignation. This ability to concentrate his mind and energies in short bursts would eventually have a dramatic impact on the election. But as the campaign got under way, the outlook for the Liberals was decidedly bleak. After years of bickering and bad publicity, the party's popularity was low and Turner's was lower still. On polls that asked respondents to rate the performances of the three party leaders, Turner invariably scored below the don't knows and the none of the aboves. Liberals told jokes about him:

Question: What do we do if Turner goes for three days without a mistake?
Answer: We get him tested for steroids.

The party's campaign literature barely mentioned him. But as bad as things were, they were about to get worse.

On Oct. 5, the bus carrying Turner, his aides and a contingent of reporters arrived in Montreal to announce how the Liberals planned to create 400,000 new day care spaces. The day had begun on a bad note. A poll by Angus Reid Associates showed the Tories with 45 percent of the decided vote, against 27 for the NDP and 26 for the Liberals. Then came news that veteran Liberal MP Keith Penner had decided not to seek re-election because, he said, it would take a miracle for Turner to win. Paul Martin, a Liberal candidate in Montreal and one of the few big names the party had been able to attract, gamely told reporters he believed in miracles. But when it came time for the day care policy, the announcement was so badly botched that it seemed those involved were trying to prove Penner right.

What got everyone into trouble were the related questions of how many day care spaces could be created and for how much money. While Turner set the price at $4 billion, his principal secretary, Peter Connolly, said it "could be $8 billion, it could be $10 billion." MP Raymond Garneau, Turner's Quebec lieutenant and the caucus finance critic, said it would cost less than $4 billion. Connolly then vowed a Liberal government would ensure that "no small child shall go in need of day care." Turner was more restrained, saying a Liberal government would create the 400,000 spaces and then reassess the programme. Because every moment of confusion had been captured on film and replayed on the evening news, the announcement was a public relations disaster. But it wasn't over.

Three long days later, in one of the most embarrassing moments of the campaign, the Liberals summoned the media for a "clarification" and announced that, yes, their programme would create 400,000 spaces, but that the cost would be a tad higher than expected, $10.1 billion over seven years. Connolly, a bluff Irishman known for cancelling appointments and for being away from Turner's office, took responsibility for the botch-up, but was back in the news a few days later for yelling and swearing at a reporter in a major Toronto hotel in full view of other patrons. Still, it wasn't over.

In mid-October, Liberals were horrified to learn that party pollster Martin Goldfarb and former Trudeau principal secretary Tom Axworthy had written a book in which they accused Turner of being out of touch with traditional Liberal values. The authors defended themselves, lamely in the eyes of many, by saying the book had been written a year earlier and that Turner had since redeemed himself by endorsing the party's election platform. At any rate, Goldfarb added, the book wouldn't do Turner or the party much damage because, as he noted, the Liberals by this time had fallen about as low as they could go. That same week, a survey by the polling firm Environics found the Liberals with 25 percent of decided support, four points behind the NDP and 17 behind the Tories.

And it still wasn't over. On Oct. 19, CBC television told its viewers that senior Liberal strategists had met several days earlier and discussed the "impact of an immediate change of leadership." While the CBC never flatly stated that a plot had been concocted, that was certainly the impression created by the report and it touched off a storm of protest. The story may in the end have worked to Turner's benefit by creating a wave of sympathy for him. This was certainly true of some reporters who began to describe Turner in a more favourable light in the wake of the CBC report. Suddenly he was showing guts, inner resolve, strength in the face of pain and adversity. The pain was genuine, the result of a pinched nerve in his back that left him with a slight but noticeable limp that invariably caught the attention of the television cameras. Night after night the TV news would show him hobbling into a meeting hall or onto a stage to talk about housing or day care, but always returning to what he described as "the cause of my life."

The cause was the free trade agreement, which he had sworn to scrap. By dint of honing and polishing his thoughts over the previous weeks and months, Turner had forged an attack that he knew by heart and which he made the cornerstone of the Liberal campaign:

> The Mulroney trade deal will fundamentally alter our way of life. The Mulroney trade deal endangers our social programmes and regional development programmes, and sacrifices our farmers, our industries, our fishermen, our miners, our lumber workers, our auto workers and our textile workers to satisfy Brian Mulroney's desire to fulfill the American dream. I will not let Brian Mulroney, by a stroke of the pen, sell out our sovereignty, our national heritage, our distinctive cultural identity. I will not let this great country surrender its birthright. I will not let Brian Mulroney destroy a 120-year-old dream called Canada, and neither will Canadians. I believe that on election day, Nov. 21, Canadians will understand that a vote for the Liberal party is a vote for a stronger, fairer, more independent,

unique, strong, proud Canada. I believe Canadians are not going to vote for Brian Mulroney, a man who would be governor of a 51st state. They are going to vote for John Turner, whose ambition is to be prime minister of a proud Canada.

Delivered to partisan crowds with an intensity Turner had rarely displayed in the previous four years, the speech left them screaming for more. But as the polls continued to show, most Canadians didn't care what Turner was saying. Indeed, only 11 days after the election began, NDP leader Ed Broadbent perceived things to be going so poorly for the Liberals that he predicted they would soon follow their British cousins into irrelevance, if not oblivion. It was a remarkably arrogant statement and one he would come to regret, but then the campaign at that point was clearly running more smoothly for the New Democrats and their highly popular leader.

For Broadbent, it was the fourth time in 13 years that he had led his party in a national election, although none of the earlier campaigns had given him and them as much hope as the current one. In mid-1987, thanks in large measure to the Liberals' internal difficulties and the Tories' sorry image, New Democrats found themselves leading in public opinion surveys for the first time since their party's creation in 1961. The bubble eventually suffered a slow leak, so that by the time the 1988 election was called the NDP was in second or third place, depending on the poll. Still, with their share of the decided support running at around 25 to 30 percent, they were well ahead of the 18-percent level that marked their finishing point in the 1984 election. In Broadbent also they had a leader whom Canadians saw as far more open, honest and credible than Mulroney or Turner.

Not surprisingly, the NDP played to its strength by using Broadbent to remind audiences of the considerable gap between what Mulroney had promised and what he had delivered across a whole range of issues. Free trade was a natural since Mulroney had emphatically rejected it during the Conservative leadership race of 1983. So was the environment. Mulroney had promised in 1984 to make it a "top priority," but had then squeezed federal agencies for funding and manpower. Acid rain, taxes, patronage and pensions — all of them were ammunition for Broadbent's assaults. To drive home the points, he would ask his audiences to pass judgement on Mulroney's promises, a technique that invariably produced a succession of hearty "No's." For example, he would describe the government's attempt to de-index pensions after Mulroney had promised they would be strengthened, and ask:

Did Brian Mulroney keep this promise?
No, the audience would roar.
Did Brian Mulroney keep his promise on free trade?
No, they would roar again.

Remarkably, although the NDP and its allies had been attacking free trade harder than the Liberals were before the election, it was the Liberals who gave it a higher profile once the campaign began. The NDP approach was to weave it into its package of policy pronouncements, which ranged from a new department of consumer affairs to a $600-million aid programme for farmers to lower federal taxes on gasoline. Anticipating accusations that it couldn't be trusted to manage the country's economy, the party was also careful to put a price tag on its pledges and explain where the money would come from.

In his first stop of the campaign, which happened to be Montreal, Broadbent predicted his next caucus would include some 20 MPs from Quebec. Spooked by the prospect of free trade, Louis Laberge, the rotund, chain-smoking President of the Quebec Federation of Labor, pledged the support of his 450,000 members to help make it happen. "We have a true chance of giving ourselves a government for the people," said Laberge, whose endorsement of the NDP made headlines in every major Quebec newspaper and prompted speculation that the New Democrats were really going to achieve their long-awaited breakthrough in the province. Not everyone was convinced. Some observers questioned how Laberge would succeed where others had failed to deliver the votes of union members. Others questioned the NDP's inexperience in Quebec where the people in charge were innocents like Donald Houle, a well-intentioned soul with virtually no track record in politics.

As inflated as they were, the NDP's expectations for Quebec were sober compared to those being floated by the Liberals. Under the 16-year reign of Pierre Trudeau, the Liberals had considered Quebec a private preserve. In 1980, they won all but one of its 75 seats. No one in the party was expecting to duplicate those results in 1988, but some truly thought they could take 30 to 40 seats. In reality, the Liberals in Quebec were on the wrong side of free trade, the wrong side of Premier Robert Bourassa, and at least parts of the party were on the wrong side of Meech Lake. It was official Liberal policy to endorse the Accord, and most Liberal MPs supported it on the two occasions it came to a vote in the House of Commons. But there were also some strong Liberal voices opposing Meech Lake, notably those of Trudeau and Jean Chrétien, and because of that and other policy positions, the party developed an image of being out of touch with Quebec, if not hostile to the interests of its francophone majority.

In contrast, the Conservatives were on the right side of Meech Lake, the right side of free trade and the right side of Bourassa. In fact, on the free trade issue, the Tories were on the right side of virtually the entire business and political elite in Quebec. This included the Parti Québécois, which believed free trade would hasten the onset of Quebec's independence. In Mulroney the Tories also had a bilingual native son who could remind Quebecers of who he was and where he had come from with the two words "chez nous," meaning "our home." If the Conservatives had a weakness in Quebec, it was on the island of Montreal, the only area in the province where they had failed to make big gains in 1984. But as the campaign unfolded and the Liberals began to collapse, Conservative campaign co-chairman Senator Michel Cogger started revising his estimates upwards. He was already confident of 50 to 55 seats, the bulk of them outside Montreal. But if the Liberals continued to lose ground, as seemed likely, it would mean big gains for the Tories in the metropolis, maybe as many as 10 to 15. Overall, Cogger thought it possible the Tories could emerge from Quebec with 65 to 70 seats, a projection supported by increasingly favourable polls.

Indeed, as the first phase of the campaign wound down, the national polls showed the Conservatives headed for a massive victory with strong support in every region of the country. Not surprisingly, the New Democrats had edged into second place while the hapless Liberals had dropped to third. Before the campaign began, Liberal strategists were talking of the need for Turner to get off to an impressive start. Now they were pinning everything on the leaders' debates scheduled for Oct. 24 and 25. Said Ray Heard, Turner's director of communications: "The debate is the single most important event in the campaign."

Election debates are much like an all-star break in professional sports. In preparation, the leaders abandon their tours in favour of cramming and coaching. The media and the country take stock of what has happened in the campaign (season) to date and to play odds makers for the coming encounter (game). The 1988 version was made all the more interesting by the fact that Mulroney, Turner and Broadbent were taking another run at each other after their first confrontation in 1984 had dramatically affected the course of that year's election.

In preparation for the 1988 debates, all three leaders hunkered down with briefing books and advisers, but only Turner conducted rehearsals in a rented television studio with aides substituting for Mulroney and Broadbent. Also present was Henry Comor, an actor, director and playwright, and one of the few professionals Turner was able to attract and keep on his staff. In layman's parlance, Comor was Turner's media coach, meaning he helped him with what he said and how he said it, especially on television. This included everything from cadence to eye contact to keeping calm, which was no easy feat for Turner. As one of Turner's aides once said, "He always seems to be churning inside." Comor was particularly effective in keeping Turner composed, an accomplishment that resulted in one wag dubbing him "the human valium."

The format for the debates was worked out over several days of bitter bargaining among representatives of the three parties. The opposition parties began by demanding two debates in each official language, but ultimately settled for one three-hour debate in French and a second one the following night in English. The three hours were divided into nine 17-minute segments, each of which allowed two of the leaders to square off while the third waited in the wings. At no time did all three have at one another.

The effect of Comor's training was evident in the French debate. Looking controlled and confident in his attacks on Mulroney, Turner emerged as the clear winner in the eyes of many Quebec commentators. Others called it a stalemate, but agreed Turner and Mulroney were the only real contenders. As for Broadbent, he was universally declared the loser, in large measure because he frequently made no sense. "Even after all those summer immersion courses in Jonquiere, his French was still so weak that he was often incomprehensible," wrote Don MacPherson of the Montreal Gazette. At times it was impossible to understand the "mush" coming out of Broadbent's mouth, said La Presse columnist Pierre Foglia.

Broadbent wasn't laboring under the same handicap the following night. On paper at least, he and Mulroney and Turner were on equal footing. In practice, however, there was no comparison as Turner put on what was probably the most compelling performance of his political career. Mulroney's strategy for the debate was to look and sound prime ministerial. Instead he appeared so cautious that his former press secretary felt compelled to tear him to shreds the next day. "A lousy, stale, uninspiring, dispassionate performance by the man who is seeking re-election. He should have done much better," ranted Michel Gratton, who had left Mulroney's office in 1987 to become a columnist for the Montreal Daily News.

No such charges could be levelled at Turner, who used the first opportunity to attack Mulroney on patronage and political morality, the very issues that Mulroney had used against him four years earlier. Referring to the scandals and controversies in Mulroney's government, Turner vowed that he would lead an administration in which his ministers would be in the cabinet room defending the public interest and "not in the court room defending themselves." Despite Mulroney's promises to do better than the previous Liberal administration, he charged, the Prime Minister had run up a "sorry" record of patronage appointments, cabinet resignations and police inquiries. Eventually the goading proved too much for Mulroney's fabled Irish temper, and he found himself in a slanging match. Unfortunately it was on free trade, and Turner was not about to be denied the cause of his life.

> Turner: I happen to believe you sold us out as a country. I happen to believe. . . .
> Mulroney: You do not have a monopoly on patriotism and I resent . . . . your implication that only you are a Canadian. I want to tell you that I come from a Canadian family and I love Canada, and that's why I did it, to promote prosperity and don't you impugn my motives.
> Turner: Once any country yields its economic levers, once a country yields its energy . . . .
> Mulroney: We have not done it.
> Turner: Once a country yields its agriculture . . . .
> Mulroney: Wrong again.
> Turner: Once a country yields itself to a subsidy war with the United States . . . .
> Mulroney: Wrong again.
> Turner: The political ability of this country to sustain the political influence of the United States, to remain as an independent nation — that is lost forever and that is the issue of this election.
> Mulroney: Mr. Turner, Mr. Turner. Let me tell you something, sir. This country is only about 120 years old, but my own father 55 years

ago went himself as a laborer with hundreds of others Canadians, and with their own hands in northeastern Quebec they built a little town, schools and churches, and they in their own way were nation building. In the same way that the waves of immigrants from the Ukraine and Eastern Europe rolled back the Prairies and in their own way, in their own time, they were nation building because they loved Canada. I today, sir, as a Canadian, believe genuinely in what I am doing. I believe it is right for Canada. I believe that in my own modest way I am nation building because I believe this benefits Canada and I love Canada.

Turner: I admire your father, (who) worked for what he did. My grandfather moved into British Columbia. My mother was a miner's daughter there. We are just as Canadian as you are Mr. Mulroney. But I tell you this. You mentioned 120 years of history. We built a country east and west and north. We built it on an infrastructure that deliberately resisted the continental pressure of the United States. For 120 years we've done it. With one signature of a pen, you've reversed that, thrown us into the north-south influence of the United States and will reduce us, I am sure, to a colony of the United States because when the economic levers go, the political independence is sure to follow.

Mulroney: Mr. Turner, the document is cancellable on six months' notice. Be serious. Be serious!

Turner: Cancellable? You are talking about our relationship with the United States . . . .

Mulroney: A commercial document that is cancellable on six months' notice.

Turner: Commercial document? That document relates to treaty. It relates to every facet of our lives. It is far more important to us than it is to the United States.

Mulroney: Mr. Turner. . .

Turner: Far more important.

Mulroney: Please be serious.

Turner: Well I am serious, and I've never been more serious in all my life.

Mulroney: Please.

Moderator: Gentlemen, we will move on to the next question from (reporter) Doug Small.

Doug Small: I would be quite happy just to let them go right on rolling on that if they had anything more to say.

Moderator: I think the issue has been exhausted.

In fact, thanks to Turner, free trade was about to turn the whole election on its head. In three short hours, the Liberal leader had redeemed himself for his disastrous performance in the 1984 debate, injected new life into the Liberal campaign, established himself as the only real alternative to Mulroney, raised the profile of the trade issue and then taken command of it. To boot, more than six million Canadians had watched at least part of the debate, with an estimated 1.8 million tuning in the night before to the French debate. It didn't take long for polls to confirm what those viewers already knew. Two days after the confrontation, a poll commissioned by CTV news showed 59 percent of eligible voters thought Turner had won, 16 percent had chosen Mulroney and a mere 11 percent Broadbent. Although he didn't do poorly in the English debate, the NDP leader had allowed Turner to dominate the trade question and push him around on other issues, notably defence. The irony for Turner was that he had done nothing new. The passion, the aggressiveness, the apparent mastery of the trade deal, all these had been on display in weeks previous. The problem then was that most Canadians had reasonably dismissed him as a klutz and were unwilling to pay him much heed. By performing well in the debate, he far exceeded expectations and caused voters to reassess their opinion of him, which they did with a vengeance.

Equally inspiring to the Liberals were the results that showed growing doubts about the free trade agreement. According to a Reid poll in late October, 36 percent of voters were strongly opposed to the pact and another 18 percent were moderately opposed. It also revealed that the Liberals had emerged as the champions of the anti-free trade forces.

The release of these polls triggered a drop in the Canadian dollar and jitters on the stock market, changes that market analysts attributed to fears for the survival of the trade deal if the Liberals won the election. For Turner, however, the blame lay with Mulroney and not the surge in Liberal support. "Frankly," he said, "if we are looking for uncertainty, I would think that the declaration made by the Prime Minister last week . . . that he treated the trade agreement as just another commercial contract subject to six months' notice must have provoked more uncertainty in the ranks of the business community than any other thing he has said in four years."

Turner's bullishness was common to virtually all Liberals, who really didn't need pollsters to tell them they were doing well. In the days following the debates, attendance at their rallies increased, party workers bubbled with new vigor, financial contributions jumped, the number of volunteers increased and, as several insiders noted, phone calls that had previously gone unanswered were miraculously being returned. This was particularly true of the business community, which was still publicly supportive of free trade, but wasn't about to ignore a possible Liberal government in the making. As for Turner, he returned to the campaign trail and his self-styled "crusade for Canada" with evangelical fervor. In the Maritimes it was a warning about the impact of free trade on regional development assistance. In Quebec and the West it was the death of the family farm. In Ontario it was the end of social programmes. "The next time I'm back here I'll be prime minister," he boldly predicted during a stop in Halifax.

Much of Turner's argumentation was suspect if not misleading. On medicare and other social benefits, for example, it had long been established in U.S. law that programmes of wide application could not be targeted for countervailing duties. And with health care costs in Canada lower than those in the U.S., it made no sense to say that Canadian companies would push to get rid of programmes in order to make themselves more competitive. However, in the era of the 10-second television clip, it was much easier to say medicare was doomed and then harvest the emotional whirlwind that followed. Indeed, as the election moved into November, the substance of the free trade pact was almost lost from the centre stage of the campaign. In its place, on the Liberal side, emerged a powerful appeal to fear and insecurity that for a time worked as well for Turner as it had for Sir John A. Macdonald and Sir Robert Borden in past elections on free trade. "It is an old debate being played out in a new way," said University of Toronto historian Michael Bliss. "Once you unleash the deep-seated Canadian fear of being taken over by the United States, it is pretty potent." Veteran journalist Bruce Hutchison agreed: "Canadians have always been viscerally frightened of becoming a colony of the United States. And by going for broke on free trade, Turner has played to those fears with great success."

Another great success was the Liberals' television advertising. In one, two images of Mulroney were joined back to back while the sound track carried two statements he had made, one in favour of free trade, the other opposing it. At the end an announcer concluded: "Say one thing, mean another. Don't let Mulroney deceive you again." A second commercial was even more memorable. Simple, but devastatingly effective, it depicted a U.S. trade negotiator erasing the Canada-U.S. border. Polling showed concerns over free trade to be particularly acute among senior citizens and low income earners, two groups that were heavily dependent on Canada's social safety net.

Watching seniors as he campaigned for free trade, Bernard Landry was reminded of the Quebec referendum. Now a university professor in Montreal, Landry was Quebec's minister of economic development in 1980 and a strong proponent of sovereignty-association. As he toured the province to promote the "Yes" side that year, he found himself in an old age home where a woman asked him if she'd still be able to get oranges in an independent Quebec. He assured her that a victory for the "Yes" forces would threaten neither her pension nor her medical care nor Quebec's ability to import oranges. But according to Landry, the woman had been so frightened by the opponents of sovereignty-association that she was unable to grasp the full meaning of what he'd said: "She told me: 'You look honest, Mr. Landry, and I believe you on the oranges. But what will we do for bananas?'" The same fears were at work in the 1988 election, he added. "I was talking to some seniors the other day and I saw exactly the same thing. It takes five minutes to scare someone to death and two hours to calm them down. And you can't get to them all." Those sentiments were echoed by Youth Minister Jean Charest. "We're trying to get to the seniors before the Liberals do. If they get to them first, there's no bringing them back."

As many Quebecers noted, the fear among seniors was not the only similarity between the election and the referendum. In both instances the "No" forces were spearheaded by federal Liberals. In some instances the same players were involved, Jean Chrétien and Monique Bégin, for example. The difference was that the Liberals in 1980 had urged Quebecers to reject the narrow confines of nationalism for the great world beyond. In the election of 1988, they wrapped themselves in the maple leaf and talked endlessly of Canada's identity and heritage. The contradiction drew a stern warning from Secretary of State Lucien Bouchard, who detected a plot by Ontario to retain its economic clout in the country. "In 1980, Ontarians came to Quebec to tell us 'You are ghettoizing yourselves. Don't do that. Open to the world instead. Do like us,'" said Bouchard, who supported the "Yes" side in the referendum. "Well, they convinced us. Quebec chose not to separate, and to become an active partner in Confederation and to open up to the world. Now they want us to stop? It gives me the impression that Quebec is the one playing straight and that Ontario has become the separatist force, the one that wants to go it alone. That makes me angry."

Angry also was Ontario Premier David Peterson when informed of Bouchard's remarks. "This is a man that tried to ruin the country over a separatist vote and now he's trying to do it over free trade," he snapped. "I think it's destructive to the fabric of this country to pit region against region." The rebuke didn't stop the sniping from Quebec. A few days later Transport Minister Benoit Bouchard appealed to "average Ontarians" to support the trade deal: "Quebec and Western Canada should also be given a crack at economic development through tariff-less trade with the United States. To reject free trade would carry heavy consequences. I want to tell Ontarians as loud and clear as I can: 'Don't forget that you are holding the key to the economic future of this country.'"

The Tory preoccupation with Ontario was understandable. Nourished by Peterson, the union movement and the *Toronto Star*, the opposition to free trade had put down deep roots in the province, particularly in the south. It was here the Liberals focussed their energy and resources, and expected to harvest their biggest yields. In early November, Liberal insiders were talking confidently of winning 60 seats in Ontario, perhaps more. Combine that with 35 in Quebec, 16 to 20 in Altantic Canada and another 30 from the West and you had the makings of a minority government, they argued. Certainly no pundit was ready to bet against them at that point. Turner's crusade to "wake up Canada" appeared strong, and polls continued to show the party tied with, or running slightly ahead of, the Tories.

But for the second time in this campaign, the momentum was about to shift, imperceptibly at first and then with the force of a Fundy tide. It actually started in late October when senior Tories began assessing the damage from the debates and Turner's assault on free trade. One question that intrigued observers was why they hadn't foreseen the predicament they were in and taken steps to avoid it. "We knew the unease (about free trade) was there," strategist Bill Neville said after the election. "But the closer you were to the agreement, the more disbelief you had that it would be possible to make people believe this agreement was going to cost them their pensions or medical services. It seemed such an outlandish assertion, I guess we didn't believe it had any credibility." They certainly did after the debates. When the election began, surveys by Tory pollster Allan Gregg showed only one third of Canadians believed free trade threatened their social programmes. After the debates, because of Turner, that number had jumped to 50 percent. "All of a sudden, John Turner, bang!, gives us a glimpse of his soul," said Gregg in a post-election interview. "He has a performance that is consistent with the leadership wants of the electorate — emotion, spontaneity and motive."

In the process, Turner re-ordered the election agenda, shifting the focus from the sleep-inducing question of who could manage economic change to the gut-wrenching question of who could save the country from free trade. But Gregg's numbers were also offering the Tories an avenue for counter attack and recovery. It was clear Turner had emerged from the debates a new man. Like Clark Kent in a telephone booth, he had gone in a loser and come out a credible leader. More important, his new-found credibility was, as Gregg could see, the bridge between the growing fear of free trade and the growing support for the Liberal party. "What we had to do was bomb the bridge," said Gregg. "And that is precisely what we proceeded to do."

The first bomb came from Finance Minister Michael Wilson, a man not usually given to strong language or excesses of emotion. But in a speech to an Ottawa luncheon crowd on Oct. 31, Wilson angrily accused Turner of lying. "John Turner in the debate Tuesday night said (Mulroney) has agreed to let the Americans have a say in the future of our social programmes such as unemployment insurance and medicare. I say to Mr. Turner, that is a lie," he charged. "Taking this lie into our senior citizens' homes is the cruellest form of campaigning that I've seen in 10 years in politics. When politicians feel that they have to prey upon the fears and emotions of some of the most defenceless people in our society today, I say that is despicable." The assault begun by Wilson was carried to other fronts. The Tories distributed five million copies of a tabloid paper promoting free-trade, and new television commercials zeroed in on Turner's competence. Questions were raised about what kind of cabinet he would be able to form. "People will have to decide whether they want Michael Wilson or John Nunziata for minister of finance" became an oft-repeated Tory line. Nunziata was a Liberal MP and a charter member of the so-called rat pack, a group of young backbenchers who made names for themselves by loudly harassing the government. It pleased the Tories no end when *The Globe and Mail's* Jeffrey Simpson described the slate of Liberal candidates as the weakest in this century: "If John Turner should win, his cabinet would surely be among the shallowest in the history of Canada, simply because he will have so little talent from which to choose."

To highlight the difference between themselves and the Liberals, Tory cabinet ministers showed up in strength for major events. Mulroney, meanwhile, accused Turner of being "deceitful" and "dishonest," and ridiculed his claim that free trade would reduce jobs: "It's pretty clear that the only job John Turner is interested in protecting is his own." Other questions were raised about the cost of the Liberal promises announced earlier in the campaign. When asked about this,

Turner's stock reply was that he couldn't be certain until he'd seen the country's books. The Tories answered by saying the books were open. And since the Liberals weren't saying how much Liberal promises would cost, the Tories gladly supplied a figure — $37 billion over four years. Moreover, they warned, the Liberal pledge to tear up the free trade deal would threaten two million jobs in Canada and might force the Americans to revoke the 1965 Canada-U.S auto pact. Remember as well, they added, that the Liberals had campaigned against wage and price controls in 1974 and then reversed themselves the following year. Maybe they were deceiving Canadians again. Maybe they really intended to implement the trade deal, but had to say they wouldn't just to get themselves elected.

Such assertions were questionable, or in some cases pure fantasy, but by this point the election had degenerated into the political equivalent of mud wrestling. Speaking on Canada AM one morning, Liberal campaign strategist Michael Kirby elegantly compared the business community's support for the Tories to an endorsement by the Ku Klux Klan. The Prime Minister was not above shaving the truth when, during a swing through Montreal, he warned that the election of a Liberal government would have the effect of "killing the free trade agreement and the Meech Lake Accord." While it was true that Turner had promised to rip up the trade pact, he had never said he would scuttle the Accord. Only days earlier, during the English-language debate, Turner had described the accord as imperfect and said there were parts of it that could be improved. In the same breath, however, he clearly stated that he would not re-open the package, a far cry from the intentions imputed to him by Mulroney.

In one of the crudest remarks of the campaign, Mulroney also asked voters to imagine a New Democrat cabinet with MP Svend Robinson as minister of defence. Robinson was an acknowledged homosexual and Mulroney insisted he meant no offence, but there probably wasn't a redneck in the country who believed him.

Meanwhile, on the centre stage of the campaign, the Conservatives were given an enormous boost by Emmett Hall, the former justice of the Supreme Court of Canada whose Royal Commission on health care in the 1960s paved the way for Canada's medicare system. He stated publicly after studying the deal, "If I had found that there was in this free trade agreement provisions which would damage medicare, I would have opposed this agreement because medicare is one of the things I hold dearest in life today." Asked if the opposition parties were deliberately lying about the deal, Hall replied: "No, I think they are doing it to get votes, to frighten the people into voting for them." Liberals and New Democrats rejected Hall's arguments, saying his contribution to the establishment of medicare didn't make him an expert on the implications of free trade. Replied the 89-year-old Hall: "I understand it, I think, better than either one of them or the two of them put together." In Quebec, a similar message was delivered by Claude Castonguay, the wildly successful businessman who served as the province's health minister in the early 1970s. "With free trade, our social programmes have many more possibilities for being maintained and even improved," he told a press conference. "More than anything else, it's the level of activity and economic prosperity that allows us to support and develop our social programmes." These endorsements, particularly the one from Hall, fitted perfectly with Gregg's plan for bombing Turner's credibility. Who better to defend medicare than the man who was credited with founding it? And if Hall was right on that issue, then Turner must be wrong and his other allegations must be suspect.

In one of the more memorable quotes of the year, poet and writer Margaret Atwood declared: "This (free trade) deal severely limits our power to introduce any new initiatives on the cultural front. It gives us not more freedom of movement but much less. Our national animal is the beaver, noted for its industry and co-operative spirit. In medieval bestiaries, it is also noted for its habit, when frightened, of biting off its own testicles and offering it to its pursuer. I hope we are not succumbing to some form of that impulse." The cultural community was no monolith, however, and many artists spoke out in favour of free trade. They included a group of 63 artists and writers whose names appeared under the following statement in newspaper ads: "There is no threat to our national identity anywhere in the agreement. Nor is there a threat to any form of Canadian cultural expression. As artists and writers, we reject the suggestion that our ability to create depends upon the denial of economic opportunities to our fellow citizens. What we make is to be seen and read by the whole world. The spirit of protectionism is the enemy of art and of thought." Among those who signed were Alex Colville, Ken Danby, Robert Fulford and Mordecai Richler.

An even stronger defence of free trade was mounted by the business community. In the 1911 election, which rang with the cry of "No truck nor trade with the Yankees," business was four-square against reciprocity. In 1988, it was overwhelmingly in favour and expressed its support in several ways — speeches, debates, letters, advertisements, information sessions with employees and inserts in newspapers. Kirby's reference to the Ku Klux Klan clearly showed he saw something sinister in this. So did Turner, who charged that "big business, led by American multinationals, are now trying to buy this election."

But as the campaign approached mid-November, some observers sensed the Liberals were beginning to wither under the Tories' attacks and the third-party endorsements of free trade. Goldfarb's polling indicated they might be able to open a second front on the issue of the national sales tax. Instead their campaign remained locked on free trade, which in time began to sound stale. They also suffered from exaggerated rhetoric, which invited scepticism and undermined their own credibility. A case in point was Turner's assertion that free trade would undermine efforts to liberalize global trade and reduce the gap between rich and poor nations. As a result, he concluded, the trade deal posed a threat to world peace. Reading this in the Montreal *Gazette* drew a chuckle from Jacques Parizeau, leader of the Parti Québécois and a respected economist. "The only thing that isn't threatened by free trade is the ozone layer," he laughed.

Another example was Monique Bégin's broad hint that free trade would lead to an increase in AIDS cases in Canada. According to Bégin, free trade would lead to private blood banks that would buy blood from drug addicts and pass on "certain illnesses." The suggestion drew a stinging rebuke from Lysiane Gagnon, columnist for *La Presse*: "For an arsenal that's already well stocked with demagogy, AIDS as a consequence of free trade reaches a new peak." The Liberals were also suffering internally from what one insider described at the time as a bout of "bloody" arrogance. As the party's fortunes increased in early November, so too did the expectations of MPs and candidates, he said. "They started talking about cabinet posts, who was going to do this, who was going to do that. This is when it turned around. We felt so bloody arrogant about winning, we stopped making the effort to win."

By the middle of November, the Conservatives' inner circle was confident of victory. Unlike the public, the Tories had access to fresh polling data every day, and that data showed them headed for a substantial victory, 170 to 180 seats in Gregg's opinion. As Operations Director Near would later explain: "We had the agenda back. People were questioning John Turner and his motives; they were looking at him and Mulroney and their competence, and there was no contest. Once the Liberals lost the free trade issue, they had nothing else left." Liberal pollster Goldfarb agreed: "We had to demonstrate that we were more than a one-issue party. As soon as we made this a referendum (on free trade), we lost the ability to tell the population that we could run the country." It was also clear, he said, that the Tory attacks on Turner had taken their toll. "They degraded Turner in their ads, with their speeches, with their spokespeople — to the point that people would not trust him."

Indeed they wouldn't. Tory polling immediately after the debates showed 55 percent of Canadians believed he opposed the trade deal out of personal conviction. By the end of the election only 27 percent held that view.

But if the Liberal campaign was flagging, they at least had the consolation of knowing they had been first and would almost certainly finish second. There was no such comfort for New Democrats, who were watching their dreams slowly turn to ash. Simply stated, the NDP had been eclipsed by the Liberals. While Turner was exhorting Canadians to, "Wake up, wake before it's too late," Broadbent was sticking doggedly to his timetable of policy announcements, including enriched pensions for seniors, a minimum tax on business, and a corporate tax to clean up the environment. These might have sold well in another election, but in the 1988 showdown they were no match for Turner's fevered warnings on free trade. Even Stephen Lewis gave the Liberal leader credit for outmanoeuvring the NDP on the issue. "I have to admit the debate was a turning point," said Lewis, a former ambassador to the United Nations and a former leader of the Ontario NDP.

In addition to trade, the New Democrats tumbled badly on language, Canada's very own tar baby. On Nov. 4, seven NDP candidates in Quebec held a press conference in which they announced that Quebec's English-speaking community had it too good and that the province's five million francophones required new tools to "keep the wolves at bay." Specifically they proposed that Quebec be the only province with access to the notwithstanding clause in the constitution, that Ottawa promote bilingualism in all provinces except Quebec, and that the "distinct society" clause in the Meech Lake Accord take precedence over the individual freedoms in the Charter of Rights. Michael Agnaieff, a senior NDP strategist in Quebec and one of the group of seven, acknowledged that the ideas marked a major departure from the party's traditional, centralist stands. "But we're working in the short, medium and long term," he added, "We are building a party." Remarkably, the seven had made their announcement with the blessing of NDP headquarters, which apparently thought it would do some good. Instead it prompted a wave of denunciations from anglophones and other NDP candidates who were infuriated by what they saw as a cynical and opportunistic attempt to court nationalist voters in Quebec. Naturally this all made headlines and left the NDP worse off than they were to begin with.

To minimize the damage inflicted by the seven, an NDP strategy meeting in Ottawa concluded that Broadbent should visit Quebec only under controlled circumstances. The advice was ignored or overruled and he was back in the province a few days later with no controls at all. Predictably, he got into trouble. The setting was a press conference on a small boat bobbing up and down on the St. Lawrence River off Quebec City. Asked about the province's controversial language law, Bill 101, Broadbent said, "I can't decide as an outsider. . . . It's not up to me to do it, it's up to the people of the province of Quebec." For someone who had hopes of leading the country, it was a truly astounding statement. Language has been a defining feature of Canada since its conception and here was a would-be candidate for prime minister telling the national media he had nothing to say about it. Making matters worse, the media remembered how Broadbent had criticized the Saskatchewan government some months earlier over a bill affecting francophone rights in that province.

In an attempt to re-orient the NDP campaign, it was decided that Broadbent would spend more time attacking Turner and denouncing both him and Mulroney as corporate lackeys. Throughout the election, Mulroney had been cast as the voice of New York's Wall Street. Henceforth Turner would be portrayed as the voice of Toronto's Bay Street, while he, Broadbent, would speak on behalf of Main Street. "The priorities of John Turner and Brian Mulroney are the same — they are the priorities of Wall Street or Bay Street. The priorities of New Democrats are your priorities," he told a Toronto audience. The problem with this new attack was that it wasn't really new; the NDP was plagiarizing itself. In the 1984 election, they had taken great delight in describing Mulroney and Turner as "Mastercard" and "VISA," or the Bobbsey twins of Bay Street. While it was fresh the first time, recycled as Wall Street, Bay Street and Main Street, it sounded flat, a reflection of the NDP campaign as a whole. Broadbent acknowledged as much in mid-November when he told reporters the NDP no longer had its sights trained on winning the election. Instead, in an echo of campaigns past, he said the key for New Democrats was to "maximize our level of support. That's the objective now."

As the election moved into its final week, it was as clear as the smile on Mulroney's face that the Tories were winning. And smile he did — a lot.

Confident of Gregg's polling data and a majority government, he eased up on free trade and returned to the theme of prosperity that carried him through the first phase of the campaign. "Prosperity means the same thing in Alberta as it does in Quebec," he told supporters. "And we are not going to allow Mr. Turner and his candidates to destroy it and take us backward. Mr. Turner wants to isolate Canada, to have us alone and vulnerable in a changing world. We have a plan to secure your future, to build a stronger, more sovereign Canada." In one of the election's more forgettable lines, Mulroney contrasted himself to Turner by saying the election was a contest between "Brian the Builder and John the Ripper." He described Liberal policies as a recipe for a recession, and warned that Turner's pledge to scuttle the trade deal would leave Canadians to "hang in the wind of American protectionism." He added: "Investors already are telling you, on the money and stock markets, what they think of Mr. Turner. They have no confidence in him and no wonder. Mr. Turner and his party offer no vision, no plan for the next four years."

On his last swing through Western Canada, Mulroney received an endorsement from an unexpected source — Calgary mayor Ralph Klein. Although he had long been a Liberal, Klein appeared at a major rally with Mulroney and urged other Liberals to vote Conservative because, he explained, free trade was good for Alberta. He said he'd been telling Liberals: "Don't vote for the party, vote for the people; don't vote for the past, vote for the future. Don't fear competition, seek it out." In Halifax, former Conservative leader Robert Stanfield heaped praise on Mulroney for the free trade agreement and the Meech Lake Accord. Describing the trade pact as an act of political courage, Stanfield stated, "I myself would have never had that courage." On Meech Lake, he said Mulroney had done "something I thought was impossible, namely to integrate Quebec into the constitutional life of this country." Stanfield said he had never thought he would see the day when Quebec would put forward a reasonable set of proposals and the other premiers would agreed to reopen constitutional talks. "Brian Mulroney conducted the most remarkable negotiations I've seen in my life," he said.

Premier Bourassa issued a final appeal for "realism," urging Quebecers to support free trade because it would be beneficial for the province. A similar message was delivered by Parizeau. Possibly the only hitch for Mulroney was having to answer for Simon Reisman. Reisman had been Canada's chief negotiator in the free trade talks, and the Tories put him on the road during the election to help meet the Liberal challenge. Belligerent and argumentative, he seemed to repel as many people as he attracted. Commenting on one of the Liberals' television commercials, he said with customary tact, "I looked at it and I almost puked." In the last week of the election, he accused Turner of being a "traitor." When pressed for comment, Mulroney allowed that Reisman had blown his "cork."

Turner, meanwhile, had finally come up with a price tag for his party's election promises, and it was a lot less than the $37 billion being tossed about by the Conservatives. In fact, Turner and his number crunchers argued that their programme would cost most Canadians nothing. Only those earning in excess of $100,000 would have to pay more. How did they reach this conclusion? First, they estimated that their promises would require $18 billion in spending. (Curiously, the C.D. Howe Institute had arrived at $26.5 billion for the same promises — a difference of $8.5 billion.) Then, on the payment side, they planned to save $350 million annually by cancelling plans for a fleet of nuclear-powered submarines. Killing free trade meant another $1.5 billion a year in import duties. On top of that, there would be revenue from a new tax on the rich, and more savings would accrue from the Liberal pledge to eliminate "government waste." Together, that might have added up to $2.5 billion a year, or $12.5 billion over five years. That was about $5 billion short of the target, but the Liberals also promised there would be extra money from the "healthy economic growth" that would necessarily follow their coming to power. John Ferguson, economics columnist for Southam News, mockingly described the plan as a "miracle of biblical proportions, a feat right up there with loaves and fishes." Turner wasn't finished, however. The following day in Newfoundland, he pledged that a Liberal government would fully finance the Hibernia offshore oil project and ensure the province received a larger share of the royalties from it. He didn't say what this would cost, but it wasn't part of the estimate released the day before. Also in Newfoundland, Turner was asked to comment on an editorial in *The Wall Street Journal* that condemned his platform as an endorsement of the "Argentine model of economic progress." His answer: "Don't cry for me, Wall Street Journal." In fairness to the Liberals, the Tories also informed the country that their promises would cost nothing. In a virtuoso display of bafflegab, Finance Minister Wilson told reporters that while the Liberals had made election promises, the Tories had made "spending commitments." And how much were the commitments worth? Zero. The difference between the Tories and the Liberals, he said, was that the Tories had made formal commitments of money through the budget while the Liberals had not made budgetary provisions for their spending. Reporters then wanted to know what they should call all the goodies the Tories announced before the election. Said Wilson: "Because it was in the spending period in the election period, you can call it a spending promise if you want. We're committed to doing it." He then explained that the Liberal spending, which he estimated at $37 billion, would come on top of all the Conservative spending. "That's the standing assumption," he said. If that was not the case, he added, then the Liberals should be asked: "Fine, what spending aren't you doing?"

Possibly the most suspenseful development of the last week was a speech by Ronald Reagan. It was known that the U.S. president would speak on trade and that his remarks would cover the agreement with Canada. The question was how far would he go? In the end, he deflated the issue by not going far at all, touching on it for a mere 20 seconds of a 30-minute speech. As far as the United States was concerned: "The free trade agreement is an example of co-operation at its best. It is a testament to the commitment of our two governments to the principles of the open market and to economic co-operation." Somehow Turner found the remarks offensive. It was, he said, a case of a "lame duck trying to rescue a dead duck," and an unprecedented intervention in a Canadian election. Asked to point out the offending passages, he replied: "In the speech there are words that our Prime Minister has used in Parliament, in favour of open trading, in favour of not going back on protectionism, in favour of this deal with Canada being a jewel and an example for the world. These words could have been written by Brian Mulroney and perhaps were." A day later Turner exploded again, this time in response to comments by British Prime Minister Margaret Thatcher. In an interview published in Washington, she said rejection of the free trade deal would make it "very difficult for any prime minister of Canada to negotiate another international agreement with another country." These remarks Turner described as "unprecedented, unwarranted and intolerable." While he doubtless believed that his tough talk was scoring points, the Tories thought he had gone too far and was helping them. "People aren't stupid," strategist Bill Neville said after the election. "Turner let his anti-American and anti-business (attitude) get out of control."

The final weekend of the campaign found the three leaders putting on a last spurt in the regions where they expected to do best — Broadbent in the West, Turner in Ontario and Mulroney in Quebec. There was also a heavy investment in advertising. Robin Sears, Deputy Campaign Director for the NDP, estimated the three parties would spend more than $1 million on ads in the last two days. Included in that sum was $180,000 paid out by the Liberals for space in every major daily Canadian newspaper. Their message was aimed at the opponents of free trade: "The only way to block it is to have all those votes go to one party, the Liberal party, vote Liberal. If you vote with any other anti-free trade party, your vote will be wasted. The Liberals are the one party that can stop free trade."

The advertisement neatly summarized what the federal election of 1988 had come down to — two parties and one issue. Abortion, defence policy, South Africa, immigration, Meech Lake, the deficit and the environment — all had been expected to figure heavily in the campaign, but none had dominated like free trade, and on that score the Liberals and Conservatives were the only players left in the ring.

CHAPTER 4

The Media and the Campaign

By Alan Frizzell and Anthony Westell

Every national election campaign is now in essence a media campaign. Television, press and radio present the candidate with the opportunity to communicate with millions of voters several times every day. However, the journalists who staff these media, interpret the candidate's message, shape the image, and may even criticize the candidate. In the circumstances it is vital for a political party to have an effective media strategy. The strategy usually employed by leaders and parties who feel themselves to be in the lead is straightforward:

— Arrange events every day so that the TV crews, pressed by deadlines and demands from home stations for footage, will have little option but to picture the leader in a favourable setting, for example, in a hardhat as he stands in a paper mill explaining to the admiring workers how they will benefit from his policies. The TV journalists may want to report on something completely different, but they cannot ignore the pictures, and even if they do, it is the pictures and not the words that will remain in the mind of the viewer;

— Ensure that in every speech or statement there is a phrase that sums up the message in a couple of seconds. This is known as a "sound bite," and it is irresistible for TV and radio reporters who have to tell the story in a minute or so and must include the voice of the candidate;

— Keep the writing press as far away as possible from the leader. If he makes himself available to the journalists, in a formal news conference or an informal "scrum," there is little or no chance that he will receive favourable notices because reporters tend not to be fans. But there is real danger that he will say something wrong or foolish on which the press will jump with enthusiasm.

The reporters will of course complain about lack of access to the leader, arguing perhaps a little arrogantly that as they represent the voters, it is the duty of the leader to submit to their interrogation. They can be bought off for a time by the attentions of the leader's aides who offer what is supposed to be inside news in the form of leaks and rumors, and by a daily supply of pre-packaged news — policy announcements and the like — known in the trade as Gainesburgers after the dogfood which looks like hamburger and comes in plastic wrappings.[1] Eventually the leader will have to meet the press, and then the tactic is to say as little as possible without actually inciting the reporters to verbal violence in the next day's papers. This sort of campaign is known as "low-bridging," presumably because a candidate on a low bridge is less visible and vulnerable than he would be on a high bridge. In the 1988 election, Prime Minister Mulroney ran a classic low-bridging campaign. His national tour was carefully organized to move him across the country from planned picture opportunity to stage-managed party rally, and the frustrated reporters hardly laid a glove upon him.

A party leader in second place has to employ a rather different strategy if he hopes to attract attention and build credibility. He will still seek to control the broadcasters by feeding them pictures and sound bites, but he must try to earn the goodwill of the press by making himself freely available to the reporters. He will hold press conferences almost daily to announce policies and answer questions about them, chat informally on the plane with journalists, and try to establish a friendly relationship by demonstrating that he is much more open, and hence useful, to the media than is his leading opponent. It is a high-risk strategy because the reporters know that it is an admission of weakness; the candidate is at their mercy, of which they have only a small supply.

Of necessity, Liberal leader John Turner employed this strategy in the 1988 campaign, and was badly bloodied in the opening weeks by highly critical reporting. The news reports focussed not on his policies but on his inability to explain them in detail, not on the improvements he had made in his campaign style since 1984 but on the weaknesses in his performance. Turner's media advisers prayed that after a few weeks the reporters would tire of the blood sport and look for "a new angle" in his plucky fight against political odds and a pinched nerve in his back. Actually, the tone of coverage did change, but it probably had more to do with Turner's rapid climb in the polls after the TV debates than with an attack of media conscience; journalists like a winner.[2]

In past campaigns, the New Democratic Party had run as the conscience of the country rather than as a party seeking to win and form a government. In addition, its leaders had usually been likeable figures on matey terms with reporters who tended to be on the liberal-left of the political spectrum. Accordingly, the media extended to the leader a sort of benign neglect. Why harass a party seeking not power but good works? This time it was a little different at the outset. The party was riding higher in the polls than ever before, and had the resources for the first time to mount a truly national campaign, including a media strategy designed to provide pictures and bites for the national news. There was a chance that it could form a minority government, and a reasonably good prospect that it could become the official opposition. Moreover, journalists are probably a little less "progressive" in attitude than they were in the 1960s and '70s. There was much talk therefore about subjecting Ed Broadbent and his policies to more critical reporting. This seemed to be occurring until the TV debates put Broadbent firmly back into third place and undermined the party's pretensions to power. Thereafter, the media coverage reflected not so much benign neglect as neglect born of lack of interest because the major show was elsewhere.

In this election, media managers came to realize that leaders' campaign tours, once the high spot of every political reporter's career, were now so tightly controlled that they were no longer an exciting story. There was always the hope of slips, blunders or worse, but in the main the media would be managed, particularly in the case of those following the Prime Minister. Nevertheless, the major policy announcements were made by leaders on tour, which was of course an inducement for news organizations to tag along although the cost was high. A ticket on a leader's plane for the entire campaign cost $12,000 to $13,000, and then there were bills for hotels and meals, and in some cases for overtime pay.[3] To assign a five-person TV crew to cover a leader throughout the campaign cost $300,000 or more. Weighing the news and the costs, even some major media organizations tended to de-emphasize the tours and to assign the most experienced journalists to report on party strategies, campaign problems, emerging issues, and the mood of the country, usually as revealed by opinion polls. The new attitude was summed up by Michael Fleming, in charge of election coverage at the Halifax Chronicle Herald which staffed the planes only in the closing weeks of the campaign:

> Leaders' tours are basically for handing out press-releases and glad-handing around. They are basically geared to television. We're looking for issues and stories, and leaders don't always provide them.[4]

This editorial scepticism had its effect on the reporters assigned to the leaders' tours, and the reporters themselves tended to be of a new breed. There was less excitement about the story and more worries about technological problems of communication with head office; most of the reporters were writing on laptop computers which did not always interface easily with telephones.[5] There was less concern about the supply of liquor and more about the cholesterol in the airline meals. Conversation might wander from the latest political gossip to the ruinous cost of overtime for the nanny at home. And of course there was much interest in what would happen after election day — that is to say, in what exotic place to take a post-campaign vacation, using the frequent-flyer bonuses which the airlines made available to the intrepid reporters flying on the leaders' chartered planes. On some legs of the tours, in fact, the media contingent divided into two groups, the old guard of veterans who smoked, drank, told rookies tall tales of campaigns past, and thought it was all good fun, and the new journalists who objected to smoking, drank Perrier, and found it all very tiring. Almost nobody thought of the tours as great news stories.

Television

Media strategies focus on television because that is where the voters are. A recent survey found:

> Television remains the primary source of news information for Canadians. In fact the public is most likely to rank this medium first for objectivity, accuracy and in-depth reporting. Of Canada's major television networks, the CBC/Radio Canada is by far the most trusted.[6]

More specifically, 47 percent say they keep up with the news through television, 31 percent through newspapers, 15 percent through radio and 4 percent through magazines. The results are markedly different when only those with a university education are counted: TV, 31; newspapers, 44; radio, 18; magazines 5.[7] And as most TV journalists are university-educated, it would be interesting to know where they get their news and how it influences their news judgement. But TV is unquestionably the major medium of communication between candidate and voter, and in the end all votes are equal.

What is not so clear is how television influences opinion in an election campaign. It is often said that it communicates images and impressions rather than facts or ideas: the viewers remember what they see much more clearly than what they hear; the response is emotional rather than rational. Joshua Meyrowitz, a U.S. media analyst, argues that television gives the viewer a sense of knowing personally the person in close-up on the screen, and:

> Recent polls show that many people will vote for a candidate they disagree with on the issues because they say they like the candidate personally. This dichotomy of response to personality and stands on the issues makes sense only in a television culture. If we read a candidate's speeches in a newspaper, it would be insane for us to say, 'This is all nonsense, but you know something, I like the guy.' Such a reaction only makes sense when we feel we have met and 'know' our leaders personally. And television gives us that feeling.[8]

The major TV events of the campaign — indeed, the major events of the entire campaign — were the two three-hour debates among the leaders, the first in French and the second in English. They were interesting, at moments exciting, because they were unpredictable; panels of journalists asked questions which prompted unscripted exchanges between the leaders. About half the electorate watched some part of the debates,[9] and many more heard or read about them in the media. They changed the course, although probably not the outcome, of the election; NDP leader Broadbent was pushed from centre stage, and Liberal leader Turner enjoyed a jump in popularity which suddenly put the Liberal party back into contention. Was it content or image that influenced public opinion?

Political journalists familiar with the leaders and the issues presumably viewed the debates more analytically than the average voter, and it is interesting to note that their first judgements were that nothing much had happened. After the French language debate, CTV's Pamela Wallin said that, "It's hard to really pick a winner." Doug Small, Ottawa bureau chief for Global, decided, "There were no knock-out punches in it. . .," a view which CBC commentators seemed to share. It was only later, by some mysterious process, that a consensus emerged that NDP leader Broadbent had lost heavily in Quebec because his French was not as good as that of his opponents.

More important was the English language debate the following night in which Prime Minister Mulroney and Turner had a sharp and passionate exchange on free trade. Again, the TV journalists participating as panelists or watching with a knowledgeable eye saw no obvious winner.

Broadcasting from booths or studios, they were not exposed to the so-called Spin Doctors employed by each of the parties to persuade any available reporters that their man had been the winner. CBC anchorman Peter Mansbridge spotted the clash of free trade as important, but observed, "Certainly I would not want to predict a winner on that exchange." The Journal later sought the opinions of four journalists across the country: two of them picked Broadbent as the clear winner over all, one said Turner had not been very good but might emerge as the winner because expectations for him had been low, and the fourth was undecided. Global's Small, who had been a panelist, thought all three had done well, and agreed with his anchorman that there had been no knock-out blow. CTV's Craig Oliver gave Turner the edge on points, and the network offered what purported to be a cross-Canada sampling of opinion including interviews with a group in Toronto which tended to the opinion that Broadbent had won. The most sensible comment that night came from CBC correspondent David Halton who declined to pick a winner on the grounds that what he had seen as a panelist in the studio was probably quite different from what the viewers had seen at home.

It was not until the following day when the press and the polls began to report on the public judgement that the TV journalists realized that Turner had scored a sensational victory and that Broadbent had been eliminated as a serious contender. As the journalists had been correct in their judgement that nothing new had been said in the debate, it was apparent that the public had been moved by images, and the media hastened to adopt this view of events. What seems to have happened was that:

— Turner attacked Mulroney on free trade with a passion which few knew he had in him, surprising the public who had been led to believe that he was a hopeless, hapless performer. He said nothing which had not been said many times before, but he said it with enormous conviction, and scores of thousands found the image compelling. Broadbent was not part of this dramatic exchange, and so was pushed to the margin of the campaign.

— Mulroney and Turner appeared as big, handsome, beautifully tailored men who would not have been out of place in *Dallas* or some such drama about the rich and famous, while Broadbent was smaller, less well-dressed, and appeared by contrast with his opponents, a supporting player rather than a star.

The voters not only liked Turner's style but they were prepared to consider seriously his leadership on free trade — an issue which in detail was as puzzling for many at the end as it had been at the beginning of the campaign. Support for the Liberals soared and opposition to free trade strengthened. In this case, it was not image overcoming ideas, but image convincing people to make up their minds on an issue on which they had previously been unsure.

TV was also responsible for the most controversial journalism of the campaign in an incident which demonstrated the medium's difficulty in dealing with complicated news. The episode actually began shortly before the election was called when Charlotte Gray, Ottawa correspondent for *Saturday Night* magazine, reported in a television commentary on the CBC's Ottawa station that there were rumours of a new revolt against Turner's leadership by members of his caucus. There had been several revolts in the past, and even more rumours, and so the story attracted little immediate attention. But among those watching were Elly Alboim, CBC-TV's respected bureau chief on Parliament Hill, and Mansbridge, normally the anchorman for the National News but also Chief of Correspondents. Alboim put the rumour in his file of things to check out with a view to doing a story at some time, probably a retrospective after the election was over.

Checking turned up no firm confirmation of the rumour, but there were hints that the inner group of Liberal strategists running the campaign felt things were going so badly that they must consider the possibility of a change of leadership, extraordinary as that would be in the middle of a campaign. But the information was not hard enough to warrant a news report and Alboim and his colleagues had more or less agreed to shelve the story when new whispers reached them. They heard that the strategists had been discussing the situation with five frontbench MPs, including some who had previously been Turner loyalists, and that as a result the five were seeking a crisis meeting with Turner to discuss what should be done, including possibly his resignation as leader. The CBC's own polling showed that things were every bit as bad as the strategists must have known from their own data: the Liberals were in third place, and the public assessment of Turner as a leader was devastating.

At this stage, the journalistic desire for a scoop, or at least not to be scooped, came into play. Alboim and his crew had been badly burned in the 1984 campaign when they held back a story intending to use it after the campaign, and then had it break in the papers. This time they decided to report what they knew, or what they thought they knew, about the Liberal crisis. They wanted to report a situation rather than a spot news event, and so they decided on an unusual format: well into the national news — it was at 9 p.m. that night of Oct. 19, because hockey was coming up at 10 p.m. — Mansbridge would do a special report on the events in the Liberal party over the past four weeks. Ironically, Turner had campaigned well that day in Vancouver, and a report on his success was featured in the regular news. Then came the acting anchorman, Sheldon Turcott, to introduce Mansbridge and his extraordinary story:

> For the last several days there has been some astonishing manoeuvring at the highest levels of the party. Some of the most senior people in the party thought the unthinkable. Deep into this election campaign, they thought about putting pressure on John Turner to quit. But CBC news has learned they've pulled back and are now prepared to work to salvage the campaign. Our chief correspondent, Peter Mansbridge, has the story of a party in crisis.

Mansbridge, filmed out-of-doors as if he were on assignment, took up the story:

> Last Thursday, four top Liberal strategists met at party headquarters in Ottawa. Michael Kirby, John Webster, Al Graham and André

Ouellet met to discuss just how poorly the Liberal campaign was going. They talked about a lot of things — the polls, the ridings where they couldn't get candidates, the poor image of the leader, even the impact of an immediate change in leadership. The next day, all four men signed documents outlining the desperate situation the party was in and sent them to John Turner at the Liberal leader's official residence, Stornoway. They did not include their thoughts about leadership, but they did ask to see Turner in a face-to-face meeting. At Stornoway, Turner read the briefing, but remained resolute, convinced the campaign was still winnable, even if he had to do it alone. He refused to meet the strategists. The next day, Saturday, Turner talked to some of them by phone, leaving them convinced he would not step down. The strategists decided that a leadership change was not an option any longer, and others impressed upon them that the campaign must go on, that dissent must end.

But then, Sunday night, came the CBC poll results, especially the leadership questions where Turner ranked dead last on every one of ten different qualities. A frenzied series of cross-country phone calls took place by strategists and senior Liberal candidates trying to assess the damage and the options. Five of the candidates, Turner's front bench in the House of Commons, called for a crisis meeting with Turner — Herb Gray from Windsor, Lloyd Axworthy from Winnipeg, Bob Kaplan from Toronto, André Ouellet, who'd been at the strategists' meeting, and Raymond Garneau from Quebec. By late Monday, Gray put in the request by phone for a meeting with Turner, but he was blocked by Principal Secretary Peter Connolly. Connolly was determined not to allow Turner to get into these kinds of discussions until he comes back to Ottawa later this week. It's not clear yet what the five MPs wanted to tell Turner, but it is known that asking Turner to step aside had been discussed by some of the group. But some also felt that if Turner was forced out the party could be left in ruins by a very public bloodbath. For the next two days, right up until late this afternoon, there was confusion and chaos. The senior aides with Turner on the campaign trail would not talk to senior strategists and candidates on the ground. Connolly didn't know who to trust any more. All this follows an incredible four-week period inside the most senior levels of the Liberal party. Here's what we know has happened. Ten days before the election call, Michael Kirby went to see John Turner in his Parliament Hill office. Kirby told Turner that private polling showed the Tories with at least 155 seats, a clear majority, going into the campaign, and one of the Liberals' biggest problems was the image of their leader. Kirby did not ask Turner to quit. He just laid out the facts. Turner's next visitor was more blunt. During a meeting punctuated with shouting, Raymond

Garneau, the party's Quebec lieutenant, told Turner he must quit, that the future of the Liberal party was at stake. But Turner said no, this was his campaign. Only Martin Goldfarb, the Liberal pollster, had good news going into the campaign. Goldfarb told Turner the election was still up for grabs. But by Day Ten of the campaign, after a few campaign fumbles, even Goldfarb was telling Turner all was lost, the Tories were sweeping and a halo of victory hovered over Brian Mulroney, a halo too firm to be knocked off.

And while all this was going on, Turner was in agonizing physical pain. He'd pinched a nerve in his back, could barely walk, could barely stand up for speeches. In Toronto, just hours before this huge Liberal fund-raiser, Turner was with his doctor, trying to find some relief for the pain. He told friends he was worried about simply making it through the campaign on physical grounds. It was the following night, last Thursday, that the four top Liberal strategists met to file their campaign assessment and talk about asking Turner to leave. But late this afternoon there were dramatic changes in this story. Liberals at all levels seemed to realize that they were heading toward a major confrontation and that the party, in the process, was only destroying itself. The strategists, with Turner and those back in Ottawa, have decided to have a special meeting on Friday to try and sort out the differences between them, and the candidates have backed off on their requests for a meeting with Turner, convinced that Turner has no intention of stepping down. But they are not happy. They're not happy with the treatment they are getting. They're not happy with the lack of consultation on major new policies like abortion, but mostly they're not happy with the performance of their party or their leader, now almost halfway through the election campaign.

The length of the item was extraordinary for a newscast and thus a signal of its importance. And to illustrate the item, the CBC showed what purported to be a copy of the memo which the strategists had sent to Turner. Taken at face value, it seemed to prove that Mansbridge knew of what he spoke, but in fact it was a fake: the CBC did not have the memo, and after initially claiming that it was a legitimate "graphic representation," Alboim later conceded that to use it had been a mistake.[10] What TV viewers took out of the report is difficult to imagine; even reading the transcript, it is hard to grasp all the angles and implications of what is, to put it mildly, a confusing account of several related events. However, the Canadian Press news service distributed nationwide an account of what the CBC had said, and *The Globe and Mail* actually carried the story further by reporting that indeed the five M.Ps had threatened to withdraw their own candidacies unless Turner resigned, but had then had second thoughts and allowed the plan to die. *The Toronto Star*, on the other hand, denied the story and later carried a long article rounding up criticisms by journalists and others about the CBC story. The *Ottawa Citizen* denounced the CBC in an editorial, and so did several columnists. Pat Gossage, the media adviser travelling with Turner, chose his words carefully when he told an Ottawa seminar organized by the Centre for Investigative Journalism:

> I think this is the most flagrant political intervention by a major news organization in a national campaign in the modern life of Canada.

It was widely noted also that none of the Liberal politicians named in the story had appeared on camera to confirm or deny the allegations. But this changed when the strategists and the five M.Ps, with varying degrees of conviction, denied the accuracy of the CBC report. Part of the difficulty, according to Senator Michael Kirby, one of the strategists concerned, was that many of the facts in the story were correct, but the construction put on them was wrong. The strategists had indeed discussed the disastrous state of the campaign and described it in a memo to Turner. They had also thought it their duty to discuss what to do if Turner decided to quit either because of his back or because he felt that it was vital to defeat free trade by defeating the Conservatives and that some other Liberal leader would have a better chance. There was, however, no thought of a coup, no plot to oust Turner in mid-campaign.[11] But even if Kirby's account of events was correct — and it will take historians to untangle the tale of who said what to whom, when and with what intent — a cynic might see little difference between plotting actively against the leader and sending him a memo couched in such bleak terms that he might feel obliged to resign. Turner's chief of staff, Peter Connolly, said later that the CBC story was an accurate and even gentle account of events, but as he was on the leader's plane and not at the crucial meetings, he seemed to be confirming the substance rather than the detail and interpretation.[12]

The CBC stuck resolutely to its story, denying that the report had said, when read carefully, that a coup had been attempted. John Owen, Chief News Editor of CBC-TV News, wrote:

> Senior journalists in the News Service, including Mr. Mansbridge, after concluding that our story was accurate, then wrestled with the dilemma of when to go on air with a story that we knew to be true, completely true. After lengthy discussions, we felt that it was irresponsible to withhold this information from our viewers.[13]

On the other hand, there were those in the CBC who questioned whether the corporation, with its large audience and semi-official status and credibility, should broadcast in the middle of an election a devastating political story which was based in part on leaks and rumour and could not be known with confidence to be the whole truth of the matter. But in the end, was the story important? Kirby claimed that it was a devastating blow to Liberal morale, and Gossage said it had the effect of isolating Turner in his plane from the strategists in Ottawa in whom he could no longer have confidence. But as far as the voters were concerned, it seemed to have little impact: a few days later Turner "won" the debates and soared in the opinion polls.

TABLE 1
Focus of Television Coverage
(Percentages of all items)*

	CBC	CTV	Global
Mulroney	19.1	17.7	21.7
Turner	18.1	19.9	22.2
Broadbent	18.6	16.6	23.8
All leaders	7.0	4.4	4.8
Other items	37.2	41.4	27.5
No. of items	(215)	(181)	(189)

*Absolute numbers of items are not comparable. In the cases of CTV and Global, seven newcasts a week were monitored; in the case of the CBC, only six are included because the *Sunday Report* and the nightly *Journal* programmes are not strictly news and are analyzed separately below. Moreover, in the monitoring process, some newscasts were not recorded. While it was possible to obtain and code the missing CBC and Global tapes, CTV refused to make 17 tapes available. Therefore the data for CTV covers only 34 days of the campaign, but the sample is large enough to compare proportions.

As we have noted, television is the major source of news for most people. To study how TV covered the election, national newscasts on the three national networks, CTV, Global and the CBC, were monitored and the election items analyzed. In total, 585 items were examined. As might be expected, most focussed on leaders (Table 1).

It is clear that the three networks gave equal attention to the three leaders. Another way of looking at coverage is to see to what extent policy issues were reported: 41 pecent of all items were about policy, and here again there was little difference among the three networks. But what issues were reported?

Free trade was the dominant issue covered on the TV news, and it received almost the same attention on all three networks. When the leaders were reported discussing policy, it was usually about free trade. No other single issue received concentrated attention (Table 2).

TABLE 2
Television Coverage of Issues
(Percentages of all items in which
policy issues were the major topic)

Economic (other than free trade)	11.8
National unity	5.4
Social issues	6.0
Women's issues	2.7
Environment	5.0
Peace/defence	2.0
Free trade	56.4
Other issues	10.7
Number of items	(296)

CBC coverage was far more extensive than that of the other networks when the nightly *Journal* and the weekly *Sunday Report* are taken into account. The *Journal* follows the news and provides background information, commentary and debate. The Sunday programme is a mixture of news and commentary. Together these programmes provided 140 items of election coverage. There was less of a focus on leaders and on free trade, and greater emphasis on party organizations, campaign strategies and personalities. However, when they did deal with policy issues, the focus was again overwhelmingly on free trade.

Considering all television items on the election, when researchers were asked to make a subjective judgement about whether each item was likely to strike a viewer as favourable toward the subject, unfavourable or neutral, more than 90 percent were assessed as being neutral.

The Press

To study in detail the coverage of the campaign by the press, seven newspapers, each a market leader in its region, were selected. These were *The Sun* in Vancouver, the *Free Press* in Winnipeg, the *Star* in Toronto, the *Gazette* and *La Presse* in Montreal, the *Chronicle-Herald* in Halifax, and the national edition of the *Globe and Mail* which is edited in Toronto but printed in centres across the country. Every journalistic item dealing with the election for every day of the campaign was analyzed and coded — 6,935 items in all, including news reports, analyses of the news, articles by columnists, editorials expressing the opinion of the paper, photographs and cartoons. These newspapers are not of course completely representative of the press in Canada, but they are widely read and influential in their markets. To some extent they set the standards for the press. Moreover this study replicates one done after the 1984 election and makes comparisons possible.

Although the campaign this time was shorter — 51 days as opposed to 57 — coverage was more extensive in most of the papers surveyed.

TABLE 3
Extent of Coverage

	V. Sun	W.FP	T.Star	M.Gaz.	M.LP	H.C-H	G&M
No. of items							
1984	739	768	1035	581	1043	631	812
1988	831	915	1378	897	1143	849	922
Col. ins							
1984	15,701	13,214	22,704	15,059	18,793	12,569	15,702
1988	13,965	17,780	28,458	17,790	19,800	10,937	17,858

For most papers, there were two major sources of news, Ottawa and their home provinces in which they reported not only the national campaign, but also the battles in the ridings. It was noticeable in 1984 that *La Presse*, the only French language paper in the group, paid far less attention to Ottawa than the

TABLE 4
Issues Covered
(Percentages of all Items Mentioning Issues)

	1984	1988
Economy/ Unemployment	28	3
National Unity	15	6
Peace/Defence	11	4
Women's Rights	11	4
Patronage	10	1
Tax Reform	5	5
Energy	4	1
Social	4	6
Free Trade	0	58
Other	12	12
Number of items	(2,193)	(2,552)

others, and far more attention to Quebec than, say, its English-language competitor in Montreal, the *Gazette*. In other words, for *La Presse* a national election was very much a Quebec affair. This was true again in 1988, when 60.7 percent of all election items in *La Presse* originated in Quebec. By contrast, only 40.8 percent of items in the *Gazette* originated in Quebec.

In analyzing coverage by type of item, it is noticeable that there has been a shift of emphasis from straight news stories to background articles and commentary. In 1984, 73 percent of items were news; in 1988 it was 61 percent. There was also a shift in the focus of the coverage. In 1984, 38.9 percent of all items about the election were concerned with the political process — party campaigns and organizations and so on; in 1988 it was 29.1 percent. In 1984, only 26 percent of items concerned policy issues; in this election it was 36.8 percent, and the issues covered changed dramatically, as the following table shows.

In the press at least, this was a one-issue campaign. Free trade dominated to the detriment of other issues, and the NDP was unsuccessful in its attempts to broaden the agenda. This was true for each of the papers (Table 5).

The Toronto Star's coverage of the free trade issue was so extensive that it occasioned comment, mainly from those who charged that the paper was not so

TABLE 5
Free Trade

	No. of items	As percentage of items about issues	As percentage of all election items
V.Sun	167	60.3	20.1
W.FP	188	54.5	20.5
T.Star	410	65.6	29.8
M.Gaz.	133	50.8	14.8
M.LP	175	48.3	15.3
H.C-H	195	60.0	23.0
G&M	207	51.6	22.5

much reporting on the issue as campaigning against the agreement. In the Dec. 4 issue of the paper, shortly after the election, the editor, John Honderich, wrote a lengthy article in which he explained and defended the paper's performance:

> For decades, the *Star* has proudly taken a leading role in promoting and identifying certain causes — among them the preservation of Canadian sovereignty and the economic and social welfare of all Canadians. Unlike many other newspapers, it has become actively engaged in policy debate. In the process, it has consciously sought to provoke public discussion with the purpose . . . of helping Canada to talk to itself . . .
>
> So in the tradition of a crusading newspaper, The Star assigned reporters, columnists and editors, at great expense and in numbers unequalled anywhere in this country, to get at the story from every conceivable angle. The intensive coverage began as soon as the agreement was unveiled and continued right up to the election.

Honderich argued that the *Star* had given prominence to all points of view, in regular columns, special articles, and by careful selection of letters from readers. He pointed out also that in publishing on its front page an editorial recommending the election of one party — in this case, the Liberals — the paper was well within Canadian custom. However, the question is not whether the *Star* gave extensive coverage to the issue, but whether its coverage was biased for or against free trade. This is difficult to determine because a report may seem to one person to be slanted against free trade, to another to be neutral, and to a third to be positive. In other words, readers approach an item in a newspaper with their own prejudices which will flavour how they interpret the item. In this study we asked coders to assess whether in their opinion the average reader would obtain a neutral, favourable, or unfavourable impression of the the actor, party or policy being discussed. The judgement is therefore subjective and, further, the measurement is not of bias: a report may be entirely accurate and yet reflect favourably or unfavourably on the subject or topic. The great majority of items, if they are news reports, should be neutral. One way to assess the balance of coverage therefore is to measure the performance of one newspaper against others (Table 6).

Thus the *Star* published more items about free trade than any other paper, and higher proportions of them were favourable or unfavourable rather than neutral. The proportion of unfavourable items was almost twice that found in the other papers in the study, and in fact no other paper came close to the *Star* in

TABLE 6
All Items on Free Trade (Percentages)

	Neutral	Favourable	Unfavourable	No. items
Toronto Star	64.6	6.1	29.3	(410)
All other papers in the sample	81.4	2.6	16.0	(1,065)

the number or proportion of items about free trade which were coded as unfavourable. Therefore, it seems fair to say that a person who read with an open mind every item on free trade in the *Star*, and who had no other sources of information would have gained an unfavourable impression of free trade. But in reality people are selective in what they read, have many sources of information, and use information to some degree to reinforce their own opinions. The *Star* also carried a large volume of advertising from groups supporting free trade, earning about $550,000 in the process — revenue known jocularly to the editors as "the wages of sin." In sum, it is unlikely that the *Star's* journalistic coverage alone determined many votes.

Free trade was such an overwhelming issue that it caused some papers to take editorial decisions which raised many eyebrows. Shortly before voting day, *The Globe and Mail* devoted its prime feature page to reprinting a number of editorials in which it had supported free trade. In Montreal, the editorial board of *The Gazette*, a member of the Southam group of papers, was opposed to free trade and attacked it on the editorial page, but the Publisher, Clark Davey, exercised his authority to write a front page article in which he endorsed the Conservative government and its free trade policy. A sister paper in the group, the *Edmonton Journal*, opposed free trade throughout the campaign, which may relieve some concerns about group ownership and control of editorial policy.

A third category of coverage — in addition to the political process and the policy issues — includes many items, such as polls, the TV debates and criticisms of the parties and the leaders. In 1984 this accounted for 34.9 percent of coverage; in 1988, it was roughly the same, 34.1 (Table 7).

The similarity is striking. Although Turner ran an open campaign and in the first weeks was the subject of critical reporting,the record overall was not as bad as in 1984 when he was in trouble from start to finish. In fact, the newspapers

TABLE 7
Other Campaign Coverage
(Percentages of items in this category)

	1984	1988
Opinion polls	14	14
TV debates	13	13
Campaign blunders	6	1
Media campaign coverage	3	6
Criticism of Turner	6	6
Criticism of Mulroney	6	7
Criticism of Broadbent	1	1
Criticism of Lib. party	4	4
Criticism of Cons. party	2	5
Criticism of NDP	1	1
Criticism of other parties	1	0
Quality of leadership	1	2
Other	42	40
Number of items	(1,957)	(2,366)

TABLE 8
Readers' Impressions of Leaders and Parties When Main Subjects
(Percentages)

	Neutral	Favourable	Unfavourable	No. of items
Mulroney	56.9	3.2	32.9	(649)
Turner	67.0	9.5	23.5	(579)
Broadbent	84.8	4.9	10.3	(406)
PC Party	58.0	5.4	36.6	(276)
Lib. Party	70.4	3.1	26.5	(196)
NDP	72.4	9.2	18.4	(76)
Other parties	90.3	5.6	4.1	(197)

were even-handed in their criticism of Turner and Mulroney. When the NDP was in a strong position in the polls, there were suggestions that the press would pay more critical attention, but this did not happen either to the party or to Broadbent. However, the picture changes when one considers items which may not have been directly critical, but created an unfavourable impression — for example, a news account which was strictly factual but reported a leader making a campaign blunder (Table 8).

In 1984 when Turner was the new prime minister and under scrutiny, only 2.9 percent of items in which he was the principal actor were favourable, and 23.7 percent were unfavourable; this time he received significantly more favourable coverage. Mulroney received the same proportion of favourable attention but the unfavourable jumped from 16.2 percent to 32.9 percent. In other words, and this may be contrary to popular impressions, Mulroney was the subject of more unfavourable coverage than Turner. The same is true when coverage of the major parties is considered: whereas in 1984 the Liberal party received far more unfavourable attention than the PC party, this time that was reversed. It may be that the press is more demanding of prime ministers and governing parties, and least demanding of leaders and parties which seem to have little chance of forming a government.

Conclusion

While it is true that the media, and television in particular, are the channels through which voters get most of their information, their influence in the political process may be overestimated. The data show that they give roughly equal exposure to the leaders and parties, although the press seems to be more critical of a prime minister and the governing party than of the alternatives. By general consent, free trade was the major issue in the election, and the media gave it extensive, even excessive, coverage, the great majority of which was thought to be neutral in its impact. As in 1984, what is striking is the similarity in the coverage provided by the three networks and by the seven papers in the study.

Of greater influence than all the work of journalists may be the election debates when leaders speak directly to the voters and in which a brief encounter can have profound impact on public opinion.

Endnotes

The content analysis on which part of this chapter is based was the work of students studying Political Reporting at the School of Journalism, Carleton University. It was probably the most extensive project of its kind ever undertaken in Canada, and the students who participated included Deanna Allen, Tory Blair, Janet Driesman, Dennis Brougham, Paul Eichhorn, Kevin Hanson, Monique Labelle, Brett Maitland, Marianne Meed, Jennifer Perry, Sarah Sacheli, Lisa Taylor, Randy Simon, Paul Wiecek, and Lydia Zajc.

1. Patrick Gossage, a media spokesman for both Pierre Trudeau and John Turner, explained media strategies employed by political leaders at an Ottawa seminar organized by the Centre for Investigative Journalism during the 1988 campaign. He advised journalists not to pay too much attention to aides during the heat of a campaign. "We lie," he said.
2. In an article on coverage of the 1988 U.S. Presidential election," The Intimidated Press", in *The New York Review of Books*, Jan. 19, 1989, Anthony Lewis wrote, "While George Bush was refusing to meet the press, Michael Dukakis at first held daily press conferences. He was rewarded by having embarrassing bits shown on the nightly news up against sound bites staged by the Bush campaign."
3. Stevie Cameron, *The Globe and Mail*, Oct. 17, 1988.
4. Ibid.
5. Many reporters were supplied with portable libraries of background information on voting histories and issues likely to arise in the campaign, stored on computer disks for use in their laptops.
6. Michael Adams, Jordan A. Levitin, "Media Bias as Viewed by the Canadian Public," in *Canadian Legislatures, 1987-8*, Robert J. Fleming, ed.; Ampersand Communications Services Inc., Ottawa, 1988.
7. Ibid.
8. Joshua Meyrowitz, "Television's Covert Challenge". reprinted from *American Theatre*, in *Dialogue*, No. 82 (4,1988) Washington, D.C.
9. Environics Research Group Ltd., in a survey for *The Globe and Mail*, Toronto.
10. In an interview with Anthony Westell.
11. Gerald Kaplan, Michael Kirby, Hugh Segal, *Election. The Issues, The Strategies, The Aftermath*. (Scarborough: Prentice-Hall, 1989) pp. 137-143.
12. At a conference to review the campaign, organized by the CBC and the School of Policy Studies, Queen's University, Feb, 1989.
13. Letter to the editor of *The Citizen*, Ottawa, Oct. 23, 1988.

CHAPTER 5

The Perils of Polling

By Alan Frizzell

It was fun being a pollster when you were the only one in town. After all, if anyone wished to disprove any of your findings, they would have to undertake another poll themselves, a costly undertaking in the cause of accuracy. True, when an election came around there was the awful risk of "getting it wrong," but that was a minor factor when compared to the rewards. And rewards there were, especially when the media discovered polling, and pollsters became commentators and experts rather than simply practitioners in the field of elementary statistics. But dark clouds began to gather over the Canadian pollsters in the 1970s. The business was becoming seriously congested, competition became fierce, the struggle for a media outlet intense. The danger was that as more and more public polls became available results would vary and lead to questions about, and criticisms of, methodology and interpretation. The image of the expert with the irrefutable data at his fingertips would be shattered. And that is what happened in the election of 1988.

For many Canadians the published polls in the election were at best an irritant, and at worst a corrupting influence on the democratic process. Calls to hot-line shows were overwhelmingly anti-poll and some candidates and journalists called for a ban on their publication during campaigns. The critics claimed that there were far too many polls and that those that were reported were inaccurate, biased and encouraged horse-race media coverage instead of a discussion of the issues in the election. The fact that the polls closest to election day accurately forecast the election outcome may have taken some of the sting out of these complaints, but it remains true that pollsters could do much better, and that if they are to avoid restrictive legislation designed to limit their activities they must develop some collective standards that will make their data more comparable and substantial.

Perhaps the pollsters could not have emerged unscathed from the election, even with perfect methodology. There has never been an election in Canada where the polls have come under such scrutiny or such criticism, and in a contest where political divisions were profound, polls which purported to show that one side or another was winning were bound to be found objectionable to some. Nevertheless, polling is a fact of life in Canadian politics. No political party plans campaign strategy without them, no government is prepared to risk major policy initiatives without gauging public opinion, and for major news organizations they are an indispensable reporting tool, both between and during elections.

It is only through media reporting of polls that the public is aware of polling numbers, and the evidence from the election indicates that the public was not

TABLE 1
Party Voting Intentions — Gallup — 1984-1988
(Percentages for Major Parties)

	PC	LIB	NDP	Other
Oct. 84	60%	21%	17%	2%
Nov. 84	55	23	20	2
Dec. 84	54	24	20	2
Jan. 85	53	25	21	1
Feb. 85	53	25	21	1
Mar. 85	56	26	17	1
Apr. 85	54	24	21	1
May. 85	45	31	22	2
June 85	44	33	21	2
July 85	40	33	26	1
Aug. 85	46	32	20	2
Sept. 85	48	29	22	1
Oct. 85	43	35	22	—
Nov. 85	40	36	24	—
Dec. 85	37	38	24	1
Jan. 86	41	36	23	—
Feb. 86	36	41	23	—
Mar. 86	41	34	25	1
Apr. 86	37	40	21	2
May. 86	37	41	21	1
June 86	32	40	27	1
July 86	36	41	21	2
Aug. 86	33	41	24	2
Sept. 86	35	36	28	1
Oct. 86	31	38	29	2
Nov. 86	31	39	29	1
Dec. 86	30	45	25	—
Jan. 87	28	41	30	1
Feb. 87	22	44	32	2
Mar. 87	24	41	34	1
Apr. 87	24	42	32	2
May. 87	26	42	30	2
June 87	24	39	35	2
July 87	23	35	41	1
Aug. 87	25	36	37	2
Sept. 87	25	36	37	2
Oct. 87	23	38	38	1
Nov. 87	25	40	33	2
Dec. 87	29	35	34	2
Jan. 88	30	36	31	3
Feb. 88	27	40	31	2
Mar. 88	28	37	31	4
Apr. 88	31	38	30	1
May. 88	28	39	31	2
June 88	31	39	29	1
July 88	35	37	27	1
Aug. 88	34	35	30	1
Sept. 88	40	26	31	3

served well by what was placed before them. This was partly due to the fact that pollsters have developed a disturbing tendency to do what they have always criticised journalists for doing; making sweeping political judgements and predictions which the limited polling data do not warrant. The dangers of this became apparent in the topsy-turvy world of Canadian politics after the 1984 election.

1984 and Beyond

The period between the 1984 and 1988 elections saw unprecedented volatility in the polls, and for the first time in Canadian politics each of the major parties found themselves at the top of the voting intentions stakes at some point and in third place on other occasions (Table 1).

The Tories ranged from a high of 60 percent support to a low of 22 percent while the Liberals had a low of 21 percent and a high of 45 percent. Given these astonishing swings, one would assume that pollsters would weigh their comments carefully. This, however, was not to be. Either because of the sin of hubris or a tendency to "Journalism Envy," pollsters were prepared to read into their numbers conclusions that would haunt them.

The fact that pollsters have come to see themselves as political commentators and gurus is worrying, especially since their prognostications are so often wrong. Newspaper columnists likewise may find that their prescriptions are inaccurate, but pollsters are supposed to work from empirical data and their conclusions might reasonably be given more weight by the public at large.

In a recent book by the Liberal pollster Martin Goldfarb a series of comments typifies this self-importance. He writes: "Like a seer or oracle, the pollster plays a role that is viewed with a combination of respect, fear, intrigue and controversy."[1] Moreover, Goldfarb argues that the pollster is no technician; he is a sage! "It is the interpretation of results — not the collection of data — that sets the good pollster apart from the ordinary one".[2] Goldfarb is not forthcoming on what special qualities the pollster has that makes such insights possible. But even this accolade to the pollster is insufficient, for he goes on to say that the pollster is not merely "primus inter pares", but simply "primus." "He is the court confidante and knows more about the inner machinations of his court than anybody else — maybe even more than the leader."[3]

Arrogance of this sort from pollsters is bound to cause trouble and that is what happened during the electoral off-season. For example, during the period when the NDP fortunes rose in the polls, Southam News pollster Angus Reid was quoted as saying that this was not temporary and that the party had become a genuine contender for power. This was despite the fact that much of the NDP strength was based on Quebec support which most analysts considered to be "vote parking" — voters registering their support in a convenient location until a real decision had to be made. The Tory pollster, Allan Gregg, in an end-of-the-year (1986) poll for *Maclean's* magazine, ordained that the Tories had six months to turn things around or face electoral defeat. Neither claim made any sense given the level of volatility in the political marketplace, and they were based on suppositions that had nothing to do with the available polling data.

There was, in addition, confusion among polls between the elections. There is regular polling by Angus Reid for Southam News, Environics Research for *The Globe and Mail* and Gallup for the *Toronto Star* and other papers. Thus results are compared and differences highlighted. This was especially true for the two most regular polls, Reid and Gallup. There were two periods when differences were particularly evident and these differences led to concern on the part of the media sponsors.

TABLE 2
Angus Reid's Two Month Lag Analysis
(Percentages for Major Parties)

	REID					GALLUP		
	PC	LIB	NDP		PC	LIB	NDP
September 87	23	38	36				
October 87	28	35	35				
November 87	30	37	32	November 87	25	40	33
December 87	—	—	—	December 87	29	35	34
January 88	31	34	34	January 88	30	36	31
February 88	32	33	33	February 88	27	40	31
March 88	34	30	34	March 88	28	37	31
				April 88	31	38	30

The first was the period May to August 1987 when NDP support rose sharply, and the second was when there was a revival of Tory support between September 1987 and April 1988. In a confidential memo to Nick Hills, the General Manager of Southam News, and Allan Christie of the *Toronto Star*, Angus Reid explained that the earlier differences were "because the Gallup organization was somewhat later than us in detecting the trend in the direction of the New Democrats. Not surprisingly, there were considerable differences between us and Gallup during this period with an average variance of 15.3 percent per month."[4] By average variance Reid meant the total of differences in levels of support for each party in polls published at the same time. Reid made no attempt to explain why Gallup would take longer to detect a trend.

When the polls differed again later in the year Reid argued that Gallup was once more late in detecting a trend, this time away from the Liberals. The issue came to a head when, in March 1988, each organization produced results that were considerably different. In an attempt to allay fears, Reid introduced a table into his memo to show that Gallup was roughly two months behind his firm in their estimates of voting intentions.[5] (Table 2)

With considerable courage Reid predicted what the next Gallup would show when published in May, based on his assumption of the two month lag. His prediction was somewhat off the mark.[6] (Table 3)

If Reid had difficulty explaining the inconsistencies, the public must have been even more baffled and it was certainly true that many journalists were becoming highly sceptical of the numbers that were being published even before the campaign began. This scepticism would carry over to the election period itself.

TABLE 3

	Reid's Gallup Estimate	Actual May Gallup
PC	33	28
LIB	33	39
NDP	33	31

TABLE 4
Election Polls
(Voting Intentions)

	Sample Size	PC	LIB	NDP	Other	Undecided
PUBLICATION DATE						
Oct. 3 Gallup	1,061	43	33	22	2	22
Oct. 5 Reid	1,512	45	26	27	2	25
Oct. 10 Gallup	1,017	41	32	46	1	13
Oct. 11 Environics	1,515	42	25	29	4	10
Oct. 14 CTV	1,100	46	27	26	1	18
Oct. 16 CBC	2,467	42	25	29	4	10
Oct. 17 Gallup	1,027	39	29	28	4	10
Oct. 21 CTV	1,100	43	25	30	2	10
Oct. 24 Gallup	1,034	40	28	29	3	19
Oct. 29 Reid	1,502	35	28	35	2	23
Oct. 29 CTV	1,100	35	39	23	3	19
Oct. 31 Gallup	1,034	38	32	27	3	11
Nov.1 Environics	1,538	31	37	26	6	13
Nov.2 Goldfarb	1,000	34	40	24	2	28
Nov. 4 CTV	1,101	40	37	20	3	16
Nov. 7 Gallup	1,041	31	43	22	4	10
Nov. 9 Environics	1,275	35	37	24	4	9
Nov. 10 Reid	1,501	39	35	24	2	22
Nov. 10 CBC	2,200	38	38	21	3	8
Nov. 11 CTV	1,100	39	39	20	2	15
Nov. 14 Gallup	1,026	35	35	26	4	8
Nov. 19 Reid	1,512	41	33	23	3	11
Nov. 19 Gallup	4,067	40	35	22	3	12
Nov. 19 CTV	2,720	43	32	20	5	15
Election Results		43	32	20	5	

The Campaign Polls

The revival of Tory fortunes in 1988 had been so staggering, and the problems of the Liberal party and its beleaguered leader so great, that for many the election appeared to be over before it started. The polls in the first two weeks of the campaign showed Tory support ranging from 42 to 46 percent. But despite this initial agreement, differences would emerge and the number of polls tended to highlight these (Table 4).

The last election was the most polled in Canadian history with a total of 24 reported national polls, an increase from the 12 conducted in 1984.

Though the polls showed general trends in party support throughout the campaign, on any given day differing poll results might be published and this gave rise to the notion that there were far too many polls during the election. However, Canada has fewer polls than most Western countries during elections. In the British election of 1987 there were 73 national polls during a four week campaign. In the 1988 U.S. election there were polls almost on a daily basis during the primary and national campaigns, running into a total of hundreds.[7]

The one election poll that seemed to be wildly out of line with the rest was the Gallup poll published on Nov.7. While all the polls after the leaders' debates showed a remarkable Liberal resurgence, and in some cases a Liberal lead, the

Gallup figures gave the Liberals an advantage of 12 percentage points. Most analysts consider that this was a "rogue poll", though they are at a loss to explain why this should be so. Lorne Bozinoff, vice-president of Gallup Canada Inc., argued that the poll was accurate and that after the debates the Liberals hit "a brief emotional high" before sliding back.[8] No other poll found any evidence of this. Gallup later argued that the poll results may have been due to random error, the elusive 20th poll, and added that it was impossible for pollsters to know if they had encountered a "rogue poll."[9] In fact there are many ways in which pollsters can gauge this, the most obvious being that in random sampling, demographic results such as sex and age breakdowns can be checked against census data to estimate the reliability of other results. Another problem with the same poll surfaced in the way the results were presented. Gallup disclosed results for the Atlantic region, Quebec, Ontario, the Prairies and B.C. Given that only 1041 respondents were interviewed, this means that the error margins for the regional results were huge.

Gallup was not the only polling group remiss in this regard. *The Globe and Mail* polling team published provincial results from a national sample of 1,275 eligible voters on Nov. 10. They estimated their Saskatchewan error margin at 13.5 percent. In an overall sample of this size a representative number of voters in that province would be 51 so that even by interviewing slightly more respondents than required, the numbers for a provincial breakdown were ludicrous.

Other problems with polling results were evident, notably in the number of undecided voters. This happened not only between organizations, but also within organizations throughout the campaign. Gallup ranged from 19 percent to 8 percent undecided, while Reid varied from 23 percent to 11 percent. In fact these differences are more apparent than real. Normally the rate of those who say they are undecided for whom to vote is anywhere from 8 to 12 percent. But another 4 to 8 percent of respondents refuse to answer a voting-intentions question, and there are also those who say they will not vote. Some polling companies report only the first of these figures while others lump all the categories together. When polling is irregular these differing practices are not much of a problem, but when polls are frequent, confusion results. Moreover, some polling firms ask respondents who are unsure about their voting choice if they are leaning to one particular party or another. The leaning respondents may or may not be included in the voting-intention numbers.

Another problem arises when one considers the nature of the vote question and its placement in the questionnaire. In the most recent Manitoba provincial election, one poll reported an undecided rate of 42 percent, largely due to the fact that the vote question was the first question asked. Most pollsters try to lead the respondent into the topic of the survey gently. Questions dealing with the respondent's interest in politics — such as, whether the respondent has been following the campaign or not — are ways of introducing the topic before directly asking about voting intentions. Angus Reid argues that this approach provides a context for the vote question. He asks about issues and perceptions of the party leaders before asking about voting intentions. Some would argue that the answers to the first questions will influence the responses to the vote question, thus causing what pollsters call "inter-item contamination."

The effect of differing techniques is to ensure that there will be differences between the polls during and between elections and when these differences emerge it should not be surprising.

During the election campaign some pollsters used their data to estimate the number of seats each party would win. This is not really difficult to do in theory; regional polling results are translated into seats on the basis of what has happened in the past. However, the regional sample sizes of most polls are so small as to make this technique risky at best, and in this election there was enough evidence of intra-regional variance to indicate that such predictions were little more than informed guesses.

It is not only in Canada that pollsters are trying to do too much with their numbers. In both the recent elections in the U.S. and the U.K. pollsters have behaved irresponsibly. In the former case there were many pre-primary polls which got the results all wrong — not surprising when one considers that actual primary turnout can be very low. What was worse was that there were polls produced in some States that had caucus elections where only a minuscule percentage of the population would actually vote, and in some cases these were presented as predictions of the likely outcome. In the 1987 British election the BBC was embarrassed by an election night prediction that the election was close and that there was a possibility of a hung parliament. This was based on a mixture of polling done the day before the election, election day polling and over-sampling in marginal constituencies. The election, of course, resulted in a landslide for Prime Minister Thatcher.

The irony of all this is that the pollsters could do a much better job without having to resort to dubious methodology or spurious prediction. All they need do is to ask more pertinent questions on issues and attitudes.

Polls and the Media
It is a sad fact that most of the media polling done in the election was concerned only with who was winning and losing. There was little examination of the issues, except for opinion questions on free trade, no explanation of why people were changing their minds or why they were voting the way they were. As usual, the exception to the rule was the CBC. The television news polls for the CBC delved into issues in detail and had a sample size that permitted regional analysis. For those reasons the CBC could use its polls to enhance other election coverage, but for most other news organizations the polling figures were so limited that this was not possible. For the media, polls are potentially an important reporting tool. They can direct election coverage and put into context the exaggerated claims of politicians. There are, however, other reasons for media polling. Since any news organization's poll is widely reported the poll becomes advertising, and most major media organizations feel that they should have their own poll as a question of status. Of the major groups, only the Sun

TABLE 5
Poll Stories as a Percentge of Election Items

	Poll as main topic	Poll mentioned in story
Vancouver Sun	5.1	9.7
Winnipeg Free Press	4.7	10.9
Globe and Mail	5.2	14.4
Toronto Star	5.4	11.7
Montreal Gazette	4.7	16.3
La Presse	7.8	11.1
Halifax Chronicle Herald	4.8	7.9

chain of newspapers and the Global television network did not commission election polling.

All media reported polling results and the similarity in the number of stories in the press about polls is striking. Though there were slightly fewer stories in those papers which did not commission polls (*Halifax Chronicle Herald* and the *Winnipeg Free Press*), the differences were small (Table 5).

These figures do not indicate that there was an overemphasis on polls, since there was only an average of around 5 percent of stories where polls were the main topic. This would leave plenty of space for the coverage of issues. But the newspapers did leave themselves open to the criticism that when they did report on the polls they did not do so very responsibly. The Canadian Daily Newspaper Publishers' Association has outlined certain basic information that should be included when polls are reported. Such factors as sample size, sponsorship, refusal rates and sample selection should all be included in the coverage. In fact there was no newspaper article in the last election that complied with all the guidelines. The stories that came closest were those in *The Globe and Mail*; these usually included a separate explanation of the methodology employed. It is difficult to understand why most newspapers don't include such information when polls have become so controversial.

The problem is even greater when polls are mentioned as secondary aspects in a story. Data which may well have been qualified when originally published are often commented on as gospel. While 73 percent of all poll stories were reported as straight news items, this was not the case for those stories where polls were the secondary topic. Forty percent of these were columns, editorials or news backgrounders. Indeed, a quarter of all news backgrounders mentioned polls at some point, indicating that poll information was used to make sense of the election campaign. Unfortunately, since almost all poll results were concerned with the horse race aspect of the election, this suggests that many news background items had a similar focus.[10]

One other notable feature of the newspaper coverage was that poll stories tended to have a higher "attention score", meaning they were more prominently displayed, than non-poll items. This was true not only where polls were the main topic of the stories, but also when they were the secondary topic.

TABLE 6
Poll Stories as a Percentage of Coverage

	Poll as main topic	Poll mentioned in story
CBC	8.9	19.9
CTV	14.9	21.0
Global	11.4	21.2

Broadcasters were much more concerned with polls than were newspapers. Global did not sponsor a poll yet it carried a higher percentage of poll items than the CBC which did. As with newspapers, there was little mention of methodological limits. The CBC did introduce some qualifications, but the other broadcasters did not.

An innovation in poll reporting in Canada was introduced by the CBC. They developed a chart of all the polls giving each party a range of support as expressed by the polls. This poll-of-polls technique is much used in other countries. The only problem with the CBC model was that the range of support for each party was colour coded and as the campaign progressed the chart took on the appearance of a Salvador Dali painting. The CBC conducted only two polls, but they were comprehensive. CTV on the other hand used their resources to conduct much less elaborate rolling polls, the main component of which was the horse race.

While there is distress in some quarters that the media conduct so much polling during elections, this will have little effect on the amount of poll coverage in the future. The media get good value for their money from pollsters, who see their work for newspapers or television as good advertising for profitable market research or government contracts. Status is gained by the media outlet and despite the complaints about horse race coverage this is a legitimate aspect of election coverage. It is also true that the two major organizations which did not sponsor polls did consider doing so, but decided against it for reasons of cost rather than from journalistic considerations. The question is not how much polling will be done, but whether or not the media will improve the quality of what they do.

Criticisms

The furor over the Gallup poll giving the Liberals a commanding lead over the Tories gave rise to the issue of accuracy of the polls. Inconsistencies among published polls are bound to fuel notions that they are not really accurate predictors. In fact pollsters have long argued that polls should not be seen as predictors but as snapshots of opinion at a given time. Moreover, there is the problem of turnout. When asked if they will vote in an election most respondents say they will, when in fact more than a quarter of the population will not vote. The latter problem can be partly solved by various techniques that predict turnout. However, the polls have been fairly accurate in predicting actual outcomes.

TABLE 7
Differences Between Gallup Results and Voting Outcomes 1945-1988

	Lib	PC	NDP	Other
1945	−2	+2	+1	−1
1949	−2	+1	+2	−1
1953	+1	0	0	−1
1957	+7	−5	−1	−1
1958	0	+2	−2	0
1962	+1	+1	−2	0
1963	−1	−1	+1	+1
1965	+4	−3	0	−1
1968	+2	−2	+1	−1
1972	0	−2	+3	−1
1974	0	0	0	0
1979	−2.5	+1.5	+1	0
1980	+4	−5	+3	−1
1984	0	0	0	0
1988	−3	+3	+2	−2

The three polls published two days before the election were close to the final outcome, and in the case of the CTV poll, bang on. Pollsters have learned that with the electorate so volatile, interviewing as close to election day as possible is necessary. Many polls increase their sample size for their last campaign poll. In the 1988 election Gallup interviewed over 4,000 respondents for its final election poll.

Politicians and business groups know how valuable polls can be. They spend considerable amounts of money on polling. But politicians are also very critical of published polls for other reasons. Bill Neville, a former journalist and now a Conservative strategist, has argued that the problem with polls is that their accuracy is almost irrelevant. Once they are out there they change the way people look at an election. There is widespread belief that polls influence the way people vote yet neither of two theories that are supposed to explain how they do this, the bandwagon and the underdog effects, applies consistently in Canadian elections. In the 1988 election campaign neither of these was consistently present.

In a poll dealing with how Canadians react to polls, *The Globe and Mail* discovered that only 13 percent of respondents admitted to being influenced in some way by them. However 64 percent thought that others were influenced by them. The survey results indicated that other influences, such as TV commercials, were much more important in influencing voting choice.[11]

In fact it could be argued that the polls should have been more influential in this election. Indeed, if a voter wanted to vote against free trade, then a knowledge of party standings would have helped to decide whether to support the Liberals or the NDP. In fact, the voting returns themselves indicate that if there was strategic voting on this issue, then there was not very much of it.

If polls do not determine voting choice in any significant way, they do influence politics, and this may explain the negative opinions of some politicians. Polls do tend to limit just how much politicians can control the agenda of an election. If an issue shows up in the polls as important to the public, journalists will question politicians about it, no matter how much those politicians would like to avoid it. Polls also influence the morale of party workers though not always in an obvious way. Politicians have admitted that poor polling results can spur the campaign workers to greater efforts. But the dangers of despondency or complacency because of poll results are real enough.

Another effect of poor poll results between elections, or at the start of a campaign, is that potential candidates may decide to sit the election out. This may explain the difficulty the Liberals encountered in getting hold of star candidates at the beginning of the 1988 campaign. In this case one might consider polls as helpful; candidates who will run only if they are sure of election may not be the best servants of their parties or of the country.

Politicians may well see polls as a nuisance, but this does not mean they do not use them for their own purposes. They do not wish to see the polls banned — just their publication restricted. In 1980, former Tory minister Sinclair Stevens wanted to ban the publication of polls during an election, and more recently, *The Globe and Mail* columnist, Jeffrey Simpson, argued for a partial ban on the publication of election polls.[12] The politician's argument is easily countered. What a politician wants is information for himself, but for nobody else.

Another argument is more difficult to deal with because it states that the democratic process is not well served by the publication of polls which tend to deflect interest away from the issues. The problem with this argument is that in Canadian politics there is evidence that voters are not overwhelmingly interested in, or informed about, the issues. The media tend to concentrate on factors other than the issues and politicians often try to avoid speaking to the issues. A ban on the publication of poll results would be unlikely to change this situation. Though there are 10 countries in the non-communist bloc where there are some restrictions on the publication of election polls, notably France and South Africa, recent attempts to do this in the U.S. and Britain have been unsuccessful.

Conclusions

There have been attempts by pollsters in the past to impose some self-discipline on their industry, but these have come to nothing. Some marketing associations do have stated standards, but these do not address all of the complaints about political polls. It might be in the pollsters' best interest if they set in motion some form of self-regulation before it is imposed upon them. In particular there is a need for some form of agreement on minimum methodological standards or even a common methodological base. A standard way of computing the undecided vote should be determined, as well as the form and placement of the voting intentions question.

Pollsters in some countries insist that media sponsors print methodological outlines and that might well be proposed in Canada. In addition, a reasonable request might be that if the media are to ensure that polling contributes to the quality of election coverage, then they should demand much more comprehensive polling that will deal with the major issues of the campaign.

Though the polls were criticized, and in some cases rightly so, they did contribute to the election process in 1988. In a period of considerable volatility they pointed out major shifts of opinion during the campaign. They did give evidence that free trade was the major issue, and that opinions on that issue were more or less evenly divided. The evidence from the polls and from academic research is that voters are less committed to enduring party loyalties, that they make voting decisions late in campaigns, and that they base their decisions on short-term factors. All this suggests that in future elections polling will be even more useful in understanding what is going on in an election, if the pollsters can put their house in order.

Endnotes

1. M. Goldfarb, T. Axworthy, *Dancing to a Different Drummer*. (Toronto; Stoddart, 1988) p. xi.
2. *Ibid*. p. xiii.
3. *Ibid*. p. xv.
4. Unpublished Memo from Angus Reid to Nic Hills and Allan Christie, April 14, 1988. p. 1.
5. *Ibid*. p. 6.
6. *Ibid*.
7. D. Butler, D. Kavanagh, *The British General Election of 1987*. (London: Macmillan, 1988) p. 125.
8. *The Globe and Mail*, November 25, 1988. p. A7.
9. This claim was made at a symposium on the election and the polls held at Queen's University on the weekend of February 25-26, 1989.
10. Carleton content analysis. See Chapter 4.
11. *The Globe and Mail*, November 25, 1988. p. A7.
12. *The Globe and Mail*, November 19 , 1988. p. A6.

CHAPTER 6

The Changeable Canadian Voter

By Lawrence LeDuc

For the past 30 years, Canadian federal politics has been a politics of volatility and change. The short span of six years saw the the elections of 1957, 1962 and 1963 produce minority governments and the election of 1958 produce the greatest landslide in our political history, the beginnings of a Conservative West, the end of the Duplessis era in Quebec, the birth of the New Democratic Party, and the sudden emergence of the Caouette Creditistes.[1] The legacy of many of these events continues to be visible in the politics of the present day, and it is in light of this that we must prepare to analyse the vote in 1988.

The succession of Lester Pearson by Pierre Trudeau in 1968 seemed at first the beginning of a new period of Liberal dominance. Trudeau's personal charisma, combined with an unbreakable Liberal hold on federal parliamentary seats in Quebec, produced Liberal majority governments in 1968, 1974, and 1980. Yet there is much that is deceptive in this interpretation of the politics of the "Trudeau era". Trudeau's first government narrowly escaped defeat in 1972, and survived the next two years as a precarious minority. Although regaining a majority in 1974, the Trudeau Liberals were then defeated by the Conservatives under Joe Clark in 1979. Returning to power once again in 1980, Trudeau retired in 1984 and in that year saw his party even more decisively defeated by the Conservatives, now led by Brian Mulroney.

Thus the political landscape since 1957 has been more suggestive of "dealignment" than of new and enduring political alignments.[2] In every election except 1958, "third" parties have polled at least 20 percent of the total vote, often in the process gaining enough parliamentary seats to deny a majority to the winner. Before Mulroney did so in 1988, no Canadian federal government since 1953 had succeeded in winning a second consecutive parliamentary majority.

In the dozen elections which form the modern Canadian political era, five federal governments have gone down to electoral defeat (St. Laurent in 1957, Diefenbaker in 1963, Trudeau in 1979, Clark in 1980, and Turner in 1984), and one more has come precariously close (Trudeau in 1972). Although the Liberals were the governing party for nearly two-thirds of the period since 1957 (20 of 31 years), their hold on power was rarely secure. Even provincial politics, often an arena of greater political stability, has not been immune from these trends in recent years. Seemingly hegemonic provincial regimes came to an end or were interrupted in Alberta, British Columbia, Ontario, New Brunswick, Newfoundland and Saskatchewan, and the rise and fall of the Parti Québécois produced a turbulent political climate in Quebec.

At the federal level, even governments which have enjoyed considerable political success have often found their standing with the mass public to be at risk. The most popular politicians of the era — Diefenbaker and Trudeau — both faded quickly in public esteem during their first term of office, turning majority governments into minorities within four years of an overwhelming victory. Virtually every federal government in the past two decades has found itself behind in the public opinion polls after less than two years in office.[3] In spite of his record majority achieved in the 1984 election, Mulroney fared little better in the affection of the public than his predecessors. In the early months of 1988, the Conservatives stood third in the Gallup poll, preferred by only 27-30 percent of a national sample. Only a quarter of the sample felt that Mulroney was the best choice for Prime Minister. The Liberals, led by the same John Turner who had brought his party to such a crushing defeat in 1984, enjoyed a comfortable lead in the polls during much of Mulroney's first term in office, even though few felt that Turner would be a better Prime Minister.[4]

Parties and Partisanship

The reasons for volatility in Canadian politics may be found in Canadians' attitudes toward government and in the nature of the party system. Earlier

TABLE 1
Attributes of Partisanship in Four National Election Studies

	1965	1974	1979	1984
Direction				
Liberal	42%	50%	44%	33%
Progressive-Conservative	28	24	30	40
NDP	12	11	13	14
Other	6	3	2	1
None	12	12	11	12
Intensity				
Very strong	23%	28%	27%	23%
Fairly strong	42	40	43	45
Weak	23	20	19	20
No party identification	12	12	11	12
Stability				
Percent who recall having identified with another party	38%	36%	32%	35%
Consistency				
Same federal and provincial direction and intensity	52%	48%	46%	45%
Different federal and provincial intensity only	23	22	21	20
Different federal and provincial identification	25	30	33	35
Summary				
Number of deviations from strong, stable, consistent partisanship[a]				
Durable partisans (0)	34%	37%	38%	34%
Flexible partisans (1)	44	35	35	39
" " (2)	18	21	22	21
" " (3)	4	7	5	6
N =	(2692)	(2343)	(2514)	(3188)

[a]From at least "fairly strong" partisanship. Variations on consistency are tabulated for direction only.

studies of public attitudes found an overwhelmingly negative view of the political world, and extensive discontent with government, parties, and politicians.[5] During the 1970s, citizens increasingly came to believe that they had little say in the affairs of government, and that their representatives tended to "lose touch" with the people soon after being elected to office.[6] Rising inflation and unemployment produced a pessimistic public outlook toward the economy, and nurtured doubt that governments were capable of finding solutions. There has been a clear tendency to place much of the blame for the problems of the country on the shoulders of those in power. Canadians of course are not in any sense unique among citizens of Western democracies in expressing discontent with government. But, while in some instances such discontent has precipitated a withdrawal from the political process or the formation of protest movements, in Canada it has more often been manifested in a willingness to "throw the rascals out" when the opportunity arose.

The Canadian party system to a considerable degree magnifies and encourages this tendency toward volatility in elections. While most Canadians express some degree of allegiance toward a political party, relatively few are strongly partisan. In the 1984 National Election Study, only 23 percent were found to be "very strong" supporters of any political party (Table 1). Many also hold different party attachments at the federal and provincial levels of government, a uniquely Canadian pattern that explains part of the volatility in federal partisanship and voting behaviour.[7] A substantial number of Canadians can be shown to have changed their party identification, or attachment, often over fairly short periods of time. Between 1974 and 1980 for example, a national panel study found that 41 percent of the sample had either changed or abandoned their party identification.[8] While some may later have returned to support their former party, this degree of movement nevertheless demonstrated the precariousness of the base of public support on which the parties depend. A classification scheme developed in *Political Choice in Canada*, estimates that slightly over a third of the electorate may be thought of as "durable" partisans — reasonably dependable, fairly strong, supporters of a particular party — while about two-thirds are "flexible" partisans, whose actual voting decisions will often be made during the course of an election campaign.[9]

As is seen in Table 1, the basic characteristics of partisanship in Canada have changed little over the 20 year period for which national survey data are available. The seemingly dominant Liberal alignments of the recent past were not in any fundamental sense more durable than the Conservative one of today. There were as many "flexible" partisans in the electorate of 1965 as are found in that of 1984 (Table 1). At the beginning of the campaign period in 1988, Canadian voters were about as open to changing their voting behaviour concerning Mulroney and his party as they had been concerning Trudeau in 1972.

Unlike the situation in some European democracies, it has not been possible to explain very much of the dynamics of Canadian politics by examining long term forces such as social class, religion, or group alignments. Ideology has been notably weak as a factor in Canadian partisanship. Twenty-five years ago, Robert

Alford described Canada as having "pure, non-class, politics" in a comparison of the Canadian party system with those of other Anglo-American democracies.[10] His description continues to have validity today, as class and class-related factors are extremely weak predictors in explaining the bases of support for Canadian parties. A few long term patterns, some of which may be fragments of past political alignments, do continue to persist. Catholics, for example, were somewhat less likely to vote Conservative, even in the Mulroney sweep of 1984, just as they have been in nearly every election since such data have been available to researchers. Linguistic and regional patterns are sometimes strong, as they were in the elections of 1979 and 1980 when Conservative support among French-Canadians was very weak. But such factors, even when taken together, can explain only on average about one tenth of the variation in support for any given party in any election. In an analysis comparing the impact of social forces in Canada with that in other countries, Canada placed 11 among 15.[11] Rather than calling upon legions of loyal supporters whose attitudes are reinforced by strong group or ideological alignments, Canadian parties must act as "brokers" between competing interests, and attempt to harness the basically negative attitudes and impulses of a dealigned electorate to serve their own short term goals.

Images and Issues

Open ended questions which have been employed in several of the National Election Studies have also shed light on the way in which Canadians see political parties. Data from three of the studies are shown in Table 2. In 1984 as in previous years, the largest components of the images which people held of the various parties were those having to do with issues and public policy, followed closely by those characterized as "style" or "performance." The parties are most commonly viewed in terms of the dominant policies or issues of the day, and/or in terms of their performance, particularly when in government. The Liberals, for example, were condemned by some for their National Energy Program, and praised by others for "doing a good job" of managing the economy while in power. Parties are much less likely to be seen in ideological terms, and references to groups, regions, etc. are also distinctly lower than the two predominant categories. For the most part, the images of parties that recur with the greatest frequency in Canada are those that tend to be most responsive to change over time. Images of parties that might be shaped by long term social or political forces are much less in evidence.

In most previous studies, party leaders have figured prominently in Canadians' perceptions of political parties. Through much of the 1970s, references to Trudeau (both positive and negative) were prominent. But in 1984, references to party leaders were considerably less frequent, in part because Mulroney, Turner, and Broadbent were less well established in the public mind as political personalities than was Trudeau (Table 2). As individuals, they also tended to be less controversial, not igniting strong passions in quite the same way that Trudeau was capable of doing, and they were therefore somewhat less dominant in shaping the public images of their parties. This is not to suggest, however, that leaders have declined in importance. What is noteworthy is that images of political parties are

TABLE 2
The Structure of Party Images, 1974-1984
(Percent Mentioning)

	1974	1979	1984
Policy/issue	61	51	51
Style/ performance	47	50	53
Leader/ leadership	38	37	23
Parties/general	35	42	41
Area/group	28	27	34
Ideology	14	15	16
N =	(2445)	(2670)	(3380)

*Based on total sample. Multiple response.
Percentages do not add to 100%.

shaped by current political trends, not by those of the past. Even when strong political leaders have been capable of reshaping their parties around their own images, their passing from the scene has often opened the door to quite rapid change. The Trudeau legacy, both in its positive and negative elements, is quickly receding from the Canadian political scene.

Each of the past four elections has seen an abrupt and dramatic shift in the issues that were considered of the greatest importance by the electorate. Although economic issues often dominate the political agenda, they are not always the same economic issues. In the 1974 election, voters were concerned about the ravages of inflation, and some took positive and negative positions on the Conservatives' proposed programme of wage and price controls. But in 1984, the unemployment issue predominated among economic references, and voters reacted to Mulroney's promise of "jobs, jobs, jobs." Other recent elections have seen the rapid interjection of entirely different categories of issues (Table 3). The activities of the PQ government in Quebec placed constitutional issues and the question of national unity squarely on the public agenda in 1979, while the debate over energy policy and the gasoline tax enacted by the Clark government produced an emphasis on natural resources issues in the 1980 election. But Canadian elections have rarely been single issue affairs, even when economic questions predominated.[12] Interspersed in the campaign rhetoric of 1984 were references to public spending, taxes, social issues such as pensions and medicare, "leadership", patronage, etc. But just as there was little discussion in 1984 of energy policy, which had seemingly been so important in the preceding election, so too was there little mention of free trade, which was to dominate the next one.

The ability of a party to link itself to a particular issue or set of issues in the mind of the electorate has been a crucial element of party political strategy in most recent election campaigns. Thus, the Conservatives' emphasis on unemployment in 1984 was intended as an indictment of the Liberals' economic record, much as inflation had been in 1974. But such a strategy is generally countered with an attempt by other parties to shift the emphasis to issues on which they may occupy better

TABLE 3
Categorization of "Most Important Issue" in Four
National Federal Elections, 1974-1984

	1974	1979	1980	1984
ECONOMIC ISSUES — The economy in general, inflation, the cost of living, taxes, wage and price controls,[b] government spending, the deficit, the budget,[c] unemployment, jobs, etc.	56%	40%	39%	57%
CONFEDERATION ISSUES — National unity, the constitution, federal/provincial relations, bilingualism, language issues, Quebec separatism, the Referendum	6	26	11	4
NATURAL RESOURCES — Oil prices, energy policy,[d] resource development, control, environmental issues	2	8	31	2
SOCIAL POLICY — Housing, health, medical care, pensions, womens' issues, etc.	12	5	2	11
OTHER ISSUES — Foreign policy, defence, peace, leaders, leadership, the parties, "time for a change", trust, patronage, majority government, the polls, the election, retrospective evaluations, all other issues	18	25	26	28
NONE, NO IMPORTANT ISSUES, DON'T KNOW	30	28	22	25
N =	(2445)	(2668)	(1786)	(3377)

[a]Percentages are rounded, and do not add to 100% because multiple responses were allowed. Up to two mentions were coded for each respondent, but a given category is counted only once
[b]8% specifically mentioned the issue of wage and price controls in 1974. Mentions of this issue were negligible in other years.
[c]Includes various references to the "Crosbie budget" in 1980. Primarily general references in other years.
[d]Includes various references to "the gasoline tax", oil prices, and Petro-Canada in 1980.
Source: Canadian National Election Studies

strategic ground. Hence, the attempt by the Liberals in 1979 to shift their campaign rhetoric away from the economy to "national unity" and "leadership" was at least partly successful. While it did not save the government from defeat, it may have denied the Conservatives a clear mandate, both in policy terms and in parliamentary seats.[13] Given the role which issues have played in election campaigns in the past, and in shaping the images of parties, it should not be surprising to find the free trade question suddenly bursting upon the scene in 1987, receding briefly as each of the three parties planned their election strategies around it, and then re-igniting after the debates.

The Dynamics of Change

Landslide elections such as those of 1958 or 1984 are generally seen as rare events in Canada. Indeed, there have been as many minority governments as parliamentary majorities during the past 30 years. But a closer examination of voting patterns finds less difference between these two seemingly different types of election outcome than might initially be supposed. The first explanation of this paradoxical observation may be found in the electoral system. British style parliamentary systems almost always distort electoral majorities, giving them an appearance of being much more sweeping than they actually are. Margaret Thatcher has decisively won each of the last three British elections, but her party has never received more than 44 percent of the total popular vote. Likewise, Pierre Trudeau's first (and largest) majority in 1968 was achieved with 46 percent of the total vote. Beyond a certain point, a relatively small shift of votes, depending on their distribution, is capable of producing a large change of seats.

Conversely, an election which produces a seemingly high degree of parliamentary stability may frequently be shown to have exhibited much greater volatility at the level of the individual voter. In 1974, for example, the Conservative share of the total vote was virtually identical to that which they had received in the 1972 election, 35 percent, and the party suffered a net decline of only eight parliamentary seats. Yet, it can be shown that beneath the surface of this result there was considerable movement of voters to and from the Conservatives between these two elections, as indeed was the case for other parties.[14] Such a pattern in federal elections is fairly commonplace. In virtually every pair of Canadian federal elections for which adequate survey data exists, it can be shown that there was considerable movement between parties by individual voters. In some pairs, gains and losses by each party among set groups of voters produced a pattern of aggregate stability. In others, the gains by one party in a particular region of the country, or among a specific group of voters, have been offset by losses among other groups or in other regions. Only in a few instances has the large degree of movement which appears common to nearly all recent federal elections in Canada been channeled in the same direction throughout the country and consistently worked to the benefit of one party at the expense of the others. Under these conditions alone will the electoral system tend to produce a large turnover of seats and overwhelming parliamentary majorities like those of 1958 or 1984.

Some evidence of the constancy of voting change in Canada may be found in Table 4, which compares data on individual vote switching in three quite different federal elections. In the 1974 federal election, which restored a Liberal majority government to power, slightly more than one voter in five (22 percent) reported having switched his/her vote from that of the previous (1972) election (Panel B). In 1984, the year of the Mulroney landslide, the comparable figure was slightly under one in three (31 percent). In the middle case, 1979, which replaced the Liberals with the minority government of Joe Clark, slightly over one voter in four (27 percent) was found to have switched from the previous (1974) election. Each of these figures is different, but it is not very different. Yet these three elections produced a diverse array of outcomes — landslide, majority, minority; Conservative, Liberal; re-election, defeat of a government. Among these three examples however, it was only in 1984 that the switching worked primarily in one direction throughout the country, in favour of the Conservatives and against the Liberals. In the other cases,

TABLE 4
Voting Change in Federal Elections: 1974-1984

	A. As % of total electorate			B. As % of voters in two elections only		
	1974	1979	1984	1974	1979	1984
Voting for the same party as in previous election	60%	55%	52%	78%	73%	69%
Voting for different parties in two elections	17	20	23	22	27	31
Previous non-voters re-entering electorate	5	7	6			
Previous voters leaving electorate	13	6	7			
New voters entering electorate	5	12	12			
N =	(2060)	(2276)	(2693)	(1586)	(1691)	(1997)

Source: Canadian National Election Studies

the level of change, even though high, was much more mixed in its electoral effects.[15]

The forces of change at work in elections are not limited to the switching of votes from one election to the next: the electorate is a continually changing entity, both in the short term as a result of abstentions and in the longer term because of the enfranchisement of new voters. This is known as the replacement effect. Such effects are not trivial, but they are relatively constant in the equation of electoral change. New voters enter the electorate in every election, in numbers varying only slightly and depending upon the interval between elections, long term population trends, etc. Turnout in elections tends to fluctuate only modestly in Canada from one election to another, and has not thus far exhibited the downward trend found in some other countries, notably the United States. On the other hand, the approximate average of 75 percent of eligible Canadians who vote in federal elections should not be taken to imply that it is always the same 75 percent. There are in every election a number of previous non-voters who return to the electorate, and a number of previous voters who leave, although the proportion of Canadians who are found not to have voted in at least one of several elections over time is quite low.[16]

Both new voters entering the electorate and those re-entering moderate change, since they do not necessarily behave the same way in any given election. In fact, when these additional sources of change are taken into account, the three elections used as examples above begin to look even more alike in terms of patterns of individual behaviour (Table 4, Panel A). The percentage of new voters entering the electorate in 1984 was about the same as in 1979, and turnout rates in these two elections were similar. Thus, former voters re-entering or leaving the electorate basically offset each other. Considered as a proportion of the total electorate, however, rather than in terms of voters only, the percentage who might be said to be stable in voting in each of these three elections ranges from 60 percent in 1974 to

52 percent in 1984, a range of only 8 across three very different elections. What differs much more than magnitude is the direction and impact of these three types of change. With fewer new voters (because of the short interval between elections) and more non-voters (reflecting the lower turnout), 1974 appears at first to be a somewhat different type of case. But the differences here are ones of degree only, since these basic types of change might be expected to be present in all elections.

A Dealigned Electorate

The growth of the electorate in Canada has been an important catalyst of change, even though younger voters have for the most part not shown characteristics of partisanship or behaviour that would distinguish them from older cohorts. But the lowering of the voting age to 18 in 1970, coupled with higher post-war birth rates, had the effect of adding over 2 million new voters to the electorate at each four or five year interval since 1968. At the time of the 1984 election, one-third of the eligible electorate was under the age of 30, and a majority of all those of voting age had entered the electorate during what are called here the Trudeau years. Although lower birth rates have now slowed down the growth of the electorate, nearly 1.5 million new voters were added to the enumeration lists in 1988. Combined with the larger number (about 2.3 million) who became eligible in 1984, one Canadian voter in five has come of voting age since Trudeau's retirement from the political scene. In 1988, about 38 percent of the electorate were "Trudeau era" voters, while the remaining 62 percent came from generations both older and younger (Figure 1). The mixture of old and new represented by the approximately 17.5 million Canadians who were eligible to participate in the 1988 election reflects both the demographic and political trends of recent years.

The combination of substantial generational change in the electorate and the overwhelming Liberal defeat of 1984 leads naturally to speculation regarding the potential for long term realignment of the Canadian party system. Continued Conservative strength in the West, the solid 1984 breakthrough in Quebec, the departure of Trudeau, the growth of NDP support, all might be factors contributing to permanent changes in the relative strength of Canadian parties.

FIGURE 1
Age/Cohort Composition of the Canadian Electorate, 1988

Entry cohort	King- St. Laurent era	Diefenbaker- Pearson era	Trudeau era	1984	1988
	26%	16%	38%	12%	8%
Age in 1988	56+	44-55	26-43	18-25	

Such a conclusion, however, is at best premature and more than likely wrong. There is little indication in Canada to date of party realignment, and considerable evidence of the persistence of dealignment in the electorate. Although the Conservatives pulled ahead of the Liberals in 1984 in terms of the total number of identifiers with the party, party identification in Canada has tended to display nearly as much volatility over time as the vote itself.[17]

Volatility in the electorate of the 1990s is very likely to continue to be as high as that of the 1970s. In part, this is because the generational changes noted above, although substantial in size, have done little to change the fundamental characteristics of the electorate. Younger voters are not greatly different from the older in terms of direction, strength, or stability of partisanship. While the Liberals have lost adherents (as well as voters) since 1974, particularly among those who entered the electorate during the Trudeau years, many could easily return in future. The persistent weakness of the Conservatives among younger voters, in 1984 as well as in each of the previous four national election studies, did not suggest the emergence of a new Conservative generation of voters. The NDP likewise failed to make any significant breakthrough among younger voters, and its overall support in elections was more unstable than that of the other two parties.[18] For many Canadians, an NDP vote represents a "protest" motivated by current grievances, rather than a lasting partisan commitment.

Overall, the Canadian electorate continues to be one with relatively weak long-term attachments to parties, low ideological commitment, and high responsiveness to short term factors such as leaders, issues, or political events. The proportion of flexible partisans in the electorate remains high, and it is high in every age cohort, every region, and virtually every significant voting group. The events leading up to the 1988 election demonstrated a number of the characteristics of the electorate documented in this chapter. Following their massive victory in the 1984 election, the Conservatives quickly slipped in the public opinion polls, falling behind the Liberals for the first time as early as the winter of 1986. Like other federal governments of recent years, the Mulroney government provoked much negative public sentiment, an improving economy notwithstanding. Yet the prospects for electoral recovery were always present, as the volatility of the polls in the pre-election period shows. However, the improvement in Conservative standing in the polls during the summer of 1988, which led to the election call, was due at least as much to the problems of the Liberals as to better public perception of the Tories. In studies of the past several federal elections, reasons given by voters for switching from one party to another tended to be more negative than positive — an expression of discontent or disillusionment with a party previously supported rather than attraction for one of the other parties.[19] Also, as the election approached, the NDP position began to fade. As has often been the case in past election campaigns, NDP strength was greatest in the between-election period, when discontent with both of the other parties was high.

Elections are major political events, and much of the movement in public attitudes which is reflected in the polls is precipitated by them and by the events which are associated with them. There is often as much shifting of party preference and of voting choice between elections that have taken place at short intervals (1972-74 or 1979-80 for example) as between those that are further apart (such as 1974-79 or 1984-88). Because its frame of reference is primarily short term, the public reacts to events as they unfold rather than to ideological or other longer term stimuli. Only a quarter to a third of the electorate (primarily the durable partisans) may be said to have their minds made up with respect to voting choice well in advance of an election. A proportion of about equal size will decide at the time that the election is called. Further movement in the polls is linked directly or indirectly to the events and stimuli which occur during the campaign itself.

The events of the 1988 election were perhaps unusual in their intensity and dramatic impact, but they were in many ways "typical" of the type of volatility which has been a feature of Canadian politics for the past three decades.

Endnotes

1. See John Meisel, *Papers on the 1962 Election* (Toronto: University of Toronto Press, 1964) or Peter Regenstreif, *The Diefenbaker Interlude* (Toronto: Longmans) for an examination of some of the issues, events, and personalities of this period.
2. A discussion of patterns of realignment and dealignment in a number of countries, including Canada, may be found in Russell Dalton, Scott Flanagan, and Paul Beck (eds.), *Electoral Change in Advanced Industrial Democracies* (Princeton University Press, 1984).
3. *The Gallup Report*, monthly surveys. A summary of these for the period 1974-83 may be found in Harold Clarke, Jane Jenson, Lawrence LeDuc, and Jon Pammett, *Absent Mandate* (Toronto, Gage, 1984), p. 186.
4. *The Gallup Report*, January-March, 1988.
5. Clarke, et al., *Absent Mandate*, ch. 2.
6. *Ibid*, pp. 38-40.
7. A more detailed discussion of the implications of provincial partisanship with respect to volatility in federal politics may be found in Harold Clarke, Jane Jenson, Lawrence LeDuc, and Jon Pammett, *Political Choice in Canada*, pp. 99-109. All references here are to the abridged edition unless otherwise noted.
8. Lawrence LeDuc, Harold Clarke, Jane Jenson, and Jon Pammett, "Partisan Instability in Canada: Evidence from a New Panel Study", *American Political Science Review*, 78 (1984), pp. 471-83.
9. Clarke, et al., *Political Choice in Canada*, ch. 5, 10.
10. Robert Alford, *Party and Society* (NY, Rand-McNally, 1963), ch. 8.
11. Richard Rose (ed.), *Electoral Behavior: a Comparative Handbook* (Glencoe, Free Press, 1974), pp. 124-27. See also William Irvine and Howard Gold, "Do Frozen Cleavages Ever Go Stale?", *British Journal of Political Science*, 10 (1980), pp. 213-25.
12. Clarke, et al., *Absent Mandate*, ch. 4. A comparison of issue volatility in Canada with that in other countries may be found in Harold Clarke, Kai Hildebrandt, Lawrence LeDuc, and Jon Pammett, "Issue Volatility and Partisan Linkages in Canada, Great Britain, the United States, and West Germany", *European Journal of Political Research*, 13 (1985), pp. 237-63.
13. Clarke, et al., *Absent Mandate*, pp. 163-67.
14. Clarke, et al., *Political Choice in Canada*, pp. 238-42.
15. See for comparison Clarke, et al., *Political Choice in Canada*, pp. 239-42, and Clarke, et al., *Absent Mandate*, pp. 152-58.
16. Clarke, et al., *Political Choice in Canada*, pp. 66-68 and 204-05.
17. *Ibid*, pp. 99-105. See also LeDuc, et al., "Partisan Instability in Canada. . .", pp. 475-79, and LeDuc, "Canada: the Politics of Stable Dealignment", in Dalton, et al., *Electoral Change in Advanced Industrial Democracies*, pp. 402-24.
18. Clarke, et al., *Political Choice in Canada*, p. 240, and Clarke, et al., *Absent Mandate*, pp. 156-158.
19. Clarke, et al., *Absent Mandate*, pp. 142-45.

CHAPTER 7

The 1988 Vote

By Jon H. Pammett

Although Canadians expressed intense interest in the 1988 election, and recognized that the choices involved were unusually important, they exercised their franchise without relish. The catalogue of public discontents with the Conservatives in their period in office has been recounted elsewhere (see Chapter One.) Before the summer of 1988, it seemed highly unlikely to all except true believers that the Conservatives could be re-elected with a majority of seats in Parliament. The public devoutly wished for an alternative — they had in fact supported the Liberals or New Democrats in the public opinion polls for much of the four-year period since the previous election. Ultimately, the Conservatives were sustained in power because of the inability of the opposition parties to provide a credible and potentially competent alternative government. Faced with a series of unattractive choices, Canadians gritted their teeth and made the best of it.

Our examination of the voting behaviour of the Canadian electorate in the 1988 election will come principally through the existence of a unique set of data. The 1984 Canadian National Election Study was an extensive post-election interview with a sample of over 3000 Canadians; it followed in the tradition of earlier Canadian National Election Studies.[1] In the one-month period immediately following the 1988 election, 1200 of the respondents from the 1984 survey were reinterviewed by telephone about the reasons for their voting behaviour and their evaluations of the issues and politicians.[2] We therefore have a 1984-88 panel study (one in which the same people are interviewed at different points in time) to observe the changes and stability in Canadian political behaviour during this crucial period. With a system of corrective weights applied, this data set becomes a representative sample of the 1988 electorate aged 22 and over. (No voters entering the eligible electorate since 1984 were interviewed.) In order to examine the behaviour of new voters in 1988, a National Exit Poll (in which voters are interviewed as they leave the polling station) will be examined in a later section of this chapter.[3] Together, these data sets will allow us an in-depth look into the motives for voting in 1988, and the patterns of the results.

The Flow of the Vote

Table 1 shows the electoral turnover from 1984 to 1988. When the total net results of the various switching patterns are computed, the vote changes favoured the opposition parties. From their overall majority of the popular vote in 1984, the Conservatives lost votes through vote-switching by their 1984

TABLE 1
Voting Behaviour 1984-1988
(total percentages)

	Conservative	1988 Liberal	NDP	Other	Did not vote
1984					
Conservative	33.2	7.9	4.2	2.5	3.2
Liberal	4.7	13.7	1.9	.7	2.0
NDP	1.5	2.0	10.0	.2	.5
Other	1.0	.2	.3	.4	.2
Did not vote	2.2	2.1	1.1	.4	3.8
					100%

Note: This entire table adds to 100 percent. The individual rows or columns do not.
Source: 1988 reinterview of 1984 National Election Study sample. (N = 1037) Panel weights applied. No new voters in 1988 are represented.

supporters to the Liberals, the New Democrats, and a group of small parties, such as the Western Reform party. Thus, the table, which percentages the total electorate with the exception of new voters entering in 1988, shows that 7.9 percent of the electorate changed from a 1984 Conservative vote to a 1988 Liberal vote, whereas 4.7 percent switched the other way. The equivalent vote exchanges between the Conservatives and the NDP were 4.2 percent versus 1.5, and between the Conservatives and other parties, 2.5 percent versus 1.0. As was often noted in previous elections, the incumbent government suffered a loss of some of its previous support.

However, the arrival in the 1988 electorate of those who had not participated in the previous election either through choice or lack of eligibility (the 'electoral replacement' process described in Chapter Six), helped the Conservatives offset the losses they suffered through vote-switching.[4] The Tories won a very slight plurality of those "transient voters" who moved into the 1988 electorate from a 1984 abstention. It is true that those who behaved in the reverse manner, deciding not to cast a ballot in 1988, were more likely to have been 1984 Conservatives (3.2 percent of the electorate, as opposed to a combined total of 2.7 percent for all the other parties). However, when combined with behaviour of newly eligible 1988 voters, who favoured the Conservatives (see the later section of this chapter) electoral replacement worked to the advantage of the Progressive Conservative party.

The combination of the Conservatives' ability to hold a substantial portion of their 1984 vote, together with an infusion of new voter support, sustained the party in power despite the tendency of electoral conversion to drain votes from it. This pattern is by no means unique in Canadian electoral history. It sustained the Liberal Party in power during the Trudeau years, in elections like 1974 when that party lost votes through conversion and yet gained the parliamentary majority that had eluded it two years earlier.[5]

Factors in the Vote Decision

Only about a third of the 1988 Canadian electorate (as opposed to half in more normal elections) claimed to have made up their minds which way to vote prior to

TABLE 2
1984-1988 Voting Pattern, By Time of Vote Decision
(row percentages)

1984-1988 Votes	Before Campaign	Early in Campaign	After Debate	In last 2 weeks
		Vote Decided		
Stable Voting				
PC-PC	36%	30	7	25
LIB-LIB	42%	26	16	16
NDP-NDP	54%	28	4	14
Switches to Conservatives				
LIB-PC	22%	28	11	40
NDP-PC	7%	50	14	29
Switches to Liberals				
PC-LIB	19%	25	20	36
NDP-LIB	10%	19	18	53
Switches to NDP				
PC-NDP	27%	19	17	38
LIB-NDP	37%	21	16	26

Note: Numbers may not add to 100 percent due to rounding.
Source: 1988 reinterview of 1984 National Election Study sample. (N=797) Panel weights applied.
Voters in both 1984 and 1988 only.

the start of the campaign. Even if we allow for the fact that some of the remainder were undoubtedly "leaning" one way or the other, the period of the campaign was of extraordinary importance. As many of the other chapters in this book indicate, the parties themselves felt that the campaign events, media coverage and advertising, were crucial to the outcome.

Table 2 shows, however, that support for the PC government was established early in the campaign. Two-thirds of those 1984 Tory voters who decided to support the party again in 1988 made up their minds either before the campaign started, or early in the campaign, at a point where the party seemed to be in a commanding position. Thus, the early Conservative "managing change" campaign, while it was altered later in response to events, did serve to consolidate important support for the party. We can also note, however, that a quarter of the 1984 Conservatives who voted the same way left their decision until the last two weeks of the campaign. Thus, the second phase of the Conservative campaign, which employed advertising attacking the credibility of Turner and the Liberals, also may have been effective, in that it may have served to bring an important group of waverers back into the fold. Liberal switching to the PCs was also high in the last weeks of the campaign. In contrast, those 1984 Liberals, and particularly New Democrats, who decided to vote the same way, made that decision even earlier in the game than Conservatives.

Vote-switching appears from Table 2 to have been much more of a last-minute decision. This is particularly apparent among those 1984 NDP voters who decided to cast a Liberal ballot in 1988. Heavily motivated, as we shall shortly see, by the desire to register most effectively their disapproval of the Free Trade

TABLE 3
Most Important Factors in Voting, 1984 and 1988

A. 1984 ELECTION

PARTY LEADERS		LOCAL CANDIDATES		PARTY AS A WHOLE	
30%		21%		49%	
ISSUES STOOD FOR	PERSONAL QUALITIES	ISSUES STOOD FOR	PERSONAL QUALITIES	ISSUES STOOD FOR	GENERAL APPROACH
56%	44%	46%	54%	37%	63%

B. 1988 ELECTION

PARTY LEADERS		LOCAL CANDIDATES		PARTY AS A WHOLE	
20%		27%		53%	
ISSUES STOOD FOR	PERSONAL QUALITIES	ISSUES STOOD FOR	PERSONAL QUALITIES	ISSUES STOOD FOR	GENERAL APPROACH
71%	29%	57%	43%	57%	43%

Source: 1984 National Election Study and 1988 reinterview of 1984 National Election Study sample. Population weights applied.

Agreement, over half of all NDP-Liberal switchers made their decision in the last two weeks of the campaign. The effect of the Turner win in the debates is apparent from these patterns, as both NDP and Conservative changes to the Liberals were heavily concentrated in the post-debate period.

The common perception that the 1988 election was much more focussed around issues than was that of 1984 is supported in these data. Table 3 gives the results from studies of both elections from the survey question which asked respondents to choose whether the party leaders, the local candidates or the parties as a whole were most important to their voting decision, and then probed for the presence or absence of an issue basis to this choice. The 1984 responses, similar to those offered to identical questions in Federal Election Studies since 1974, showed that parties as a whole were more important to electoral choice than leaders (or especially, than candidates), and that a majority of the party answers normally reflect a consideration of the party's "general approach to government" rather than its "position on specific issues." In the 1988 survey, those choosing party as most important were more likely to cite an issue basis for their choice. Important as the underlying issues were to those who cast a vote based on party, they were even more crucial to those citing leaders. Over 70 percent of those saying that party leader was most important to their voting decision stated that it was the leader's issue positions rather than his "personal qualities" that motivated the choice. Significantly, those picking leader as most important factor were substantially fewer than usual in 1988, reflecting the

TABLE 4
Ratings of the Conservative Government
(mean /4)

RATED ON:	ALL VOTERS FOR:			SWITCHERS TO:	
	CONS	LIB	NDP	CONS	LIB/NDP
OVERALL PERFORMANCE	2.2	2.8	3.1	2.3	2.8
FREE TRADE	2.1	3.4	3.5	2.1	3.4
LEADERSHIP	2.2	2.8	3.1	2.4	2.8
UNEMPLOYMENT	2.3	2.8	3.1	2.3	2.8
NATIONAL UNITY	2.3	2.9	3.2	2.4	3.0
THE DEFICIT	2.5	3.0	3.3	2.7	3.1
HONESTY	2.7	3.3	3.5	3.0	3.4
DAY CARE	2.8	3.3	3.4	3.0	3.3
ENVIRONMENT	2.8	3.2	3.4	3.0	3.2
ABORTION	3.0	3.4	3.4	3.0	3.2

Note: ratings signify 1 = excellent 2 = good 3 = fair 4 = poor
Source: 1988 reinterview of 1984 National Election Study. Population weights applied.

lack of enthusiasm for all the leaders. As a result, the role of local candidates in motivating electoral decision-making in 1988 was at a higher level than in the 1984 election. In previous elections, however, those voting with local candidates uppermost in their minds had been concerned with their personal appeal. In 1988 it was candidates' issue positions which took precedence.

Canadians gave the Conservatives mixed reviews for their overall 1984-88 performance as the Government of Canada. There is a substantial relationship, as might be expected, between these ratings and the party that people voted for in 1988. (Table 4) Conservative voters gave the government an overall rating which was close to "good" on a four-point scale, while Liberal voters thought it closer to "fair" and NDP voters were slightly harsher. Probing more deeply into the specifics of the Conservative record reveals considerable variation in public approval. Even among Conservative partisans, "good" ratings were delivered to the government only in the areas of dealing with free trade and unemployment, fostering national unity, and providing leadership for the country. The improved state of the national economy encouraged such a positive judgement on the economic issues, as did the Meech Lake Accord in the realm of unity.

Judgments of the Conservative government in a number of other issue-areas were not nearly so favourable, even among their own supporters. On social issues such as day care, on the question of protection of the environment, on the sensitive matter of abortion legislation, and in "running an honest government" even those who voted Conservative rendered a less-than-enthusiastic verdict. Liberals and New Democrats, of course, were more critical. But overall, the Canadian public rated the Mulroney government 2.75/4 for its performance during the four years preceeding the election, somewhat akin to giving a student a 'C+' on an examination. In such an atmosphere, the government could hope for reelection only if the alternatives were even less acceptable.

The Leaders
When considered as a group, Canadian political party leaders reached a nadir of popularity in 1988. Public attitudes towards leaders have been measured in the

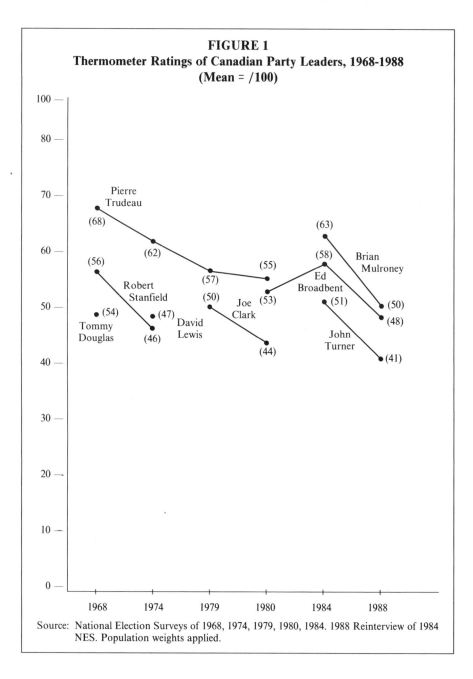

FIGURE 1
Thermometer Ratings of Canadian Party Leaders, 1968-1988
(Mean = /100)

Source: National Election Surveys of 1968, 1974, 1979, 1980, 1984. 1988 Reinterview of 1984 NES. Population weights applied.

National Election Studies since 1968 by a technique known as the "thermometer," in which interviewees are told to rate their feelings of warmth or coolness toward the politicians who lead the parties in terms of a thermometer which ranges from 0 degrees at its coldest end to 100 degrees at its warmest.

Using this measure (Figure 1 and, later, Table 8) judgements about Canadian political leaders have ranged in general downwards since the heady period of the late 1960s when Trudeaumania swept the land.[6] The downward slide of Trudeau's image reflects the perhaps-inevitable disillusionment which sets in after a public figure has become a known quantity.

Despite this overall trend, the depth of public displeasure with the leaders in 1988 was extraordinary. Since measurement using the thermometer began, we have never before experienced a federal election in which *no* leader scored above the neutral mark (50). Sitting Prime Ministers have, it is true, not fared well. We have to go back ten years to 1979 to find an incumbent PM rated above the neutral point (Trudeau at 57). Joe Clark in 1980, and John Turner in 1984 were rated poorly. But Brian Mulroney's nosedive in public appeal is unprecedented: he fell fully 13 points (from 63 to 50) in 4 years, eclipsing any of the other declines registered previously, such as Robert Stanfield's 10 point drop between 1968 and 1974.

As can be clearly seen in Figure 1, the public also judged John Turner and Ed Broadbent harshly. Both the Liberal and NDP leaders fell a full 10 points in public estimation between 1984 and 1988. In Broadbent's case, the fall from grace (58 to 48 on the thermometer) must have been particularly upsetting, since he had maintained a substantially more favourable public image than any other NDP leader, and in fact led "best Prime Minister" polls at various points during the four years. Broadbent's supposed personal drawing power was made the centerpiece of the NDP campaign. And John Turner in 1988 was, quite simply, the least popular Canadian political leader in 20 years (eclipsing at 41 thermometer points the old record established by Joe Clark in 1980), and quite likely one of the least approved in Canadian history.

The depth of public antipathy to Turner presents a considerable irony, since he was generally acknowledged to have waged a passionate election campaign in his crusade against the Free Trade Agreement. Evaluations of the leaders' performance in the debates held in mid-campaign showed Turner a clear winner (Table 5). On a scale of 0 to 10, Canadians gave Turner a mean score of 6.8, a full point higher than Mulroney, and almost two points ahead of Broadbent. This perception of Turner's superiority in the leader debates was not just held by

TABLE 5
Evaluations of Leader Debate 1988
(mean /10)

DEBATE PERFORMANCE	MULRONEY	TURNER	BROADBENT
OVERALL	5.8	6.8	4.9
PC VOTERS	6.4	6.1	4.5
LIB VOTERS	5.4	7.8	4.8
NDP VOTERS	5.0	7.1	6.2
OTHER VOTERS	5.5	5.6	4.5

Note: rating scale: 0 = very poor 10 = very good performance
Source: 1988 reinterview of 1984 National Election Study. Population weights applied.

Liberal voters—those who ended up voting NDP preferred Turner's debate performance to that of their own leader by a wide margin, and even Conservative voters were willing to grant Turner almost as much credibility as the Prime Minister in the TV extravaganza. Obviously, then, the debate wasn't everything, even though Turner's performance visibly improved Liberal morale, placed the NDP on the defensive in the race for second place, and made the election a lot closer than it otherwise would have been.

The public distaste for all the leaders is reflected in the unusually low level of "leader personality effects" on the election outcome. We have already noted the drop in those citing "party leader" as the most important factor in their voting decision. (Table 3) The number of voters doing so declined to a mere 20 percent, and of those, most said that the issue stands of the leaders were more important than the leaders' "personal qualities." Of the relatively small group of people who cited the personalities of the leaders as the most important factor in deciding their votes, the Conservatives showed a slight advantage, coming primarily from 1984 Tory voters deciding to remain with that party and citing Mulroney's personal characteristics as the prime reason. However, comparisons of 1988 with previous years show that the "leadership edge" of Mulroney was insignificant this time, compared with his own in 1984, and with Pierre Trudeau in previous elections.[7] Local candidate personality effects were substantially more important to the Conservative victory in 1988 than were those of leader, perhaps because they had so many incumbent members.

The Issues

The fact that discussion of issues dominated the election campaign in 1988 was not in itself unusual, but the concentration on a single issue was less normal. Elections dominated by single issues have occurred before, but those in most recent memory have been issues of a broad "problem" sort. (see Chapter Six, Table 3) In 1974, many people agreed that "the problem of inflation" was an urgent priority for government to attack, though much discussion took place about the feasibility of various proposals for so doing such as wage and price controls, and even whether such a world-wide phenomenon would be tractable to the policy manouevres of a single nation. The 1984 election witnessed a comparable amount of public agreement in identifying unemployment as a problem for government, encapsulated by Mr. Mulroney's definition of the important election issues as "jobs, jobs, jobs."

The concentration on free trade as the election issue of 1988 was, however, so total as to approach a genuine consensus. The issue was mentioned as "most important election issue" by 82 percent of the electorate, and many of those who failed to cite it in their first opportunity mentioned it as second choice. (Table 6) Unemployment as a political issue had faded from view, with only a scattering of people thinking that the 8 percent unemployment rate of 1988 merited the same government attention as the 11 percent rate of 1984. And inflation, the number-one bogey of the seventies, had gone so far away from the public mind that not one single person in the sample identified it as an election issue in 1988, despite

TABLE 6
Most Important Election Issues 1988

	MOST IMPORTANT	ALL[a] MENTIONS
ECONOMIC ISSUES		
free trade	82%	88%
state of economy generally	1	2
inflation	0	0
taxes	1	4
govt spending, deficit	2	7
unemployment	1	2
CONFEDERATION ISSUES		
national unity, intergov. relations	1	6
bilingualism, language	—	2
RESOURCE ISSUES		
environment	2	9
SOCIAL ISSUES		
housing, welfare, medicare, education, pensions, etc	2	14
OTHER ISSUES		
foreign policy, defence	0	1
leadership	2	5
party evaluations	1	1
trust in govt/patronage	1	1
all others	1	3
NO ISSUES	5	X

[a]Percentage of those mentioning an issue. Two mentions possible.
Source: 1988 reinterview of 1984 National Election Study.
Population weights applied. (N = 1203)

the fact that, at 4 percent, the inflation rate was by no means insignificant by overall postwar standards.

Free trade dominated the 1988 issue agenda so totally that hardly anyone could escape it. Only 5 percent of the survey respondents, therefore, stated that there was "no issue" in 1988, a number substantially lower than the 25 to 30 percent that normally cannot identify an issue. Two other issue areas did, however, manage to shove their way onto the agenda in 1988. Social issues, which had undergone a slow slide in the public identification of election questions, continued the modest resurgence they had begun in 1984, in part because of opposition party attempts to identify social programmes as potentially at risk from the Free Trade Agreement. Secondly, environmental issues achieved more importance in the public issue agenda than ever before.

Free trade was not only an unusually dominant issue, it was an unusually specific one. Unlike inflation or unemployment, where all parties could agree that the problem existed and promise to do something about it if elected, free trade was the product of a specific agreement negotiated on the government's initiative with a foreign country. As such, free trade had at least the potential to engender public discussion on specific matters of public policy, and to spark an

TABLE 7
Effects of Issues in 1988 Election
(% of total voters)

VOTING PATTERN	CONS	LIB	NDP	OTHER
A. FREE TRADE				
switch to	3.7	7.5	3.2	1.3
remain	16.5	7.8	6.1	.1
84 nonvote to	1.3	1.6	.9	.3
total	21.5	16.9	10.2	1.7
B. ALL OTHER ISSUES				
switch to	.6	.7	.4	.6
remain	3.0	1.0	.9	.2
84 nonvote to	.1	0	.1	.1
total	3.7	1.7	1.4	.9

Note: The table displays voting patterns for those citing issues as the most important factor in their voting decision. It divides people according to which issue they considered most important.
Source: 1988 reinterview of 1984 National Election Study. (N = 937) Panel weights applied. Voters in 1988 only.

overall public decision on the correct direction of that policy. And politicians of all parties seemed to help this process along, since the Liberals held up passage of the bill implementing the agreement by their insistence that an election be held on the issue, the Conservative government obliged by calling one, and even the NDP revised its initial strategy to go along with the general mood to call the 1988 election "a referendum on free trade."

Table 7 (Panel A) estimates the potential impact of the free trade issue on the 1988 election outcome by examining the voting patterns of those who said that issues were the most important factor in their voting decision and who designated the subject as the most important election issue. Patterns of vote-switching based on the free trade issue went substantially against the Conservatives, with almost as many people switching to the NDP on the issue as to the PCs, and substantially more choosing the Liberals. The table also shows, however, that a large bloc of issue-oriented voters, constituting 16.5 percent of the total, remained with their 1984 Conservative vote choice, and cited free trade as the most important issue reason for doing so. There was a small group of Conservative voters who did not favour the Free Trade Agreement, but they were more or less cancelled out in the total picture by those Liberal and NDP voters who thought the FTA might be a good idea after all.

Was the 1988 election a referendum on the Free Trade Agreement, and did the reelected government receive a policy mandate on the issue? The totals in Table 7 show that about half of the voters in 1988 claimed to be making up their minds primarily on the basis of the free trade issue. Looking at the electorate as a whole, the results cannot be interpreted as reflecting a clear public statement on the issue. The results show that just over a fifth of voters (21.5 percent) voted primarily on issues, cited free trade as the most important issue, and voted Conservative. Since both the Liberal and New Democratic parties opposed the

agreement, the equivalent issue-oriented votes for those two parties based on free trade could be added together in evaluating the public judgement on the issue. If one does so, just over a quarter of Canadians (16.9 percent voting Liberal and 10.2 percent voting NDP) disagreed with the FTA. Thus, no pro-FTA policy mandate can be claimed by the Progressive Conservative party, despite the fact that they won the election. Of course, if one compares the Conservative voting on the issue in Table 7 with each of the other parties separately, the PCs have an edge on the issue.

The political parties decided on their interpretation of this question right away, with the Conservatives claiming a mandate on free trade, and the Liberals announcing that "the public had chosen" their opponents and that they would no longer seek to delay unduly passage of the legislation, which was in fact put in place by the end of the year. The parties' logic in adopting this position reflected their judgement of public reaction to any other course of action, and hence a belief that the public at large considered the issue decided by the election result rather than by the more detailed consideration of voting patterns based specifically on the issue, such as we have engaged in here. No doubt this judgement was an accurate reading of the mood of Canadians—efforts to further harass and block the agreement would have produced a public opinion backlash against the opposition. Strictly speaking, however, the public judgement on free trade was not clear-cut, supporting yet again the position that elections are a very poor mechanism for genuine public consultation on specific public policy issues.[8]

Regional Voting Patterns

Canadian federal elections are often a composite of many different trends in separate parts of the country. In recent elections, for example, the province of Quebec has produced solid support for a party, the Liberals, favoured by relatively few in the Western region of Canada. In this respect, then, the 1984 Conservative landslide produced a "national" electoral result for the first time since at least 1968, and arguably since 1958. Conservatives came from all provinces in large numbers. In 1988 there was the re-emergence of a distinctive regional pattern in the results.

Election night 1988 saw a poor showing for the Progressive Conservative party in the periphery of the country, both East and West. Indeed, there are reports of panic having struck the party officials when initial reports of the Maritime results showed substantial Liberal victories. Quebec was solidly Conservative, and the party even did well in Ontario, where doubts had existed all during the campaign about how they would fare. In the West, Saskatchewan and particularly British Columbia gave substantial gains to the NDP. Thus, contrary to many of the assumptions made in the long era in which the Liberals formed the government, Canadian regional patterns of party support were not tied to the public's view of that party as the representative of central Canada. Rather, it appeared much more as if the periphery of the country was expressing doubt about the incumbent federal government, whatever its partisan stripe.

TABLE 8
Leader and Issue Ratings, By Province, 1984 and 1988

A. LEADER THERMOMETER RATINGS (MEAN /100)

	MULRONEY		TURNER		BROADBENT	
	1984	1988	1984	1988	1984	1988
CANADA	63	50	51	41	58	48
NEWFOUNDLAND	67	58	57	47	60	52
PR ED ISLAND	69	55	54	37	62	42
NOVA SCOTIA	61	53	51	41	57	45
NEW BRUNSWICK	64	47	56	45	63	44
QUEBEC	66	56	51	42	55	42
ONTARIO	62	46	50	41	60	53
MANITOBA	57	48	52	45	56	46
SASKATCHEWAN	67	50	52	45	58	52
ALBERTA	70	59	47	31	53	40
BR COLUMBIA	58	43	54	44	57	58

B. FREE TRADE AGREEMENT

	SUPPORT-OPPOSITION (Mean /4)*	VOTE IMPORTANCE (Mean /3)**
CANADA	2.4	1.7
NEWFOUNDLAND	2.4	1.9
PR ED ISLAND	2.5	1.8
NOVA SCOTIA	2.3	1.9
NEW BRUNSWICK	2.8	1.9
QUEBEC	2.1	1.8
ONTARIO	2.6	1.6
MANITOBA	2.2	1.9
SASKATCHEWAN	2.9	1.7
ALBERTA	2.0	1.7
BR COLUMBIA	2.6	1.6

*1 = strongly favour 2 = somewhat favour 3 = somewhat oppose 4 = strongly oppose
**1 = a great deal of effect on vote 2 = some 3 = not much
Source: 1984 National Election Study and 1988 reinterview. Population weights applied.

The pattern of regional support for the Conservative government in 1988 looked surprisingly similar (Alberta excepted) to that for the Liberals in the Trudeau era.

With the exception of British Columbia, the regional patterns of leader approval on the thermometer measure provide little explanation for the differential patterns of party support. John Turner was not discernibly more popular in provinces where the Liberals did well than where they failed. Ed Broadbent was the most popular leader in Ontario, where the NDP failed to enhance substantially their total of seats in Parliament, as he was in British Columbia, where they did. Brian Mulroney was just about as personally popular in much of the Maritime region as he was in Quebec or even Alberta, and yet we have noted the Conservative failure in Atlantic Canada. The amount of variation in leader popularity displayed in Table 8 is very similar to that in the Trudeau era, with the gap in mean thermometer ratings between most popular and least popular provincial scores being 16 in the cases of Mulroney and Turner, and 18 for Broadbent.

TABLE 9
Gender and Vote, 1988

VOTE	MEN	WOMEN
A. VOTES OF MEN AND WOMEN, 1988		
Conservative	52%	43%
Liberal	25	32
NDP	19	21
Other	5	5
B. VOTE SWITCHING 1984-88		
% switching votes	25.8	27.4
% switching to Conservatives	8.8	6.3
% switching to Lib/NDP	12.5	14.1

C. VOTE BY FAMILY INCOME AND GENDER, 1988

Family Income ($ thousand)	29 AND UNDER	30-49	50 AND OVER
MALE VOTERS			
voted Conservative	42%	49%	61%
voted Liberal	27	20	21
voted NDP	24	24	15
voted for other parties	8	6	3
FEMALE VOTERS			
voted Conservative	43%	43%	44%
voted Liberal	32	36	29
voted NDP	23	16	24
voted for other parties	3	4	3

D. FREE TRADE AGREEMENT

	SUPPORT/OPPOSITION (Mean /4)	VOTE IMPORTANCE (Mean /3)
MEN	2.2	1.7
WOMEN	2.6	1.7

Note: Numbers may not add to 100 percent due to rounding.
Source: 1988 reinterview of 1984 National Election Study.
Population weights applied. 1988 voters only.

Issue concerns show similar identification of important issues across the provinces, with the exceptions of an enhanced concern for the environment in British Columbia and Quebec, a concern which was aimed in an anti-government direction only in the former province. Opinions on free trade are, however, consistent with regional voting patterns in many places. Saskatchewan, British Columbia, New Brunswick and Ontario all show higher than average opposition to the Free Trade Agreement (Table 8B) Given the overall importance of free trade opinion to the voting decision, these issue concerns provide more explanation of regional voting patterns than do those resting on other factors.

Gender and Vote in 1988

The 1988 federal election saw the emergence of a gender gap in Canadian voting, but one relatively modest in size. Whereas in 1984 the differential in the Progressive Conservative vote between men and women was 3 percent, this increased to 9 percent in 1988 (Table 9A). The propensity for women to switch their votes from 1984 to 1988 was higher than that for men, and was more likely to be directed away from the Conservatives. (Table 9B) Women's voting patterns were less likely to be related to income than were men's. (Table 9C) Men who lived in households making over $50,000 a year voted PC at a 61 percent rate, compared to 42 percent of those in households earning under $30,000. Women show no such variation by level of income, although those who had business or professional occupations were more partial to free trade and the Conservative party than were women in other occupational categories, including housewives. The male-female differentials referred to here are equivalent for both French and English speakers, even though francophone women supported the Conservatives at a higher rate than did anglophones (a finding also true for men.)

Women rated the Conservative Party lower than did men on the thermometer (a mean score of 51 as opposed to 55 for men). Women were also less favourable to Prime Minister Mulroney, giving him a mean thermometer score of 47, compared to 53 for men. When asked for their evaluation of the performance of the Progressive Conservative government in a series of issue areas (specified in Table 4), the women's judgements were consistently harsher. Of particular relevance to the voting decision was women's rating of the Free Trade Agreement, well below men in terms of a mean score (Table 9D).

New Voters in 1988

At the outset of this chapter, when discussing the flows of the vote from 1984 to 1988, we noted that, although our reinterview of the 1984 National Election Study contained no new voters, we could look with a different data set at the behaviour of those who joined the active electorate in 1988. Table 10 displays the electoral choices made by young people, as well as some of their opinions. Although the Conservatives did slightly less well among new voters than among those who had participated before, they still fared much better than the other parties. Thus, going along with their slight plurality of the transient vote from 1984, the Conservatives saw the electoral replacement process operate in their favour. In so doing, they mirrored the performance of the Trudeau Liberals, in that while switching often went against that party while in power, they gained, and often sustained their governmental position, through recruiting new cadres of support at every election. If a disproportionate number of these new recruits were subsequently to desert the party, there were still newer support groups to recruit. The same thing may indeed be happening to the Conservative party in the present, and if so, they may be able to establish as dominant a position as the Liberals of an earlier era.

TABLE 10
Behaviour of New and Established Voters, 1988

	NEW VOTERS	OTHER VOTERS
A. Voted: Conservative	41%	44%
Liberal	28	33
NDP	29	19
Other parties	3	4
B. Cited issues as most important factor in voting decision	62%	50%
C. Cited free trade as most important issue	84%	69%
D. Opposed to free trade	55%	51%
E. Made vote decision in last week	34%	25%
F. Best Prime Minister:		
Mulroney	51%	49%
Broadbent	33	30
Turner	16	20
G. Party Identification:		
Conservative	34%	37%
Liberal	35	26
NDP	10	15

Note: Numbers may not add to 100 percent due to rounding.
Source: Carleton Journalism Exit Poll, 1988. Population weights applied. Voters only. (N = 1813)

However, there are rays of hope for the Liberal party in the current crop of new voters. For one thing, more of them claim to identify with the Liberal party than any other, indicating that attractive leadership could translate these feelings into votes in the future. (Table 10G) Indeed, more attractive leadership could likely have translated these party identifications into Liberal votes in 1988 as well — the 1988 young voters were more issue-oriented than other members of the electorate, and were also more anti-free trade. (Table 10C and D) They made their vote decisions late in the campaign. (Table 10E) However, their rating of Turner as the leader who would make the best Prime Minister was even lower than the rest of the electorate. Leadership, then, while not looming large in an overall interpretation of the 1988 election, did play an important role in drying up a possible reservoir of Liberal votes, and salvaging them for the Conservatives.

Conclusion
The 1988 Canadian federal election was marked by public indifference to the claims of the parties and the performance of the leaders. It was decided by the ultimate judgement that the potential alternative governments offered by the opposition parties were not credible. Despite John Turner's performance in the leadership debate, and despite Ed Broadbent's high approval rating in the inter-election period, the electorate did not trust them or their parties to form a government. Despite lukewarm feelings towards the Conservatives and also towards Prime Minister Mulroney, many voting choices went their way by

default. Electoral replacement worked ultimately in the Conservatives' favour, with young voters choosing not to opt for an unknown or risky future.

The free trade gamble paid off; while it certainly did not win the Conservatives more votes than it lost through switching, it provided a reason for a large proportion of 1984 voters to stay with that party. Though many Canadians had doubts or second thoughts about free trade (indeed, the country was split on its desirability), it was a comprehensive policy initiative with a vision of an economic future, which was more than the other parties could credibly claim. So in the end it came down to a choice to sustain known quantities instead of opting for a very uncertain and potentially disastrous future.

Endnotes

1. The 1984 Canadian National Election Study was financed by the Social Sciences and Humanities Research Council of Canada, and organized by Ronald Lambert, Steven Brown, James Curtis, Barry Kay and John Wilson. Previous studies were conducted after the1965, 1968, 1974, 1979 and 1980 elections, and are referred to occasionally in this chapter. The most extensive reports of these studies are contained in Harold D. Clarke, Jane Jenson, Lawrence LeDuc and Jon H. Pammett, *Absent Mandate* (Toronto: Gage, 1984) and *Political Choice in Canada* (Toronto: McGraw-Hill Ryerson, 1979).
2. The 1988 reinterview of the 1984 Canadian National Election Study sample was organized by Ronald Lambert, Steven Brown, James Curtis, Barry Kay, Lawrence LeDuc and Jon Pammett, and was conducted by the Carleton University Journalism Survey Centre under the direction of Alan Frizzell.
3. The 1988 Exit Poll was organized by Alan Frizzell, and carried out by the Carleton University Journalism Survey Centre. Interviews were carried out with voters leaving the polling booths in two constituencies from each province in Canada.
4. The distinction between electoral conversion and replacement is developed in *Political Choice in Canada* and *Absent Mandate*, both *op cit.*
5. See *Political Choice in Canada*, chapter 12.
6. See the analyses of leader images in *Absent Mandate*, ch 5.
7. See *Absent Mandate*, p 162. 8. Jon H. Pammett, "Political Education and Democratic Participation," in Jon H. Pammett and Jean-Luc Pepin, eds, *Political Education in Canada* (Halifax: Institute for Research on Public Policy, 1988) pp 209-218.

Conclusion

The election of 1988 was one of the most dramatic in Canadian history. A single issue, free trade, dominated debate and aroused political passions to a degree seldom seen in Canada. There was an abrupt change of party fortunes in the middle of the campaign, and then a gradual return to the status quo ante under the influence of advertising which attacked opponents with unusual ferocity. In these circumstances, the results have been subjected to a variety of shorthand explanations. To some commentators it was mainly a referendum on free trade, and that topic was certainly the focus of media coverage. To others, it was basically a question of leadership, despite the fact that none of the candidates commanded much popular enthusiasm.

The analyses in this book desmonstrate that neither of these simple explanations is viable. Free trade was certainly in the minds of many voters when they made their decision, but it was only one factor, and analyses of voting show that opinion was divided into roughly equal parts. While the election result cannot be interpreted as an endorsement of free trade, under the Canadian parliamentary system the outcome was a mandate for the Conservatives to govern, and this included the implementation of their trade policy.

The evidence on leadership also is inconclusive. Fewer voters cited leaders as the most important factor in their decision than in previous surveys. As a group, the leaders of the three major parties were less popular than at any time in recent history, and in fact analysis of voting behaviour shows that Canadians have become more sceptical of political leadership. In other words, we may have seen a change in public attitude towards leadership rather than a reflection on the quality of that leadership. Nevertheless, Prime Minister Mulroney had a relative advantage over his opponents, and that was a factor in the outcome.

The most persuasive conclusion is that the verdict in 1988, to return the Conservative government with a reduced majority, was determined in the same way as most recent Canadian elections — by a combination of decisions based on current rather than longer term considerations. These considerations were often negative, a lack of confidence in the alternatives rather than a positive statement of support for the government. For many voters in 1988, the Conservative party was the least objectionable choice, the safest choice despite the uncertainties of free trade, the party with some semblance of acceptable leadership and managerial experience and skill. It was the election in which the idea that the governing party was "The best of a bad bunch" overtook the 1984 belief that it was "Time for a change."

The predominance of short-term forces provides no support for the notion that the election constitutes a basic realignment of political support, establishing a new Conservative hegemony for the 1990s and beyond. Instead, large groups of voters chose between the parties on the basis of candidates, issues and images of the day rather than on established party loyalties or socially-determined alignments. Evidence for this is apparent from the considerable swings in public opinion between the elections and during the campaign. In these circumstances, the campaign was obviously important, and here the Conservatives scored. They had more money, more experience and a better organization than their opponents, and on the whole they managed things well, keeping Mulroney out of trouble while Turner floundered and his campaign organization was riven by feuds. The key to a breakthrough for the NDP was in Quebec, but the party's credibility was weakened by Broadbent's limited ability in French and by the inexperience of its leaders in the province. The Conservative campaign was a testimonial to media management and the effective use of polls and advertising to find and attack the weak spots of their opponents.

APPENDIX

The Results

Nationally

TABLE A1
Federal Election Results*
(X = less than 1%)

		1945	1949	1953	1957	1958	1962	1963	1965
LIB	VOTE %	41	49.5	49	41	34	37	41	40
	SEATS	125	193	171	105	49	100	129	131
PC	VOTE %	27	30	31	39	54	37	33	32
	SEATS	67	41	51	112	208	116	95	97
**NDP	VOTE %	16	13	11	11	9.5	13	14	18
	SEATS	28	13	23	25	8	19	17	21
SC	VOTE %	4	4	5	7	3	12	12	8
	SEATS	13	10	15	19	0	30	24	5
OTHER	VOTE %	12	4	3	3	X	1	X	2
	SEATS	12	5	5	4	0	0	0	11
% TURNOUT		75	74	67.5	74	79	79	79	75
TOTAL NUMBER OF SEATS 245		262	265	265	265	265	265	265	

		1968	1972	1974	1979	1980	1984	1988
LIB	VOTE %	46	39	43	40	44	28	32
	SEATS	155	109	141	114	147	40	83
PC	VOTE %	31	35	35	36	33	50	43
	SEATS	72	107	95	136	103	211	169
NDP	VOTE %	17	18	15	18	20	18	20
	SEATS	23	31	16	26	32	30	43
SC	VOTE %	4	8	5	5	2	1	X
	SEATS	14	15	11	6	0	0	0
OTHER	VOTE %	2	X	2	1	1	3	5
	SEATS	1	2	1	0	0	1	0
% TURNOUT		76	77	71	76	69	76	75
TOTAL NUMBER OF SEATS		264	264	264	282	282	282	295

*Reports of the Chief Electoral Officer
**CCF up to and including the 1958 election

By Province

TABLE A2
Election Results by Province 1984 and 1988*
(X = less than 1%)

			1984				1988		
		LIB	PC	NDP	OTHERS	LIB	PC	NDP	OTHERS
NFLD.	VOTE %	36	58	6	X	45	42	12	X
	SEATS	3	4	0	0	5	2	0	0
P.E.I.	VOTE %	41	52	6	X	50	41	7	1
	SEATS	1	3	0	0	4	0	0	0
N.S.	VOTE %	34	51	15	X	47	41	11	1
	SEATS	2	9	0	0	6	5	0	0
N.B.	VOTE %	32	54	14	X	45	40	9	5
	SEATS	1	9	0	0	5	5	0	0
QUE.	VOTE %	35	50	9	5	30	53	14	3
	SEATS	17	58	0	0	12	63	0	0
ONT.	VOTE %	30	48	21	1	39	38	20	3
	SEATS	14	67	13	1	43	46	10	0
MAN.	VOTE %	22	43	27	8	36	37	21	5
	SEATS	1	9	4	0	5	7	2	0
SASK.	VOTE %	18	42	38	2	18	36	44	1
	SEATS	0	9	5	0	0	4	10	0
ALTA.	VOTE %	13	69	14	4	14	52	17	17
	SEATS	0	21	0	0	0	25	1	0
B.C.	VOTE %	16	47	35	2	21	34	37	7
	SEATS	1	19	8	0	1	12	19	0
YUKON/ NWT	VOTE %	24	47	23	4	30	30	37	3
	SEATS	0	3	0	0	2	0	1	0
TOTAL	VOTE %	28	50	19	3	32	43	20	5
	SEATS	40	211	30	1	83	169	43	0

*Reports of the Chief Electoral Officer

By Region

TABLE A3
Election Results by Region 1945-1968 (Seats)*

	1945	1949	1953	1957	1958	1962	1963	1965	1968
ATLANTIC									
LIB	19	25	27	12	8	14	20	15	7
PC	6	7	5	21	25	18	13	18	25
CCF/NDP	1	1	1	—	—	1	—	—	—
SC	—	—	—	—	—	—	—	—	—
OTHER	1	1	—	—	—	—	—	—	—
TOTAL	27	34	33	33	33	33	33	33	32
QUEBEC									
LIB	53	66	66	63	25	35	47	56	56
PC	2	2	4	9	50	14	8	8	4
CCF/NDP	—	—	—	—	—	—	—	—	—
SC	—	—	—	—	—	26	20	9	14
OTHER	10	5	5	3	—	—	—	2	—
TOTAL	65	73	75	75	75	75	75	75	74
ONTARIO									
LIB	34	56	50	20	14	43	52	51	64
PC	48	25	33	61	67	35	27	25	17
CCF/NDP	—	1	1	3	3	6	6	9	6
SC	—	—	—	—	—	—	—	—	—
OTHER	—	1	1	1	1	1	—	—	1
TOTAL	82	83	85	85	85	85	85	85	88
WEST									
LIB	19	43	27	10	1	7	10	9	29
PC	11	7	9	21	66	49	47	46	25
CCF/NDP	27	10	21	22	5	12	11	12	16
SC	13	10	15	19	—	4	4	5	—
OTHER	1	1	—	—	—	—	—	—	—
TOTAL	71	71	72	72	72	72	72	72	70

*Reports of the Chief Electoral Officer

TABLE A3
Election Results by Region 1972-1988 (Seats)*

	1972	1974	1979	1980	1984	1988
ATLANTIC						
LIB	10	13	12	19	7	20
PC	22	17	18	13	25	12
NDP	—	1	2	—	—	—
SC	—	—	—	—	—	—
OTHER	—	1	—	—	—	—
TOTAL	32	32	32	32	32	32
QUEBEC						
LIB	56	60	67	74	17	12
PC	2	3	2	1	58	63
NDP	—	—	—	—	—	—
SC	15	11	6	—	—	—
OTHER	1	—	—	—	—	—
TOTAL	74	74	75	75	75	75
ONTARIO						
LIB	36	55	32	52	14	43
PC	40	25	57	38	67	46
NDP	11	8	6	5	13	10
SC	—	—	—	—	—	—
OTHER	1	—	—	—	1	—
TOTAL	88	88	95	95	95	99
WEST						
LIB	7	13	3	2	2	6
PC	43	50	57	49	58	48
CCF/NDP	20	7	17	26	17	32
SC	—	—	—	—	—	—
OTHER	—	—	—	—	—	—
TOTAL	70	70	77	77	77	86

*Reports of the Chief Electoral Officer

By Province 1974-88

TABLE A4.1
Election Results by Province 1974-1988*
(X = less than 1%)

	LIBERAL					PC				
	1988	1984	1980	1979	1974	1988	1984	1980	1979	1974
NFLD.										
VOTE %	45	36	47	38	47	42	58	36	31	44
SEATS	5	3	5	4	4	2	4	2	2	3
P.E.I.										
VOTE %	50	41	47	40	46	41	52	46	53	49
SEATS	4	1	2	0	1	0	3	2	4	3
N.S.										
VOTE %	47	34	40	36	41	41	51	39	45	47
SEATS	6	2	5	2	2	5	9	6	8	8
N.B.										
VOTE %	45	32	50	45	47	40	54	33	40	33
SEATS	5	1	7	6	6	5	9	3	4	3
QUEBEC										
VOTE %	30	35	68	62	54	53	50	13	13	21
SEATS	12	17	74	67	60	63	58	1	2	3
ONTARIO										
VOTE %	39	30	42	37	45	38	48	36	42	35
SEATS	43	14	52	32	55	46	67	38	57	25
MAN.										
VOTE %	36	22	28	24	27	37	43	38	44	48
SEATS	5	1	2	2	2	7	9	5	7	9
SASK.										
VOTE %	18	18	24	20	31	36	42	39	42	36
SEATS	0	0	0	0	3	4	9	7	10	8
ALTA.										
VOTE %	14	13	21	21	25	52	69	66	67	61
SEATS	0	0	0	0	0	25	21	21	21	19
B.C.										
VOTE %	21	16	22	23	33	34	47	41	45	42
SEATS	1	1	0	1	8	12	19	16	20	12
YUKON/NWT										
VOTE %	30	24	37	33	28	30	47	32	37	39
SEATS	2	0	0	0	0	0	3	2	2	1
TOTAL										
VOTE %	32	28	44	40	43	43	50	33	36	35
SEATS	83	40	147	114	141	169	211	103	136	95

*Reports of the Chief Electoral Officer

TABLE A4.2
Election Results by Province 1974-1988*
(X = less than 1%)

	NDP					ALL OTHERS				
	1988	1984	1980	1979	1974	1988	1984	1980	1979	1974
NFLD.										
VOTE %	12	6	17	31	9	X	X	X	X	X
SEATS	0	0	0	1	0	0	0	0	0	0
P.E.I.										
VOTE %	7	6	7	7	5	1	X	X	X	X
SEATS	0	0	0	0	0	0	0	0	0	0
N.S.										
VOTE %	11	15	21	19	11	1	X	X	X	X
SEATS	0	0	0	1	1	0	0	0	0	0
N.B.										
VOTE %	9	14	16	15	9	5	X	1	X	11
SEATS	0	0	0	0	0	0	0	0	0	1
QUEBEC										
VOTE %	14	9	9	5	7	3	5	10	20	18
SEATS	0	0	0	0	0	0	0	0	6	11
ONTARIO										
VOTE %	20	21	22	21	19	3	1	X	1	1
SEATS	10	13	5	6	8	0	1	0	0	0
MAN.										
VOTE %	21	27	34	33	24	5	8	X	X	1
SEATS	2	4	7	5	2	0	0	0	0	0
SASK.										
VOTE %	44	38	36	37	32	1	2	1	1	1
SEATS	10	5	7	4	2	0	0	0	0	0
ALTA.										
VOTE %	17	14	10	10	9	17	4	3	3	5
SEATS	1	0	0	0	0	0	0	0	0	0
B.C.										
VOTE %	37	35	35	32	23	7	2	2	1	2
SEATS	19	8	12	8	2	0	0	0	0	0
YUKON/NWT										
VOTE %	37	23	31	29	33	3	4	X	1	X
SEATS	1	0	1	1	1	0	0	0	0	0
TOTAL										
VOTE %	20	19	20	18	15	5	3	3	6	6
SEATS	43	30	32	26	16	0	1	0	6	12

*Reports of the Chief Electoral Officer

By Constituency

KEY

PC	Progressive Conservatives
LIB	Liberals
NDP	New Democratic Party
GREEN	Green
REFORM	Reform Party
CONFED RWP	Confederation of Regions Western Party
CHRISTIAN	Christian Heritage Party
LIBERTARIAN	Libertarian Party
RHINO	Rhinoceros Party
COMMONWEALTH	Party for Commonwealth of Canada
COMMUNIST	Communist Party
SC	Social Credit
PN	Parti Nationaliste
INDEPENDENT	Independent

CONSTITUENCY RESULTS**	1988	1984
ONTARIO		
ALGOMA	1988	1984
PC	23.5%	34.7%
LIB	53.2%	38.3%
NDP	23.3%	25.8%
NO AFFILIATION	—	1.3%
TOTAL	31,490	36,885
BRAMPTON	1988	1984
PC	51.6%	—
LIB	24.6%	—
NDP	18.0%	—
CHRISTIAN	4.7%	—
LIBERTARIAN	1.0%	—
TOTAL	57,095	—
BRAMPTON-GEORGETOWN	1988	1984
PC	—	56.2%
LIB	—	27.4%
NDP	—	15.7%
GREEN	—	0.5%
COMMUNIST	—	0.2%
TOTAL	—	85,035
BRAMPTON-MALTON	1988	1984
PC	41.5%	—
LIB	34.4%	—
NDP	22.5%	—
LIBERTARIAN	0.9%	—
COMMUNIST	0.4%	—
NO AFFILIATION	0.3%	—
TOTAL	39,546	—

CONSTITUENCY RESULTS	1988	1984
BRANT	1988	1984
PC	29.7%	41.5%
LIB	24.2%	13.9%
NDP	41.5%	44.2%
CHRISTIAN	3.8%	—
GREEN	0.6%	—
LIBERTARIAN	0.2%	—
COMMONWEALTH	0.1%	—
SC	—	0.4%
TOTAL	47,351	52,275
BRUCE-GREY	1988	1984
PC	40.9%	64.7%
LIB	38.9%	23.3%
NDP	19.0%	12.0%
GREEN	0.7%	—
COMMONWEALTH	0.5%	—
TOTAL	48,311	42,654
BURLINGTON	1988	1984
PC	51.6%	61.9%
LIB	27.1%	18.8%
NDP	16.1%	19.3%
CHRISTIAN	4.5%	—
LIBERTARIAN	0.6%	—
TOTAL	50,496	60,670
CAMBRIDGE	1988	1984
PC	40.4%	60.2%
LIB	26.8%	14.5%
NDP	28.1%	24.1%
CHRISTIAN	4.5%	—
INDEPENDENT	0.3%	—
RHINO	—	0.9%
COMMONWEALTH	—	0.3%
TOTAL	50,961	38,134

CONSTITUENCY RESULTS	1988	1984
CARLETON-GLOUCESTER	1988	1984
PC	37.3%	—
LIB	48.1%	—
NDP	9.7%	—
CHRISTIAN	4.2%	—
RHINO	0.7%	—
TOTAL	64,269	—
COCHRANE-SUPERIOR	1988	1984
PC	23.6%	32.4%
LIB	40.1%	41.7%
NDP	36.4%	25.9%
TOTAL	29,839	29,621
DURHAM	1988	1984
PC	46.5%	—
LIB	29.1%	—
NDP	20.0%	—
CHRISTIAN	3.2%	—
LIBERTARIAN	0.6%	—
GREEN	0.6%	—
TOTAL	51,787	—
DURHAM-NORTHUMBERLAND	1988	1984
PC	—	59.3%
LIB	—	20.8%
NDP	—	18.6%
RHINO	—	0.8%
LIBERTARIAN	—	0.5%
TOTAL	—	42,077
ELGIN	1988	1984
PC	38.6%	67.1%
LIB	34.3%	19.6%
NDP	20.8%	13.4%
CHRISTIAN	6.2%	—
TOTAL	40,623	34,745
ERIE	1988	1984
PC	38.5%	55.8%
LIB	36.5%	27.1%
NDP	20.9%	17.1%
CHRISTIAN	4.1%	—
TOTAL	39,116	34,381
ESSEX-KENT	1988	1984
PC	32.3%	58.0%
LIB	49.4%	28.8%
NDP	18.4%	13.2%
TOTAL	37,750	32,163
ESSEX-WINDSOR	1988	1984
PC	14.3%	31.6%
LIB	41.3%	29.1%
NDP	44.1%	39.3%
NO AFFILIATION	0.2%	—
TOTAL	42,893	47,685

CONSTITUENCY RESULTS	1988	1984
GLENGARRY-PRESCOTT-RUSSELL	1988	1984
PC	19.1%	33.0%
LIB	70.7%	53.1%
NDP	9.1%	13.9%
LIBERTARIAN	0.7%	—
COMMONWEALTH	0.4%	—
TOTAL	49,868	49,065
GREY-SIMCOE	1988	1984
PC	—	59.8%
LIB	—	24.0%
NDP	—	15.4%
LIBERTARIAN	—	0.9%
TOTAL	—	39,049
GUELPH	1988	1984
PC	. —	49.9%
LIB	—	29.2%
NDP	—	19.5%
RHINO	—	0.7%
LIBERTARIAN	—	0.7%
TOTAL	—	47,051
GUELPH-WELLINGTON	1988	1984
PC	43.2%	—
LIB	31.9%	—
NDP	19.5%	—
CHRISTIAN	3.3%	—
GREEN	1.0%	—
LIBERTARIAN	0.5%	—
RHINO	0.4%	—
NO AFFILIATION	0.1%	—
TOTAL	59,523	—
HALDIMAND-NORFOLK	1988	1984
PC	37.6%	59.0%
LIB	38.0%	26.3%
NDP	15.1%	13.3%
CHRISTIAN	8.9%	—
LIBERTARIAN	0.4%	—
INDEPENDENT	—	1.4%
TOTAL	44,500	46,251
HALTON	1988	1984
PC	—	60.6%
LIB	—	22.5%
NDP	—	14.6%
GREEN	—	2.4%
TOTAL	—	62,859
HALTON-PEEL	1988	1984
PC	54.6%	—
LIB	31.6%	—
NDP	13.0%	—
LIBERTARIAN	0.9%	—
TOTAL	52,223	—

CONSTITUENCY RESULTS	1988	1984
HAMILTON EAST	1988	1984
PC	21.4%	30.5%
LIB	49.8%	37.9%
NDP	28.0%	31.0%
NO AFFILIATION	0.4%	—
COMMUNIST	0.4%	0.2%
SC	—	0.3%
COMMONWEALTH	—	0.2%
TOTAL	37,416	38,364
HAMILTON MOUNTAIN	1988	1984
PC	30.5%	32.4%
LIB	32.9%	18.2%
NDP	32.8%	49.2%
CHRISTIAN	3.5%	—
COMMONWEALTH	0.2%	0.2%
NO AFFILIATION	0.1%	—
TOTAL	51,492	52,420
HAMILTON-WENTWORTH	1988	1984
PC	41.9%	52.0%
LIB	34.0%	28.8%
NDP	15.8%	18.0%
CHRISTIAN	7.2%	—
RHINO	1.2%	—
GREEN	—	0.7%
LIBERTARIAN	—	0.4%
COMMONWEALTH	—	0.2%
TOTAL	57,013	49,217
HAMILTON WEST	1988	1984
PC	33.9%	40.4%
LIB	37.8%	30.2%
NDP	25.5%	28.0%
CHRISTIAN	2.1%	—
INDEPENDENT	0.4%	—
COMMUNIST	0.2%	0.4%
LIBERTARIAN	—	0.7%
COMMONWEALTH	—	0.3%
TOTAL	43,860	41,052
HASTINGS-FRONTENAC-LENNOX AND ADDINGTON	1988	1984
PC	40.0%	56.3%
LIB	38.0%	27.5%
NDP	17.3%	15.1%
CHRISTIAN	3.7%	—
INDEPENDENT	1.1%	1.2%
TOTAL	43,158	35,543
HURON-BRUCE	1988	1984
PC	42.6%	64.8%
LIB	35.3%	23.8%
NDP	16.5%	11.0%
CHRISTIAN	5.6%	—
LIBERTARIAN	—	0.4%
TOTAL	47,050	37,004

CONSTITUENCY RESULTS	1988	1984
KENORA RAINY RIVER	1988	1984
PC	21.6%	35.3%
LIB	38.3%	27.6%
NDP	34.8%	37.1%
CHRISTIAN	4.2%	—
RHINO	1.1%	—
TOTAL	34,782	35,946
KENT	1988	1984
PC	35.0%	48.8%
LIB	40.0%	34.8%
NDP	20.1%	16.4%
CHRISTIAN	4.9%	—
TOTAL	39,560	37,444
KINGSTON AND THE ISLANDS	1988	1984
PC	35.8%	55.1%
LIB	40.6%	27.7%
NDP	20.1%	12.6%
CHRISTIAN	2.9%	—
LIBERTARIAN	0.5%	0.6%
NO AFFILIATION	—	3.0%
GREEN	—	1.0%
TOTAL	56,919	47,180
KITCHENER	1988	1984
PC	41.8%	46.8%
LIB	36.1%	28.3%
NDP	21.6%	24.3%
LIBERTARIAN	0.4%	0.5%
NO AFFILIATION	0.2%	—
TOTAL	53,640	57,019
LAMBTON-MIDDLESEX	1988	1984
PC	40.4%	54.6%
LIB	41.5%	33.7%
NDP	12.1%	11.7%
CHRISTIAN	5.9%	—
TOTAL	41,699	41,215
LANARK-CARLETON	1988	1984
PC	48.0%	—
LIB	35.6%	—
NDP	14.7%	—
CONFED RWP	1.7%	—
TOTAL	56,999	—
LANARK-RENFREW-CARLETON	1988	1984
PC	—	53.8%
LIB	—	34.2%
NDP	—	11.7%
COMMONWEALTH	—	0.3%
TOTAL	—	45,372

CONSTITUENCY RESULTS	1988	1984
LEEDS-GRENVILLE	1988	1984
PC	38.9%	61.5%
LIB	43.4%	23.3%
NDP	11.1%	14.0%
CHRISTIAN	3.4%	—
CONFED RWP	3.2%	—
GREEN	—	0.8%
LIBERTARIAN	—	0.4%
TOTAL	46,416	43,842
LINCOLN	1988	1984
PC	38.6%	49.1%
LIB	37.7%	27.3%
NDP	17.5%	22.2%
CHRISTIAN	5.3%	—
INDEPENDENT	0.5%	—
INDEPENDENT	0.2%	—
INDEPENDENT	0.1%	0.2%
NO AFFILIATION	0.1%	0.3%
GREEN	—	0.6%
SC	—	0.2%
TOTAL	51,702	53,609
LONDON EAST	1988	1984
PC	37.5%	47.2%
LIB	37.7%	25.9%
NDP	24.4%	26.9%
NO AFFILIATION	0.4%	—
TOTAL	51,860	38,426
LONDON-MIDDLESEX	1988	1984
PC	38.3%*	47.0%
LIB	38.3%	28.3%
NDP	23.0%	24.7%
NO AFFILIATION	0.4%	—
TOTAL	48,354	39,541
LONDON WEST	1988	1984
PC	45.7%	51.4%
LIB	37.5%	32.3%
NDP	16.1%	16.3%
LIBERTARIAN	0.7%	—
TOTAL	62,155	67,129
MARKHAM	1988	1984
PC	53.1%	—
LIB	31.8%	—
NDP	9.0%	—
NO AFFILIATION	5.3%	—
LIBERTARIAN	0.8	—
TOTAL	69,066	—
MISSISSAUGA EAST	1988	1984
PC	41.5%	—
LIB	45.6%	—
NDP	11.2%	—
LIBERTARIAN	0.7%	—
CONFED RWP	0.5%	—
INDEPENDENT	0.4%	—
COMMONWEALTH	0.2%	—
TOTAL	50,564	—

CONSTITUENCY RESULTS	1988	1984
MISSISSAUGA NORTH	1988	1984
PC	—	49.5%
LIB	—	34.9%
NDP	—	14.5%
GREEN	—	0.6%
LIBERTARIAN	—	0.5%
TOTAL	—	95,194
MISSISSAUGA SOUTH	1988	1984
PC	51.9%	56.4%
LIB	34.7%	28.9%
NDP	12.0%	14.7%
RHINO	0.7%	—
LIBERTARIAN	0.6%	—
COMMONWEALTH	0.1%	—
TOTAL	47,175	58,404
MISSISSAUGA WEST	1988	1984
PC	48.2%	—
LIB	41.5%	—
NDP	9.7%	—
LIBERTARIAN	0.7%	—
TOTAL	68,516	—
NEPEAN	1988	1984
PC	41.5%	—
LIB	47.2%	—
NDP	10.8%	—
COMMONWEALTH	0.5%	—
TOTAL	56,442	—
NEPEAN-CARLETON	1988	1984
PC	—	55.9%
LIB	—	28.0%
NDP	—	14.8%
GREEN	—	1.0%
INDEPENDENT	—	0.3%
TOTAL	—	74,491
NIAGARA FALLS	1988	1984
PC	39.5%	55.1%
LIB	35.0%	19.8%
NDP	21.3%	23.8%
CHRISTIAN	4.0%	—
COMMONWEALTH	0.2%	—
GREEN	—	0.9%
SC	—	0.4%
TOTAL	43,257	41,463
NICKEL BELT	1988	1984
PC	20.8%	31.2%
LIB	23.5%	29.6%
NDP	44.8%	38.6%
CONFED RWP	10.5%	—
RHINO	0.5%	0.7%
TOTAL	38,898	44,410

CONSTITUENCY RESULTS	1988	1984
NIPISSING	1988	1984
PC	39.8%	47.2%
LIB	41.1%	39.8%
NDP	17.2%	13.0%
CONFED RWP	1.4%	—
INDEPENDENT	0.5%	—
TOTAL	37,679	36,540
NORTHUMBERLAND	1988	1984
PC	41.0%	62.3%
LIB	41.1%	24.7%
NDP	14.4%	12.0%
CHRISTIAN	2.4%	
LIBERTARIAN	0.4%	0.4%
RHINO	0.4%	
CONFED RWP	0.2%	—
GREEN	—	0.7%
TOTAL	45,288	38,627
OAKVILLE-MILTON	1988	1984
PC	54.0%	—
LIB	35.1%	—
NDP	8.7%	—
CHRISTIAN	1.7%	
LIBERTARIAN	0.5%	—
TOTAL	64,873	—
ONTARIO	1988	1984
PC	48.9%	56.1%
LIB	32.3%	23.2%
NDP	17.9%	20.7%
LIBERTARIAN	0.7%	—
COMMONWEALTH	0.2%	—
TOTAL	71,443	62,677
OSHAWA	1988	1984
PC	33.8%	38.8%
LIB	20.5%	18.1%
NDP	44.3%	42.3%
LIBERTARIAN	1.1%	0.6%
COMMONWEALTH	0.3%	0.1%
COMMUNIST	—	0.1%
TOTAL	41,534	59,320
OTTAWA-CARLETON	1988	1984
PC	—	44.7%
LIB	—	39.7%
NDP	—	13.9%
RHINO	—	0.8%
INDEPENDENT	—	0.4%
GREEN	—	0.4%
COMMONWEALTH	—	0.1%
TOTAL	—	77,539

CONSTITUENCY RESULTS	1988	1984
OTTAWA CENTRE	1988	1984
PC	26.5%	34.3%
LIB	36.5%	29.6%
NDP	34.9%	34.4%
GREEN	0.6%	0.6%
RHINO	0.6%	0.7%
INDEPENDENT	0.3%	0.1%
INDEPENDENT	0.2%	0.1%
LIBERTARIAN	0.2%	
NO AFFILIATION	0.1%	—
COMMONWEALTH	0.1%	—
COMMUNIST	—	0.2%
INDEPENDENT	—	0.1%
TOTAL	49,638	51,919
OTTAWA SOUTH	1988	1984
PC	35.1%	—
LIB	50.8%	—
NDP	13.5%	—
LIBERTARIAN	0.3%	—
COMMONWEALTH	0.2%	—
NO AFFILIATION	0.1%	—
TOTAL	54,576	—
OTTAWA-VANIER	1988	1984
PC	23.2%	28.8%
LIB	59.2%	49.1%
NDP	16.0%	21.5%
RHINO	1.0%	—
NO AFFILIATION	0.5%	—
NO AFFILIATION	0.1%	—
INDEPENDENT	—	0.6%
TOTAL	48,265	43,601
OTTAWA WEST	1988	1984
PC	38.7%	48.8%
LIB	49.4%	35.4%
NDP	11.2%	15.2%
COMMUNIST	0.3%	—
NO AFFILIATION	0.3%	—
INDEPENDENT	—	0.5%
TOTAL	47,376	54,494
OXFORD	1988	1984
PC	39.7%	57.1%
LIB	37.0%	28.7%
NDP	16.0%	13.5%
CHRISTIAN	6.5%	—
LIBERTARIAN	0.4%	0.7%
COMMONWEALTH	0.3%	—
TOTAL	48,715	44,925
PARRY SOUND-MUSKOKA	1988	1984
PC	43.3%	57.2%
LIB	31.1%	24.1%
NDP	25.7%	17.9%
INDEPENDENT	—	0.8%
TOTAL	39,753	39,723

CONSTITUENCY RESULTS	1988	1984
PERTH	1988	1984
PC	—	54.9%
LIB	—	29.1%
NDP	—	16.0%
TOTAL	—	34,940
PERTH-WELLINGTON-WATERLOO	1988	1984
PC	39.1%	—
LIB	37.0%	—
NDP	19.0%	—
CHRISTIAN	4.4%	—
LIBERTARIAN	0.5%	—
TOTAL	45,972	—
PETERBOROUGH	1988	1984
PC	40.7%	52.7%
LIB	30.3%	22.8%
NDP	27.6%	20.7%
LIBERTARIAN	0.5%	2.9%
RHINO	0.4%	0.6%
GREEN	0.4%	—
INDEPENDENT	—	0.3%
TOTAL	55,056	51,469
PRINCE EDWARD-HASTINGS	1988	1984
PC	36.2%	54.3%
LIB	43.1%	26.7%
NDP	14.5%	18.5%
CHRISTIAN	4.5%	—
CONFED RWP	1.2%	—
LIBERTARIAN	0.5%	—
INDEPENDENT	—	0.5%
TOTAL	45,345	38,714
RENFREW	1988	1984
PC	32.1%	—
LIB	54.3%	—
NDP	12.5%	—
CONFED RWP	1.1%	—
TOTAL	47,038	—
RENFREW-NIPISSING-PEMBROKE	1988	1984
PC	—	45.0%
LIB	—	45.1%
NDP	—	9.8%
TOTAL	—	43,219
ST. CATHERINES	1988	1984
PC	40.7%	49.7%
LIB	33.3%	18.5%
NDP	25.5%	30.6%
COMMUNIST	0.5%	0.2%
GREEN	—	0.7%
SC	—	0.2%
COMMONWEALTH	—	0.1%
TOTAL	48,167	53,530

CONSTITUENCY RESULTS	1988	1984
SARNIA-LAMBTON	1988	1984
PC	45.0%	54.6%
LIB	31.8%	25.7%
NDP	22.2%	19.4%
RHINO	1.0%	—
INDEPENDENT	—	0.2%
INDEPENDENT	—	0.1%
TOTAL	42,861	44,058
SAULT STE. MARIE	1988	1984
PC	32.7%	38.6%
LIB	32.0%	29.3%
NDP	35.3%	31.5%
COMMONWEALTH	—	0.6%
TOTAL	41,385	34,031
SIMCOE CENTRE	1988	1984
PC	45.4%	—
LIB	33.3%	—
NDP	16.2%	—
CHRISTIAN	4.3%	—
CONFED RWP	0.8%	—
TOTAL	51,802	—
SIMCOE NORTH	1988	1984
PC	44.1%	55.0%
LIB	37.8%	26.6%
NDP	18.1%	17.1%
GREEN	—	0.8%
LIBERTARIAN	—	0.5%
TOTAL	49,597	45,282
SIMCOE SOUTH	1988	1984
PC	—	58.1%
LIB	—	26.3%
NDP	—	15.7%
TOTAL	—	52,891
STORMONT-DUNDAS	1988	1984
PC	29.3%	46.0%
LIB	46.0%	41.2%
NDP	12.7%	12.8%
CONFED RWP	12.0%	—
TOTAL	42,853	45,733
SUDBURY	1988	1984
PC	22.0%	32.3%
LIB	42.0%	41.3%
NDP	27.8%	25.7%
CONFED RWP	8.0%	—
COMMUNIST	0.2%	0.2%
RHINO	—	0.6%
TOTAL	42,538	43,613
THUNDER BAY-ATIKOKAN	1988	1984
PC	31.2%	34.0%
LIB	32.7%	24.6%
NDP	35.9%	41.5%
COMMUNIST	0.2%	—
TOTAL	36,629	35,459

CONSTITUENCY RESULTS	1988	1984
THUNDER BAY-NIPIGON	**1988**	**1984**
PC	25.6%	28.3%
LIB	40.2%	34.0%
NDP	34.1%	37.2%
LIBERTARIAN	—	0.5%
TOTAL	38,147	37,418
TIMISKAMING	**1988**	**1984**
PC	36.6%	53.9%
LIB	33.5%	22.1%
NDP	25.5%	23.5%
CONFED RWP	3.9%	—
INDEPENDENT	0.5%	
SC	—	0.5%
TOTAL	30,712	28,503
TIMMINS-CHAPLEAU	**1988**	**1984**
PC	30.8%	37.5%
LIB	32.5%	32.2%
NDP	36.6%	29.9%
NO AFFILIATION	—	0.4%
TOTAL	31,751	31,887
VICTORIA-HALIBURTON	**1988**	**1984**
PC	46.8%	60.9%
LIB	34.8%	20.2%
NDP	17.2%	17.5%
LIBERTARIAN	0.6%	0.7%
SC	0.4%	—
COMMONWEALTH	0.2%	—
GREEN	—	0.7%
TOTAL	47,568	49,606
WATERLOO	**1988**	**1984**
PC	45.1%	56.4%
LIB	36.3%	24.6%
NDP	17.4%	18.2%
LIBERTARIAN	1.1%	0.9%
TOTAL	59,745	56,608
WELLAND	**1988**	**1984**
PC	—	42.0%
LIB	—	33.0%
NDP	—	24.0%
GREEN	—	0.7%
COMMUNIST	—	0.3%
TOTAL	—	43,836
WELLAND-ST. CATHERINES-THOROLD	**1988**	**1984**
PC	34.6%	—
LIB	37.8%	—
NDP	26.7%	—
GREEN	0.6%	—
NO AFFILIATION	0.2%	—
COMMUNIST	0.1%	—
TOTAL	47,212	—

CONSTITUENCY RESULTS	1988	1984
WELLINGTON-DUFFERIN-SIMCOE	**1988**	**1984**
PC	—	68.5%
LIB	—	16.7%
NDP	—	14.8%
TOTAL	—	43,754
WELLINGTON-GREY-DUFFERIN-SIMCOE	**1988**	**1984**
PC	50.9%	—
LIB	30.2%	—
NDP	15.1%	—
CHRISTIAN	3.4%	—
LIBERTARIAN	0.3%	—
TOTAL	51,224	—
WINDSOR-LAKE ST. CLAIR	**1988**	**1984**
PC	19.4%	—
LIB	37.2%	—
NDP	43.4%	—
TOTAL	43,560	—
WINDSOR-WALKERVILLE	**1988**	**1984**
PC	—	34.1%
LIB	—	29.1%
NDP	—	36.8%
TOTAL	—	39,724
WINDSOR WEST	**1988**	**1984**
PC	14.3%	24.3%
LIB	56.2%	40.6%
NDP	28.9%	34.2%
NO AFFILIATION	0.3%	—
COMMUNIST	0.3%	0.3%
RHINO	—	0.7%
TOTAL	42,398	33,601
YORK NORTH	**1988**	**1984**
PC	42.6%	31.7%
LIB	42.7%	20.4%
NDP	13.2%	11.4%
NO AFFILIATION	—	36.5%
LIBERTARIAN	1.5%	—
TOTAL	87,825	88,266
YORK-PEEL	**1988**	**1984**
PC	—	62.2%
LIB	—	20.8%
NDP	—	15.5%
INDEPENDENT	—	0.8%
LIBERTARIAN	—	0.7%
TOTAL	—	60,301
YORK-SIMCOE	**1988**	**1984**
PC	47.2%	—
LIB	35.1%	—
NDP	13.2%	—
CHRISTIAN	3.9%	—
LIBERTARIAN	0.6%	—
TOTAL	56,664	—

CONSTITUENCY RESULTS	1988	1984	CONSTITUENCY RESULTS	1988	1984
METROPOLITAN			DON VALLEY WEST	1988	1984
TORONTO BEACHES	1988	1984	PC	53.3%	59.9%
PC	—	33.9%	LIB	36.8%	25.8%
LIB	—	22.2%	NDP	8.3%	13.2%
NDP	—	40.6%	LIBERTARIAN	0.8%	1.2%
GREEN	—	1.6%	INDEPENDENT	0.6%	—
LIBERTARIAN	—	1.0%	COMMUNIST	0.1%	—
INDEPENDENT	—	0.4%	COMMONWEALTH	0.1%	—
NO AFFILIATION	—	0.3%			
COMMONWEALTH	—	0.1%	TOTAL	51,896	49,907
TOTAL	—	36,717			
			EGLINTON-		
BEACHES-WOODBINE	1988	1984	LAWRENCE	1988	1984
PC	29.2%	—	PC	30.9%	40.3%
LIB	33.2%	—	LIB	51.0%	43.0%
NDP	35.2%	—	NDP	15.6%	14.9%
LIBERTARIAN	0.8%	—	LIBERTARIAN	1.3%	0.8%
GREEN	0.7%	—	COMMUNIST	0.5%	0.5%
INDEPENDENT	0.6%	—	NO AFFILIATION	0.3%	—
INDEPENDENT	0.2%	—	COMMONWEALTH	0.3%	—
COMMONWEALTH	0.1%	—	INDEPENDENT	—	0.5%
TOTAL	44,813	—	TOTAL	40,078	43,379
BROADVIEW-			ETOBICOKE CENTRE	1988	1984
GREENWOOD	1988	1984	PC	48.4%	56.8%
PC	22.4%	34.7%	LIB	40.5%	29.8%
LIB	38.9%	18.3%	NDP	9.6%	12.8%
NDP	36.0%	45.6%	LIBERTARIAN	0.7%	0.6%
LIBERTARIAN	1.1%	—	GREEN	0.4%	—
GREEN	0.7%	0.7%	COMMUNIST	0.2%	—
RHINO	0.6%	0.7%	COMMONWEALTH	0.1%	—
COMMONWEALTH	0.3%	—	NO AFFILIATION	0.1%	—
TOTAL	40,643	33,044	TOTAL	50,268	59,875
DAVENPORT	1988	1984			
PC	18.6%	21.1%	ETOBICOKE-		
LIB	58.9%	53.7%	LAKESHORE	1988	1984
NDP	18.8%	22.5%	PC	47.1%	44.8%
LIBERTARIAN	1.7%	1.0%	LIB	—	30.3%
RHINO	0.8%	—	NDP	43.4%	23.7%
COMMUNIST	0.7%	0.7%	LIBERTARIAN	6.8%	0.7%
NO AFFILIATION	0.5%	—	GREEN	1.5%	—
GREEN	—	1.0%	NO AFFILIATION	0.9%	—
TOTAL	27,913	24,686	COMMUNIST	0.3%	0.5%
			TOTAL	45,217	44,439
DON VALLEY EAST	1988	1984			
PC	44.7%	54.4%	ETOBICOKE NORTH	1988	1984
LIB	37.9%	34.0%	PC	34.6%	40.5%
NDP	15.1%	10.7%	LIB	45.3%	38.9%
LIBERTARIAN	1.3%	0.7%	NDP	17.3%	19.9%
INDEPENDENT	0.6%	0.3%	CHRISTIAN	1.7%	—
COMMUNIST	0.4%	—	LIBERTARIAN	0.9%	0.7%
TOTAL	41,874	54,644	NO AFFILIATION	0.1%	—
			TOTAL	49,889	56,106
DON VALLEY NORTH	1988	1984			
PC	43.4%	—			
LIB	41.9%	—			
NDP	11.8%	—			
INDEPENDENT	1.4%	—			
LIBERTARIAN	1.4%	—			
TOTAL	40,412	—			

CONSTITUENCY RESULTS	1988	1984
PARKDALE-HIGH PARK	**1988**	**1984**
PC	36.4%	40.2%
LIB	43.5%	36.5%
NDP	17.7%	20.9%
LIBERTARIAN	1.0%	0.6%
RHINO	0.6%	—
INDEPENDENT	0.5%	—
COMMUNIST	0.4%	0.3%
GREEN	—	1.5%
TOTAL	45,136	39,475
ROSEDALE	**1988**	**1984**
PC	41.4%	52.8%
LIB	41.2%	26.1%
NDP	15.1%	17.8%
LIBERTARIAN	0.7%	0.7%
GREEN	0.7%	1.9%
RHINO	0.5%	—
COMMUNIST	0.2%	0.4%
INDEPENDENT	0.2%	—
COMMONWEALTH	0.1%	0.3%
TOTAL	54,887	43,963
ST. PAUL'S	**1988**	**1984**
PC	47.5%	47.6%
LIB	40.8%	37.9%
NDP	10.0%	12.6%
GREEN	0.7%	1.2%
LIBERTARIAN	0.7%	0.5%
COMMUNIST	0.3%	0.2%
COMMONWEALTH	—	0.1%
TOTAL	53,029	43,977
SCARBOROUGH-AGINCOURT	**1988**	**1984**
PC	42.4%	—
LIB	44.3%	—
NDP	11.6%	—
NO AFFILIATION	1.0%	—
LIBERTARIAN	0.7%	—
TOTAL	43,906	—
SCARBOROUGH CENTRE	**1988**	**1984**
PC	40.6%	46.7%
LIB	39.7%	33.3%
NDP	18.9%	19.3%
LIBERTARIAN	0.8%	0.8%
TOTAL	42,440	42,782
SCARBOROUGH EAST	**1988**	**1984**
PC	43.3%	55.6%
LIB	39.0%	28.1%
NDP	16.4%	13.6%
LIBERTARIAN	0.7%	1.1%
GREEN	0.5%	1.2%
COMMUNIST	0.2%	0.3%
COMMONWEALTH	—	0.2%
TOTAL	41,929	47,390

CONSTITUENCY RESULTS	1988	1984
SCARBOROUGH-ROUGE RIVER	**1988**	**1984**
PC	37.6%	—
LIB	47.1%	—
NDP	13.6%	—
LIBERTARIAN	1.1%	—
GREEN	0.6%	—
TOTAL	48,341	—
SCARBOROUGH WEST	**1988**	**1984**
PC	35.7%	40.9%
LIB	36.8%	29.4%
NDP	26.4%	27.5%
LIBERTARIAN	1.1%	0.8%
GREEN	—	0.9%
COMMONWEALTH	—	0.3%
COMMUNIST	—	0.2%
TOTAL	41,745	41,616
SPADINA	**1988**	**1984**
PC	—	23.8%
LIB	—	35.0%
NDP	—	39.0%
LIBERTARIAN	—	1.1%
RHINO	—	0.9%
INDEPENDENT	—	0.3%
TOTAL	—	33,927
TRINITY	**1988**	**1984**
PC	—	22.8%
LIB	—	43.6%
NDP	—	29.8%
GREEN	—	1.5%
LIBERTARIAN	—	1.1%
COMMUNIST	—	0.9%
COMMONWEALTH	—	0.3%
TOTAL	—	22,507
TRINITY-SPADINA	**1988**	**1984**
PC	21.3%	—
LIB	37.4%	—
NDP	38.5%	—
LIBERTARIAN	1.2%	—
RHINO	1.1%	—
INDEPENDENT	0.3%	—
NO AFFILIATION	0.1%	—
TOTAL	40,379	—
WILLOWDALE	**1988**	**1984**
PC	43.4%	43.5%
LIB	47.0%	42.8%
NDP	8.8%	13.0%
RHINO	0.5%	—
LIBERTARIAN	0.3%	0.6%
TOTAL	51,510	51,528

CONSTITUENCY RESULTS	1988	1984
YORK CENTRE	1988	1984
PC	22.4%	27.4%
LIB	60.5%	51.2%
NDP	15.3%	19.8%
LIBERTARIAN	1.8%	0.6%
NO AFFILIATION	—	0.6%
NO AFFILIATION	—	0.5%
TOTAL	41,243	40,658
YORK EAST	1988	1984
PC	—	47.3%
LIB	—	35.5%
NDP	—	16.3%
LIBERTARIAN	—	0.5%
COMMUNIST	—	0.4%
TOTAL	—	46,492
YORK-SCARBOROUGH	1988	1984
PC	—	48.6%
LIB	—	35.7%
NDP	—	13.2%
LIBERTARIAN	—	1.1%
INDEPENDENT	—	0.7%
INDEPENDENT	—	0.7%
TOTAL	—	100,375
YORK SOUTH-WESTON	1988	1984
PC	21.6%	28.6%
LIB	53.7%	37.7%
NDP	23.1%	31.0%
LIBERTARIAN	0.8%	0.8%
COMMUNIST	0.5%	0.5%
COMMONWEALTH	0.3%	—
NO AFFILIATION	—	1.4%
TOTAL	39,304	37,666
YORK WEST	1988	1984
PC	19.1%	30.9%
LIB	59.6%	44.6%
NDP	18.2%	22.0%
LIBERTARIAN	1.5%	0.9%
NO AFFILIATION	0.8%	—
INDEPENDENT	0.4%	0.7%
COMMUNIST	0.4%	0.4%
GREEN	—	0.6%
TOTAL	33,424	39,564
QUEBEC ABITIBI	1988	1984
PC	57.6%	52.0%
LIB	16.2%	28.0%
NDP	26.3%	8.0%
RHINO	—	5.1%
PN	—	4.3%
SC	—	2.6%
TOTAL	38,666	44,706

CONSTITUENCY RESULTS	1988	1984
ARGENTEUIL-PAPINEAU	1988	1984
PC	56.4%	55.9%
LIB	27.1%	32.1%
NDP	14.1%	7.1%
RHINO	2.3%	2.5%
PN	—	1.5%
INDEPENDENT	—	0.9%
TOTAL	40,895	37,734
BEAUCE	1988	1984
PC	68.7%	53.1%
LIB	25.9%	43.1%
NDP	5.4%	2.6%
PN	—	1.2%
TOTAL	52,709	47,137
BEAUHARNOIS-SALABERRY	1988	1984
PC	58.4%	63.1%
LIB	26.7%	26.1%
NDP	11.9%	6.2%
GREEN	1.5%	—
RHINO	1.5%	2.8%
PN	—	1.8%
TOTAL	49,937	43,743
BELLECHASSE	1988	1984
PC	65.0%	57.8%
LIB	26.2%	34.4%
NDP	6.5%	4.0%
GREEN	2.4%	—
RHINO	—	2.5%
PN	—	1.2%
TOTAL	42,513	42,111
BERTHIER-MASKINONGÉ-LANAUDIÈRE	1988	1984
PC	—	69.6%
LIB	—	26.2%
NDP	—	2.7%
PN	—	1.4%
COMMONWEALTH	—	0.2%
TOTAL	—	44,801
BERTHIER-MONTCALM	1988	1984
PC	56.3%	—
LIB	25.9%	—
NDP	11.3%	—
GREEN	4.0%	—
NO AFFILIATION	2.5%	—
TOTAL	52,153	—

CONSTITUENCY RESULTS	1988	1984
BLAINVILLE-DEUX-MONTAGNES	1988	1984
PC	62.0%	47.1%
LIB	21.0%	38.8%
NDP	14.1%	9.2%
RHINO	2.7%	2.5%
COMMONWEALTH	0.2%	0.1%
PN	—	1.7%
SC	—	0.4%
NO AFFILIATION	—	0.2%
INDEPENDENT	—	0.0%
TOTAL	65,772	61,246
BONAVENTURE-ILES-DE-LA-MADELEINE	1988	1984
PC	58.6%	50.1%
LIB	35.6%	44.2%
NDP	5.8%	3.4%
PN	—	1.4%
COMMONWEALTH	—	0.9%
TOTAL	26,435	30,951
BROME-MISSISQUOI	1988	1984
PC	54.0%	53.1%
LIB	32.9%	38.4%
NDP	13.1%	5.6%
PN	—	2.4%
LIBERTARIAN	—	0.3%
COMMONWEALTH	—	0.2%
TOTAL	41,762	40,851
CHAMBLY	1988	1984
PC	47.0%	51.8%
LIB	19.9%	29.7%
NDP	31.6%	11.2%
RHINO	1.4%	3.8%
COMMONWEALTH	0.1%	0.3%
PN	—	3.2%
TOTAL	54,780	60,855
CHAMPLAIN	1988	1984
PC	64.7%	60.0%
LIB	16.2%	31.6%
NDP	19.1%	6.8%
PN	—	1.6%
TOTAL	46,051	45,773
CHARLESBOURG	1988	1984
PC	60.1%	52.4%
LIB	26.6%	31.6%
NDP	13.4%	10.2%
RHINO	—	3.6%
PN	—	1.5%
SC	—	0.7%
COMMONWEALTH	—	0.1%
TOTAL	59,190	71,728

CONSTITUENCY RESULTS	1988	1984
CHARLEVOIX	1988	1984
PC	80.0%	63.6%
LIB	14.2%	32.0%
NDP	4.3%	2.8%
RHINO	1.4%	—
PN	—	1.6%
TOTAL	42,143	37,199
CHÂTEAUGUAY	1988	1984
PC	44.8%	46.6%
LIB	32.8%	37.8%
NDP	16.5%	11.1%
NO AFFILIATION	3.4%	—
RHINO	2.5%	—
PN	—	3.6%
LIBERTARIAN	—	0.6%
COMMONWEALTH	—	0.3%
TOTAL	50,117	45,752
CHICOUTIMI	1988	1984
PC	70.4%	60.8%
LIB	18.4%	29.3%
NDP	11.2%	6.0%
RHINO	—	2.2%
PN	—	1.7%
TOTAL	43,616	36,678
DRUMMOND	1988	1984
PC	53.5%	56.2%
LIB	34.7%	33.6%
NDP	11.7%	6.2%
PN	—	2.5%
NO AFFILIATION	—	0.8%
SC	—	0.7%
TOTAL	44,523	42,136
FRONTENAC	1988	1984
PC	73.6%	71.2%
LIB	19.9%	23.1%
NDP	5.1%	2.7%
GREEN	1.5%	—
RHINO	—	2.1%
PN	—	1.0%
TOTAL	35,146	39,690
GASPÉ	1988	1984
PC	57.7%	60.9%
LIB	34.6%	32.5%
NDP	5.2%	3.4%
RHINO	1.8%	—
INDEPENDENT	0.6%	1.0%
PN	—	2.2%
TOTAL	28,424	31,422
GATINEAU	1988	1984
PC	—	50.9%
LIB	—	34.4%
NDP	—	12.9%
PN	—	1.5%
COMMONWEALTH	—	0.3%
TOTAL	—	50,820

CONSTITUENCY RESULTS	1988	1984
GATINEAU-LA LIÈVRE	1988	1984
PC	39.4%	—
LIB	43.3%	—
NDP	15.4%	—
RHINO	1.2%	—
NO AFFILIATION	0.7%	—
TOTAL	54,302	—
HULL-AYLMER	1988	1984
PC	31.9%	37.0%
LIB	49.8%	40.6%
NDP	15.4%	19.6%
RHINO	1.4%	—
NO AFFILIATION	1.2%	—
NO AFFILIATION	0.3%	—
PN	—	2.4%
COMMONWEALTH	—	0.4%
TOTAL	46,591	42,039
JOLIETTE	1988	1984
PC	55.1%	73.9%
LIB	24.8%	17.1%
NDP	14.3%	4.2%
GREEN	4.5%	—
NO AFFILIATION	1.0%	—
COMMONWEALTH	0.3%	0.1%
RHINO	—	2.9%
PN	—	1.2%
SC	—	0.4%
COMMUNIST	—	0.2%
TOTAL	50,661	52,547
JONQUIÈRE	1988	1984
PC	63.6%	49.6%
LIB	15.6%	38.4%
NDP	20.8%	5.1%
PN	—	4.4%
RHINO	—	2.5%
TOTAL	33,816	36,700
KAMOURASKA-RIVIÈRE-DU-LOUP	1988	1984
PC	58.5%	53.2%
LIB	29.7%	35.0%
NDP	9.3%	4.2%
GREEN	2.0%	—
NO AFFILIATION	0.6%	0.6%
RHINO	—	5.4%
PN	—	1.6%
TOTAL	34,875	36,929
LABELLE	1988	1984
PC	—	55.6%
LIB	—	28.4%
NDP	—	9.2%
RHINO	—	3.1%
PN	—	3.0%
SC	—	0.5%
COMMONWEALTH	—	0.2%
TOTAL	—	50,892

CONSTITUENCY RESULTS	1988	1984
LAC-SAINT-JEAN	1988	1984
PC	66.3%	61.8%
LIB	15.4%	31.0%
NDP	18.2%	5.2%
PN	—	2.0%
TOTAL	34,843	40,898
LANGELIER	1988	1984
PC	46.6%	43.1%
LIB	28.2%	35.8%
NDP	20.1%	11.7%
GREEN	3.6%	—
NO AFFILIATION	0.8%	—
INDEPENDENT	0.6%	—
RHINO	—	6.6%
PN	—	2.4%
SC	—	0.5%
TOTAL	52,638	39,157
LA PRAIRIE	1988	1984
PC	53.0%	41.6%
LIB	33.5%	39.6%
NDP	10.7%	13.5%
RHINO	2.4%	2.9%
COMMONWEALTH	0.3%	0.3%
PN	—	2.2%
TOTAL	58,123	63,671
LAURENTIDES	1988	1984
PC	55.2%	—
LIB	28.0%	—
NDP	13.8%	—
RHINO	2.5%	—
COMMONWEALTH	0.4%	—
TOTAL	56,164	—
LÉVIS	1988	1984
PC	57.4%	49.6%
LIB	22.2%	26.5%
NDP	19.6%	18.5%
SC	0.8%	0.3%
RHINO	—	2.5%
PN	—	2.5%
TOTAL	58,621	65,192
LONGUEUIL	1988	1984
PC	53.3%	47.7%
LIB	22.6%	32.4%
NDP	19.6%	10.6%
RHINO	3.8%	4.2%
NO AFFILIATION	0.4%	—
COMMONWEALTH	0.3%	0.1%
PN	—	5.0%
TOTAL	54,539	60,661
LOTBINIÈRE	1988	1984
PC	52.7%	48.5%
LIB	29.9%	43.4%
NDP	17.4%	4.2%
RHINO	—	2.0%
PN	—	1.9%
TOTAL	50,434	46,539

CONSTITUENCY RESULTS	1988	1984
LOUIS-HÉBERT	1988	1984
PC	59.8%	46.0%
LIB	24.8%	35.3%
NDP	13.0%	11.8%
RHINO	2.4%	3.1%
INDEPENDENT	—	1.8%
PN	—	1.7%
SC	—	0.3%
TOTAL	62,452	64,006
MANICOUAGAN	1988	1984
PC	61.6%	71.6%
LIB	22.9%	24.5%
NDP	14.4%	2.4%
COMMONWEALTH	1.0%	0.3%
PN	—	1.4%
TOTAL	27,770	39,424
MATAPÉDIA-MATANE	1988	1984
PC	50.2%	52.7%
LIB	36.4%	32.7%
NDP	13.4%	3.0%
PN	—	11.6%
TOTAL	31,799	30,355
MÉGANTIC-COMPTON-STANSTEAD	1988	1984
PC	60.3%	60.0%
LIB	30.0%	30.6%
NDP	8.3%	6.3%
SC	1.4%	0.9%
GREEN	—	1.1%
PN	—	1.0%
COMMONWEALTH	—	0.1%
TOTAL	38,557	42,823
MONTMORENCY-ORLÉANS	1988	1984
PC	60.5%	47.0%
LIB	22.9%	39.7%
NDP	15.2%	8.1%
NO AFFILIATION	1.3%	—
RHINO	—	3.3%
PN	—	1.2%
SC	—	0.6%
TOTAL	48,868	48,383
PONTIAC-GATINEAU-LABELLE	1988	1984
PC	53.6%	62.0%
LIB	30.2%	28.6%
NDP	16.2%	7.6%
PN	—	1.5%
COMMONWEALTH	—	0.4%
TOTAL	38,318	35,111

CONSTITUENCY RESULTS	1988	1984
PORTNEUF	1988	1984
PC	57.4%	51.1%
LIB	26.5%	38.0%
NDP	12.2%	6.5%
GREEN	3.9%	—
RHINO	—	2.6%
PN	—	1.4%
SC	—	0.5%
TOTAL	38,328	46,604
QUÉBEC-EST	1988	1984
PC	55.7%	48.1%
LIB	25.9%	34.9%
NDP	14.3%	10.2%
RHINO	1.9%	4.1%
GREEN	1.7%	—
NO AFFILIATION	0.4%	—
PN	—	1.9%
SC	—	0.6%
COMMONWEALTH	—	0.2%
TOTAL	52,931	41,111
RICHELIEU	1988	1984
PC	68.9%	59.2%
LIB	19.3%	30.8%
NDP	6.8%	4.5%
GREEN	4.1%	—
RHINO	1.0%	2.0%
PN	—	3.0%
SC	—	0.4%
COMMONWEALTH	—	0.2%
TOTAL	46,590	48,540
RICHMOND-WOLFE	1988	1984
PC	47.5%	39.4%
LIB	41.0%	51.4%
NDP	9.6%	4.7%
RHINO	1.9%	—
PN	—	3.8%
SC	—	0.8%
TOTAL	40,972	35,154
RIMOUSKI-TÉMISCOUATA	1988	1984
PC	62.6%	59.8%
LIB	27.8%	33.4%
NDP	6.4%	2.9%
INDEPENDENT	3.2%	—
PN	—	2.0%
RHINO	—	1.8%
COMMONWEALTH	—	0.2%
TOTAL	37,977	42,656
ROBERVAL	1988	1984
PC	76.4%	61.9%
LIB	12.1%	34.8%
NDP	9.5%	2.3%
RHINO	2.1%	—
PN	—	1.1%
TOTAL	34,977	37,157

CONSTITUENCY RESULTS	1988	1984
SAINT-HUBERT	1988	1984
PC	48.9%	—
LIB	29.1%	—
NDP	18.0%	—
RHINO	2.3%	—
GREEN	1.4%	—
COMMONWEALTH	0.3%	—
TOTAL	52,289	—
SAINT-HYACINTHE-BAGOT	1988	1984
PC	52.6%	47.4%
LIB	33.9%	44.1%
NDP	13.4%	4.5%
RHINO	—	2.1%
PN	—	1.9%
COMMONWEALTH	—	0.1%
TOTAL	47,993	48,545
SAINT-JEAN	1988	1984
PC	56.3%	59.8%
LIB	29.8%	28.8%
NDP	11.8%	7.1%
RHINO	2.2%	2.4%
PN	—	2.0%
COMMONWEALTH	—	0.1%
TOTAL	49,198	51,490
SAINT-MAURICE	1988	1984
PC	45.3%	35.4%
LIB	24.6%	58.9%
NDP	30.1%	3.5%
PN	—	2.2%
TOTAL	41,372	40,843
SHEFFORD	1988	1984
PC	43.2%	42.9%
LIB	48.2%	47.5%
NDP	8.5%	6.7%
PN	—	2.9%
TOTAL	49,630	53,632
SHERBROOKE	1988	1984
PC	63.3%	51.5%
LIB	22.6%	33.8%
NDP	11.7%	9.8%
RHINO	1.9%	2.4%
NO AFFILIATION	0.3%	—
COMMUNIST	0.3%	0.2%
PN	—	1.6%
SC	—	0.5%
COMMONWEALTH	—	0.2%
TOTAL	54,556	43,171
TÉMISCAMINGUE	1988	1984
PC	46.3%	50.2%
LIB	14.2%	34.0%
NDP	37.8%	5.4%
RHINO	1.7%	3.6%
PN	—	5.3%
SC	—	1.6%
TOTAL	41,284	40,501

CONSTITUENCY RESULTS	1988	1984
TERREBONNE	1988	1984
PC	52.8%	60.3%
LIB	18.5%	26.2%
NDP	10.7%	8.9%
INDEPENDENT	15.5%	—
RHINO	2.5%	—
PN	—	4.2%
COMMONWEALTH	—	0.4%
TOTAL	66,998	72,668
TROIS-RIVIÈRES	1988	1984
PC	68.9%	63.9%
LIB	15.8%	24.3%
NDP	12.8%	4.6%
RHINO	1.9%	2.4%
NO AFFILIATION	0.6%	—
PN	—	4.4%
COMMUNIST	—	0.3%
TOTAL	42,642	41,982
VERCHÈRES	1988	1984
PC	66.0%	56.0%
LIB	17.3%	28.0%
NDP	13.8%	9.5%
RHINO	2.6%	3.2%
COMMONWEALTH	0.2%	0.2%
PN	—	3.1%
TOTAL	48,931	69,067
ISLAND OF MONTREAL AND ÎLE JÉSUS AHUNTSIC	1988	1984
PC	42.4%	—
LIB	41.1%	—
NDP	11.0%	—
GREEN	2.2%	—
RHINO	2.0%	—
NO AFFILIATION	0.7%	—
COMMUNIST	0.4%	—
COMMONWEALTH	0.2%	—
TOTAL	51,161	—
ANJOU-RIVIÈRE-DES-PRAIRIES	1988	1984
PC	51.5%	—
LIB	32.7%	—
NDP	12.6%	—
GREEN	2.3%	—
NO AFFILIATION	0.9%	—
TOTAL	53,259	—
BOURASSA	1988	1984
PC	43.3%	40.6%
LIB	41.5%	44.0%
NDP	11.0%	8.1%
RHINO	2.0%	3.5%
GREEN	0.9%	—
SC	0.4%	0.5%
COMMUNIST	0.4%	—
NO AFFILIATION	0.3%	0.2%
COMMONWEALTH	0.2%	0.3%
PN	—	2.5%
NO AFFILIATION	—	0.2%
TOTAL	43,782	46,017

CONSTITUENCY RESULTS	1988	1984
DOLLARD	1988	1984
PC	—	45.9%
LIB	—	37.7%
NDP	—	11.6%
RHINO	—	2.2%
PN	—	1.7%
LIBERTARIAN	—	0.7%
COMMONWEALTH	—	0.2%
TOTAL	—	56,856

DUVERNAY	1988	1984
PC	60.7%	50.4%
LIB	22.9%	31.1%
NDP	14.8%	8.5%
SC	0.9%	0.3%
COMMONWEALTH	0.7%	0.1%
PN	—	5.4%
RHINO	—	3.5%
INDEPENDENT	—	0.8%
TOTAL	55,028	59,331

GAMELIN	1988	1984
PC	—	44.5%
LIB	—	37.3%
NDP	—	10.1%
RHINO	—	3.5%
PN	—	2.8%
GREEN	—	1.5%
COMMONWEALTH	—	0.2%
TOTAL	—	46,879

HOCHELAGA-MAISONNEUVE	1988	1984
PC	39.1%	41.2%
LIB	34.2%	38.0%
NDP	20.6%	11.2%
RHINO	3.0%	5.8%
GREEN	1.9%	—
NO AFFILIATION	0.7%	—
COMMONWEALTH	0.3%	0.2%
COMMUNIST	0.3%	0.3%
PN	—	3.4%
TOTAL	41,570	32,139

LACHINE	1988	1984
PC	—	51.7%
LIB	—	32.2%
NDP	—	12.0%
RHINO	—	2.1%
PN	—	1.1%
LIBERTARIAN	—	0.5%
INDEPENDENT	—	0.3%
INDEPENDENT	—	0.2%
TOTAL	—	47,049

CONSTITUENCY RESULTS	1988	1984
LACHINE-LAC-SAINT-LOUIS	1988	1984
PC	45.4%	—
LIB	44.1%	—
NDP	7.9%	—
GREEN	1.5%	—
LIBERTARIAN	0.6%	—
NO AFFILIATION	0.4%	—
COMMONWEALTH	0.2%	—
TOTAL	57,036	—

LASALLE	1988	1984
PC	—	46.7%
LIB	—	39.1%
NDP	—	9.6%
RHINO	—	2.7%
PN	—	1.7%
COMMONWEALTH	—	0.3%
TOTAL	—	49,725

LASALLE-ÉMARD	1988	1984
PC	42.7%	—
LIB	45.5%	—
NDP	10.6%	—
NO AFFILIATION	0.6%	—
COMMUNIST	0.4%	—
COMMONWEALTH	0.2%	—
TOTAL	51,465	—

LAURIER	1988	1984
PC	—	28.7%
LIB	—	34.6%
NDP	—	17.1%
RHINO	—	12.1%
PN	—	3.4%
GREEN	—	2.8%
SC	—	0.7%
COMMUNIST	—	0.5%
COMMONWEALTH	—	0.2%
TOTAL	—	26,898

LAURIER-SAINTE-MARIE	1988	1984
PC	29.7%	—
LIB	39.1%	—
NDP	21.6%	—
RHINO	5.2%	—
GREEN	3.5%	—
COMMUNIST	0.4%	—
NO AFFILIATION	0.3%	—
COMMONWEALTH	0.2%	—
TOTAL	40,840	—

LAVAL	1988	1984
PC	49.1%	47.6%
LIB	34.4%	35.7%
NDP	15.6%	12.7%
COMMONWEALTH	0.9%	0.5%
PN	—	3.6%
TOTAL	54,691	64,486

CONSTITUENCY RESULTS	1988	1984
LAVAL-DES-RAPIDES	1988	1984
PC	53.7%	39.3%
LIB	28.7%	43.9%
NDP	14.2%	10.1%
GREEN	2.9%	—
COMMONWEALTH	0.4%	0.2%
RHINO	—	3.7%
PN	—	2.9%
TOTAL	52,015	51,916
MERCIER	1988	1984
PC	54.8%	—
LIB	23.0%	—
NDP	18.2%	—
RHINO	2.9%	—
COMMUNIST	0.5%	—
NO AFFILIATION	0.3%	—
COMMONWEALTH	0.2%	—
TOTAL	56,192	—
MONTRÉAL-MERCIER	1988	1984
PC	—	46.4%
LIB	—	35.8%
NDP	—	9.1%
PN	—	4.7%
RHINO	—	3.8%
COMMONWEALTH	—	0.3%
TOTAL	—	54,080
MONTRÉAL-SAINTE-MARIE	1988	1984
PC	—	34.7%
LIB	—	43.4%
NDP	—	11.2%
RHINO	—	7.4%
PN	—	3.1%
COMMONWEALTH	—	0.2%
TOTAL	—	31,509
MOUNT ROYAL	1988	1984
PC	32.0%	39.1%
LIB	59.9%	47.5%
NDP	5.4%	9.9%
RHINO	1.1%	1.6%
GREEN	1.0%	—
INDEPENDENT	0.4%	0.2%
COMMONWEALTH	0.2%	0.2%
NO AFFILIATION	0.1%	—
PN	—	0.8%
LIBERTARIAN	—	0.7%
TOTAL	45,699	47,854
NOTRE-DAME-DE-GRÂCE	1988	1984
PC	27.9%	—
LIB	54.6%	—
NDP	12.3%	—
GREEN	2.0%	—
RHINO	1.6%	—
CHRISTIAN	0.9%	—
LIBERTARIAN	0.5%	—
NO AFFILIATION	0.2%	—
COMMONWEALTH	0.1%	—
TOTAL	42,014	—

CONSTITUENCY RESULTS	1988	1984
NOTRE-DAME-DE-GRÂCE-LACHINE EAST	1988	1984
PC	—	38.4%
LIB	—	43.4%
NDP	—	14.0%
RHINO	—	2.4%
PN	—	1.4%
COMMONWEALTH	—	0.3%
TOTAL	—	41,238
OUTREMONT	1988	1984
PC	38.4%	29.3%
LIB	34.7%	40.9%
NDP	20.5%	18.9%
GREEN	2.9%	2.5%
RHINO	2.4%	4.2%
COMMUNIST	0.4%	0.5%
NO AFFILIATION	0.4%	—
COMMONWEALTH	0.3%	0.4%
PN	—	3.3%
TOTAL	45,790	35,458
PAPINEAU	1988	1984
PC	—	36.9%
LIB	—	39.0%
NDP	—	13.1%
RHINO	—	5.9%
PN	—	3.6%
SC	—	0.5%
COMMUNIST	—	0.5%
COMMONWEALTH	—	0.4%
NO AFFILIATION	—	0.3%
TOTAL	—	32,707
PAPINEAU-SAINT-MICHEL	1988	1984
PC	33.2%	—
LIB	46.0%	—
NDP	15.1%	—
RHINO	2.5%	—
GREEN	1.2%	—
COMMUNIST	0.6%	—
NO AFFILIATION	0.5%	—
NO AFFILIATION	0.4%	—
COMMONWEALTH	0.4%	—
TOTAL	39,400	—
PIERREFONDS-DOLLARD	1988	1984
PC	49.8%	—
LIB	40.2%	—
NDP	7.0%	—
RHINO	1.5%	—
INDEPENDENT	0.8%	—
LIBERTARIAN	0.5%	—
COMMONWEALTH	0.1%	—
TOTAL	55,317	—

CONSTITUENCY RESULTS	1988	1984
ROSEMONT	1988	1984
PC	37.8%	42.2%
LIB	29.2%	38.7%
NDP	20.2%	10.9%
NO AFFILIATION	4.6%	0.3%
RHINO	3.7%	4.3%
GREEN	3.1%	—
COMMUNIST	0.3%	0.4%
SC	0.3%	0.4%
NO AFFILIATION	0.3%	0.3%
NO AFFILIATION	0.3%	—
COMMONWEALTH	0.3%	0.2%
PN	—	2.7%
TOTAL	45,259	37,377
SAINT-DENIS	1988	1984
PC	30.4%	31.3%
LIB	47.2%	48.4%
NDP	14.7%	11.8%
RHINO	2.8%	4.1%
GREEN	2.6%	—
NO AFFILIATION	0.8%	—
SC	0.6%	—
COMMUNIST	0.5%	0.7%
COMMONWEALTH	0.5%	0.3%
PN	—	2.5%
INDEPENDENT	—	0.8%
TOTAL	42,249	38,710
SAINT-HENRI-WESTMOUNT	1988	1984
PC	39.3%	35.2%
LIB	41.6%	45.3%
NDP	13.1%	14.6%
GREEN	2.3%	—
RHINO	1.7%	3.2%
NO AFFILIATION	1.0%	—
NO AFFILIATION	0.5%	—
LIBERTARIAN	0.4%	—
NO AFFILIATION	0.1%	—
PN	—	1.6%
COMMONWEALTH	—	0.1%
TOTAL	39,887	40,281
SAINT-JACQUES	1988	1984
PC	—	37.5%
LIB	—	39.6%
NDP	—	14.8%
RHINO	—	4.4%
PN	—	2.7%
COMMUNIST	—	0.6%
COMMONWEALTH	—	0.4%
TOTAL	—	27,433
SAINT-LAURENT	1988	1984
PC	41.5%	—
LIB	46.3%	—
NDP	9.6%	—
GREEN	1.7%	—
NO AFFILIATION	0.7%	—
COMMONWEALTH	0.3%	—
TOTAL	44,114	—

CONSTITUENCY RESULTS	1988	1984
SAINT-LÉONARD	1988	1984
PC	37.2%	—
LIB	50.3%	—
NDP	10.2%	—
GREEN	1.8%	—
NO AFFILIATION	0.5%	—
TOTAL	45,796	—
SAINT-LÉONARD-ANJOU	1988	1984
PC	—	39.3%
LIB	—	41.4%
NDP	—	12.7%
RHINO	—	3.6%
PN	—	2.8%
COMMONWEALTH	—	0.2%
TOTAL	—	59,232
SAINT-MICHEL-AHUNTSIC	1988	1984
PC	—	38.0%
LIB	—	42.5%
NDP	—	12.0%
RHINO	—	3.8%
PN	—	3.1%
COMMUNIST	—	0.5%
COMMONWEALTH	—	0.2%
TOTAL	—	40,652
VAUDREUIL	1988	1984
PC	55.7%	54.5%
LIB	30.0%	29.6%
NDP	11.3%	11.6%
GREEN	1.7%	—
RHINO	1.2%	2.1%
COMMONWEALTH	0.1%	0.2%
PN	—	1.5%
LIBERTARIAN	—	0.5%
TOTAL	54,596	68,825
VERDUN-SAINT-PAUL	1988	1984
PC	45.3%	43.5%
LIB	34.3%	41.2%
NDP	14.8%	9.8%
GREEN	3.0%	—
RHINO	2.0%	3.3%
COMMONWEALTH	0.3%	0.3%
NO AFFILIATION	0.2%	—
PN	—	2.0%
TOTAL	44,380	39,927
NOVA SCOTIA ANNAPOLIS VALLEY-HANTS	1988	1984
PC	44.2%	53.9%
LIB	40.0%	28.5%
NDP	12.5%	16.0%
CHRISTIAN	2.8%	—
NO AFFILIATION	0.4%	—
RHINO	—	1.7%
TOTAL	47,007	43,792

CONSTITUENCY RESULTS	1988	1984
CAPE BRETON-EAST		
RICHMOND	1988	1984
PC	20.8%	32.8%
LIB	66.2%	55.8%
NDP	13.0%	10.2%
RHINO	—	1.2%
TOTAL	34,441	36,319
CAPE BRETON		
HIGHLANDS-CANSO	1988	1984
PC	44.0%	50.1%
LIB	50.9%	38.8%
NDP	5.1%	11.1%
TOTAL	39,911	38,705
CAPE BRETON-THE		
SYDNEYS	1988	1984
PC	28.8%	37.5%
LIB	63.2%	44.1%
NDP	7.9%	18.3%
TOTAL	37,831	36,382
CENTRAL NOVA	1988	1984
PC	48.6%	61.0%
LIB	38.4%	26.0%
NDP	13.0%	13.0%
TOTAL	39,241	35,182
CUMBERLAND-		
COLCHESTER	1988	1984
PC	46.2%	57.3%
LIB	41.6%	29.6%
NDP	9.3%	13.1%
CHRISTIAN	2.5%	—
INDEPENDENT	0.5%	—
TOTAL	44,134	42,196
DARTMOUTH	1988	1984
PC	41.8%	—
LIB	46.2%	—
NDP	10.9%	—
LIBERTARIAN	0.9%	—
NO AFFILIATION	0.2%	—
TOTAL	47,539	—
DARTMOUTH-		
HALIFAX EAST	1988	1984
PC	—	55.0%
LIB	—	26.1%
NDP	—	19.0%
TOTAL	—	50,136
HALIFAX	1988	1984
PC	38.0%	44.8%
LIB	43.0%	34.4%
NDP	17.7%	20.5%
LIBERTARIAN	0.6%	—
COMMUNIST	0.3%	—
INDEPENDENT	0.3%	—
COMMONWEALTH	0.2%	—
NO AFFILIATION	—	0.4%
TOTAL	52,250	41,940

CONSTITUENCY RESULTS	1988	1984
HALIFAX WEST	1988	1984
PC	44.8%	54.3%
LIB	38.6%	24.3%
NDP	16.3%	20.8%
COMMONWEALTH	0.4%	—
INDEPENDENT	—	0.6%
TOTAL	55,452	55,797
SOUTH SHORE	1988	1984
PC	46.4%	56.7%
LIB	42.6%	29.0%
NDP	10.2%	14.3%
LIBERTARIAN	0.8%	—
TOTAL	39,923	39,419
SOUTH WEST NOVA	1988	1984
PC	41.5%	50.6%
LIB	50.0%	41.9%
NDP	5.7%	7.6%
CHRISTIAN	2.8%	—
TOTAL	42,113	40,724
NEW BRUNSWICK		
BEAUSEJOUR	1988	1984
PC	27.2%	—
LIB	58.6%	—
NDP	10.2%	—
CONFED RWP	3.9%	—
TOTAL	38,644	—
CARLETON-		
CHARLOTTE	1988	1984
PC	47.2%	61.6%
LIB	41.6%	24.1%
NDP	7.7%	14.3%
CONFED RWP	3.5%	—
TOTAL	33,921	32,224
FREDERICTON	1988	1984
PC	43.0%	—
LIB	39.7%	—
NDP	10.3%	—
CONFED RWP	5.8%	—
RHINO	0.7%	—
INDEPENDENT	0.5%	—
TOTAL	47,680	—
FUNDY-ROYAL	1988	1984
PC	46.7%	56.6%
LIB	36.3%	25.0%
NDP	11.0%	18.5%
CONFED RWP	6.1%	—
TOTAL	45,261	45,990
GLOUCESTER	1988	1984
PC	42.7%	55.1%
LIB	51.7%	38.4%
NDP	5.5%	5.1%
INDEPENDENT	—	1.4%
TOTAL	39,135	42,674

CONSTITUENCY RESULTS	1988	1984
MADAWASKA-VICTORIA	**1988**	**1984**
PC	48.2%	51.9%
LIB	43.8%	41.9%
NDP	8.0%	6.2%
TOTAL	30,573	31,624
MIRAMICHI	**1988**	**1984**
PC	32.4%	—
LIB	50.8%	—
NDP	6.1%	—
CONFED RWP	10.7%	—
TOTAL	27,696	—
MONCTON	**1988**	**1984**
PC	34.0%	57.2%
LIB	46.9%	27.8%
NDP	9.7%	14.6%
CONFED RWP	7.3%	—
CHRISTIAN	1.8%	—
NO AFFILIATION	0.3%	—
INDEPENDENT	—	0.5%
TOTAL	50,779	52,365
NORTHUMBERLAND-MIRAMICHI	**1988**	**1984**
PC	—	53.9%
LIB	—	37.7%
NDP	—	8.4%
TOTAL	—	31,765
RESTIGOUCHE	**1988**	**1984**
PC	40.0%	45.7%
LIB	49.4%	39.7%
NDP	10.6%	14.7%
TOTAL	30,890	30,865
SAINT JOHN	**1988**	**1984**
PC	43.1%	52.2%
LIB	38.6%	25.5%
NDP	12.5%	21.2%
CONFED RWP	4.6%	—
LIBERTARIAN	0.7%	0.8%
INDEPENDENT	0.4%	—
SC	—	0.3%
TOTAL	39,006	31,809
WESTMORLAND-KENT	**1988**	**1984**
PC	—	38.0%
LIB	—	41.8%
NDP	—	20.3%
TOTAL	—	35,228
YORK-SUNBURY	**1988**	**1984**
PC	—	58.9%
LIB	—	23.1%
NDP	—	17.2%
INDEPENDENT	—	0.9%
TOTAL	—	42,806

CONSTITUENCY RESULTS	1988	1984
MANITOBA		
BRANDON-SOURIS	**1988**	**1984**
PC	46.7%	52.2%
LIB	30.7%	14.6%
NDP	13.5%	15.6%
REFORM	4.2%	—
CHRISTIAN	3.6%	—
CONFED RWP	0.9%	17.5%
INDEPENDENT	0.3%	—
TOTAL	37,137	36,044
CHURCHILL	**1988**	**1984**
PC	20.5%	33.7%
LIB	23.0%	18.0%
NDP	56.4%	45.6%
INDEPENDENT	—	1.6%
LIBERTARIAN	—	1.2%
TOTAL	25,132	23,769
DAUPHIN-SWAN RIVER	**1988**	**1984**
PC	41.4%	42.6%
LIB	19.6%	15.5%
NDP	33.4%	36.3%
REFORM	3.4%	—
CONFED RWP	1.1%	5.7%
NO AFFILIATION	1.1%	—
TOTAL	35,581	28,133
LISGAR	**1988**	**1984**
PC	—	49.4%
LIB	—	14.1%
NDP	—	6.5%
CONFED RWP	—	28.6%
RHINO	—	1.4%
TOTAL	—	31,445
LISGAR-MARQUETTE	**1988**	**1984**
PC	53.9%	—
LIB	22.1%	—
NDP	6.8%	—
REFORM	8.7%	—
CHRISTIAN	5.6%	—
CONFED RWP	1.5%	—
RHINO	1.3%	—
TOTAL	32,420	—
PORTAGE-INTERLAKE	**1988**	**1984**
PC	38.7%	—
LIB	30.2%	—
NDP	18.6%	—
REFORM	11.8%	—
LIBERTARIAN	0.7%	—
TOTAL	34,343	—

CONSTITUENCY RESULTS	1988	1984
PORTAGE-MARQUETTE	1988	1984
PC	—	49.4%
LIB	—	13.4%
NDP	—	14.3%
CONFED RWP	—	22.3%
LIBERTARIAN	—	0.7%
TOTAL	—	31,147
PROVENCHER	1988	1984
PC	55.5%	58.3%
LIB	32.5%	14.1%
NDP	7.3%	20.1%
REFORM	3.6%	—
CONFED RWP	1.0%	6.8%
LIBERTARIAN	—	0.7%
TOTAL	34,214	34,462
ST. BONIFACE	1988	1984
PC	33.5%	39.7%
LIB	51.6%	34.0%
NDP	10.7%	22.9%
REFORM	2.7%	—
LIBERTARIAN	0.9%	—
INDEPENDENT	0.4%	—
NO AFFILIATION	0.1%	—
CONFED RWP	—	3.4%
TOTAL	46,815	49,239
SELKIRK	1988	1984
PC	38.2%	—
LIB	26.7%	—
NDP	29.8%	—
CHRISTIAN	2.5%	—
REFORM	1.3%	—
CONFED RWP	0.8%	—
RHINO	0.7%	—
NO AFFILIATION	0.1%	—
TOTAL	46,687	—
SELKIRK-INTERLAKE	1988	1984
PC	—	40.7%
LIB	—	10.4%
NDP	—	38.7%
CONFED RWP	—	9.8%
LIBERTARIAN	—	0.5%
TOTAL	—	33,812
WINNIPEG-ASSINIBOINE	1988	1984
PC	—	52.4%
LIB	—	30.8%
NDP	—	13.4%
CONFED RWP	—	2.6%
LIBERTARIAN	—	0.9%
TOTAL	—	52,650

CONSTITUENCY RESULTS	1988	1984
WINNIPEG-BIRDS HILL	1988	1984
PC	—	39.6%
LIB	—	10.4%
NDP	—	45.8%
CONFED RWP	—	2.1%
RHINO	—	1.1%
INDEPENDENT	—	1.1%
TOTAL	—	52,181
WINNIPEG-FORT GARRY	1988	1984
PC	—	40.7%
LIB	—	45.7%
NDP	—	12.7%
LIBERTARIAN	—	0.7%
COMMUNIST	—	0.3%
TOTAL	—	46,573
WINNIPEG NORTH	1988	1984
PC	24.6%	30.2%
LIB	38.3%	24.8%
NDP	34.1%	43.3%
REFORM	1.9%	—
INDEPENDENT	0.5%	0.6%
COMMUNIST	0.5%	0.7%
NO AFFILIATION	0.2%	—
INDEPENDENT	—	0.4%
TOTAL	42,750	42,041
WINNIPEG NORTH CENTRE	1988	1984
PC	18.3%	28.3%
LIB	41.3%	22.5%
NDP	35.8%	46.1%
REFORM	1.4%	—
LIBERTARIAN	1.4%	—
INDEPENDENT	0.8%	2.1%
COMMUNIST	0.6%	—
NO AFFILIATION	0.3%	—
INDEPENDENT	—	1.0%
TOTAL	29,210	22,891
WINNIPEG-ST. JAMES	1988	1984
PC	40.8%	42.5%
LIB	44.8%	20.4%
NDP	10.2%	33.4%
REFORM	3.7%	—
NO AFFILIATION	0.3%	—
COMMUNIST	0.2%	0.3%
CONFED RWP	—	2.8%
LIBERTARIAN	—	0.6%
TOTAL	41,693	29,453
WINNIPEG SOUTH	1988	1984
PC	45.9%	—
LIB	44.5%	—
NDP	6.3%	—
REFORM	2.9%	—
LIBERTARIAN	0.5%	—
TOTAL	49,762	—

CONSTITUENCY RESULTS	1988	1984
WINNIPEG SOUTH CENTRE	1988	1984
PC	28.6%	—
LIB	58.5%	—
NDP	10.5%	—
REFORM	1.8%	—
LIBERTARIAN	0.3%	—
NO AFFILIATION	0.3%	—
TOTAL	42,140	—
WINNIPEG-TRANSCONA	1988	1984
PC	25.6%	—
LIB	31.9%	—
NDP	41.1%	—
INDEPENDENT	0.7%	—
INDEPENDENT	0.4%	—
NO AFFILIATION	0.3%	—
TOTAL	42,206	—

BRITISH COLUMBIA BURNABY	1988	1984
PC	—	35.1%
LIB	—	16.3%
NDP	—	48.0%
GREEN	—	0.6%
TOTAL	—	58,991
BURNABY-KINGSWAY	1988	1984
PC	30.0%	—
LIB	22.2%	—
NDP	43.2%	—
REFORM	2.7%	—
LIBERTARIAN	1.0%	—
GREEN	0.4%	—
INDEPENDENT	0.3%	—
INDEPENDENT	0.2%	—
TOTAL	58,193	—
CAPILANO	1988	1984
PC	—	56.5%
LIB	—	26.8%
NDP	—	12.5%
GREEN	—	1.5%
INDEPENDENT	—	1.3%
RHINO	—	1.2%
LIBERTARIAN	—	0.4%
TOTAL	—	50,694
CAPILANO-HOWE SOUND	1988	1984
PC	47.0%	—
LIB	29.6%	—
NDP	14.2%	—
REFORM	8.1%	—
RHINO	0.7%	—
LIBERTARIAN	0.4%	—
TOTAL	43,217	—

CONSTITUENCY RESULTS	1988	1984
CARIBOO-CHILCOTIN	1988	1984
PC	36.7%	54.5%
LIB	25.1%	13.0%
NDP	35.8%	30.6%
REFORM	1.7%	—
RHINO	0.7%	—
GREEN	—	1.0%
SC	—	0.9%
TOTAL	31,421	37,705
COMOX-ALBERNI	1988	1984
PC	28.3%	—
LIB	16.6%	—
NDP	42.8%	—
REFORM	9.9%	—
GREEN	1.1%	—
CHRISTIAN	1.0%	—
COMMUNIST	0.3%	—
TOTAL	49,331	—
COMOX-POWELL RIVER	1988	1984
PC	—	43.4%
LIB	—	9.5%
NDP	—	44.6%
GREEN	—	0.9%
CONFED RWP	—	0.7%
SC	—	0.6%
COMMUNIST	—	0.4%
TOTAL	—	61,173
COWICHAN-MALAHAT-THE ISLANDS	1988	1984
PC	—	42.1%
LIB	—	10.8%
NDP	—	45.1%
GREEN	—	0.7%
LIBERTARIAN	—	0.6%
CONFED RWP	—	0.5%
INDEPENDENT	—	0.1%
INDEPENDENT	—	0.1%
TOTAL	—	54,498
DELTA	1988	1984
PC	44.3%	—
LIB	19.9%	—
NDP	29.3%	—
REFORM	4.5%	—
CHRISTIAN	1.6%	—
INDEPENDENT	0.3%	—
LIBERTARIAN	0.2%	—
TOTAL	44,640	—
ESQUIMALT-JUAN-DE-FUCA	1988	1984
PC	25.1%	—
LIB	12.0%	—
NDP	50.9%	—
REFORM	10.4%	—
GREEN	1.0%	—
INDEPENDENT	0.3%	—
NO AFFILIATION	0.2%	—
CONFED RWP	0.1%	—
TOTAL	44,469	—

CONSTITUENCY RESULTS	1988	1984
ESQUIMALT-SAANICH	1988	1984
PC	—	48.3%
LIB	—	14.5%
NDP	—	35.1%
GREEN	—	0.8%
CONFED RWP	—	0.5%
SC	—	0.5%
LIBERTARIAN	—	0.3%
COMMUNIST	—	0.1%
TOTAL	—	65,790
FRASER VALLEY EAST	1988	1984
PC	38.8%	59.9%
LIB	21.2%	14.8%
NDP	28.0%	23.9%
CHRISTIAN REFORM	8.3%	—
RHINO	3.1%	—
LIBERTARIAN	0.6%	—
	—	1.4%
TOTAL	42,874	53,529
FRASER VALLEY WEST	1988	1984
PC	45.8%	54.7%
LIB	19.6%	12.7%
NDP	25.6%	30.2%
CHRISTIAN REFORM	4.7%	—
LIBERTARIAN	3.5%	—
RHINO	0.7%	0.6%
GREEN	—	0.7%
CONFED RWP	—	0.4%
COMMUNIST	—	0.3%
NO AFFILIATION	—	0.2%
	—	0.1%
TOTAL	51,412	65,759
KAMLOOPS	1988	1984
PC	32.4%	—
LIB	13.2%	—
NDP	52.3%	—
REFORM	1.1%	—
GREEN	0.6%	—
COMMUNIST	0.2%	—
NO AFFILIATION	0.2%	—
TOTAL	41,155	—
KAMLOOPS-SHUSWAP	1988	1984
PC	—	36.3%
LIB	—	8.3%
NDP	—	54.1%
RHINO	—	0.6%
GREEN	—	0.4%
CONFED RWP	—	0.2%
INDEPENDENT	—	0.1%
TOTAL	—	56,423
KOOTENAY EAST	1988	1984
PC	38.5%	—
LIB	12.1%	—
NDP	43.2%	—
REFORM	4.1%	—
CHRISTIAN	2.2%	—
TOTAL	34,487	—

CONSTITUENCY RESULTS	1988	1984
KOOTENAY EAST-REVELSTOKE	1988	1984
PC	—	46.5%
LIB	—	11.5%
NDP	—	40.8%
INDEPENDENT	—	1.2%
TOTAL	—	38,993
KOOTENAY WEST	1988	1984
PC	—	47.4%
LIB	—	7.4%
NDP	—	45.2%
TOTAL	—	33,324
KOOTENAY WEST-REVELSTOKE	1988	1984
PC	36.0%	—
LIB	15.6%	—
NDP	46.5%	—
GREEN	1.9%	—
TOTAL	35,201	—
MISSION-COQUITLAM	1988	1984
PC	39.5%	—
LIB	13.1%	—
NDP	43.8%	—
REFORM	1.7%	—
CHRISTIAN	1.6%	—
LIBERTARIAN	0.4%	—
TOTAL	50,877	—
MISSION-PORT MOODY	1988	1984
PC	—	47.5%
LIB	—	11.0%
NDP	—	40.2%
GREEN	—	0.8%
SC	—	0.5%
TOTAL	—	64,541
NANAIMO-ALBERNI	1988	1984
PC	—	45.8%
LIB	—	9.9%
NDP	—	42.9%
GREEN	—	0.9%
COMMUNIST	—	0.4%
NO AFFILIATION	—	0.1%
TOTAL	—	59,834
NANAIMO-COWICHAN	1988	1984
PC	9.6%	—
LIB	34.0%	—
NDP	49.3%	—
REFORM	6.0%	—
GREEN	0.9%	—
COMMUNIST	0.3%	—
TOTAL	55,377	—

CONSTITUENCY RESULTS	1988	1984
NEW WESTMINSTER-BURNABY	1988	1984
PC	31.5%	—
LIB	19.3%	—
NDP	43.6%	—
REFORM	3.0%	—
SC	1.3%	—
GREEN	0.6%	—
LIBERTARIAN	0.6%	—
COMMUNIST	0.2%	—
TOTAL	57,157	—
NEW WESTMINSTER-COQUITLAM	1988	1984
PC	—	40.0%
LIB	—	12.7%
NDP	—	46.2%
RHINO	—	0.9%
COMMUNIST	—	0.3%
TOTAL	—	45,769
NORTH ISLAND-POWELL RIVER	1988	1984
PC	24.4%	—
LIB	16.2%	—
NDP	51.8%	—
CHRISTIAN	3.5%	—
REFORM	1.8%	—
GREEN	1.2%	—
RHINO	0.7%	—
COMMUNIST	0.3%	—
TOTAL	45,188	—
NORTH VANCOUVER	1988	1984
PC	37.6%	—
LIB	27.2%	—
NDP	23.9%	—
REFORM	8.9%	—
GREEN	0.9%	—
RHINO	0.7%	—
LIBERTARIAN	0.5%	—
COMMUNIST	0.2%	—
NO AFFILIATION	0.1%	—
NO AFFILIATION	0.1%	—
TOTAL	49,186	—
NORTH VANCOUVER-BURNABY	1988	1984
PC	—	43.6%
LIB	—	28.7%
NDP	—	25.7%
RHINO	—	0.8%
GREEN	—	0.4%
LIBERTARIAN	—	0.4%
COMMUNIST	—	0.2%
NO AFFILIATION	—	0.1%
CONFED RWP	—	0.1%
TOTAL	—	49,855

CONSTITUENCY RESULTS	1988	1984
OKANAGAN CENTRE	1988	1984
PC	37.3%	—
LIB	17.1%	—
NDP	30.2%	—
REFORM	14.5%	—
GREEN	0.9%	—
TOTAL	52,302	—
OKANAGAN NORTH	1988	1984
PC	—	56.1%
LIB	—	15.5%
NDP	—	26.8%
SC	—	1.6%
TOTAL	—	64,032
OKANAGAN-SHUSWAP	1988	1984
PC	36.2%	—
LIB	15.9%	—
NDP	43.5%	—
REFORM	3.1%	—
GREEN	1.2%	—
NO AFFILIATION	0.2%	—
TOTAL	42,551	—
OKANAGAN-SIMILKAMEEN	1988	1984
PC	—	52.2%
LIB	—	15.6%
NDP	—	29.3%
CONFED RWP	—	1.3%
SC	—	0.8%
GREEN	—	0.8%
TOTAL	—	51,849
OKANAGAN-SIMILKAMEEN-MERRITT	1988	1984
PC	35.5%	—
LIB	17.4%	—
NDP	38.6%	—
REFORM	5.8%	—
GREEN	1.6%	—
SC	1.0%	—
TOTAL	43,195	—
PORT MOODY-COQUITLAM	1988	1984
PC	36.2%	—
LIB	15.5%	—
NDP	44.2%	—
REFORM	3.0%	—
GREEN	0.7%	—
LIBERTARIAN	0.5%	—
TOTAL	53,983	—

CONSTITUENCY RESULTS	1988	1984
PRINCE GEORGE-BULKLEY VALLEY	**1988**	**1984**
PC	31.7%	49.3%
LIB	24.9%	13.4%
NDP	38.2%	34.6%
CHRISTIAN	3.2%	—
REFORM	1.6%	—
INDEPENDENT	0.5%	0.4%
LIBERTARIAN	—	1.3%
RHINO	—	1.1%
TOTAL	37,335	38,339
PRINCE-GEORGE-PEACE RIVER	**1988**	**1984**
PC	39.6%	62.4%
LIB	11.9%	9.9%
NDP	33.3%	24.1%
REFORM	14.5%	—
INDEPENDENT	0.5%	—
CONFED RWP	0.3%	1.0%
RHINO	—	1.1%
SC	—	1.0%
LIBERTARIAN	—	0.4%
TOTAL	35,115	33,879
RICHMOND	**1988**	**1984**
PC	44.0%	—
LIB	22.8%	—
NDP	27.2%	—
REFORM	3.3%	—
CHRISTIAN	1.2%	—
LIBERTARIAN	0.8%	—
GREEN	0.4%	—
COMMUNIST	0.2%	—
TOTAL	58,025	—
RICHMOND-SOUTH DELTA	**1988**	**1984**
PC	—	55.4%
LIB	—	19.4%
NDP	—	23.8%
GREEN	—	0.6%
INDEPENDENT	—	0.4%
CONFED RWP	—	0.4%
TOTAL	—	68,892
SAANICH-GULF ISLANDS	**1988**	**1984**
PC	33.5%	—
LIB	17.6%	—
NDP	35.4%	—
REFORM	%	—
NO AFFILIATION	0.3%	—
LIBERTARIAN	0.3%	—
NO AFFILIATION	0.3%	—
COMMUNIST	0.1%	—
TOTAL	65,447	—

CONSTITUENCY RESULTS	1988	1984
SKEENA	**1988**	**1984**
PC	28.3%	36.2%
LIB	14.6%	16.6%
NDP	52.7%	45.8%
CHRISTIAN	3.6%	—
REFORM	0.9%	—
RHINO	—	1.4%
TOTAL	31,910	30,956
SURREY NORTH	**1988**	**1984**
PC	32.8%	—
LIB	24.9%	—
NDP	37.0%	—
REFORM	2.3%	—
CHRISTIAN	1.6%	—
LIBERTARIAN	0.5%	—
RHINO	0.4%	—
GREEN	0.3%	—
NO AFFILIATION	0.2%	—
TOTAL	53,881	—
SURREY-WHITE ROCK	**1988**	**1984**
PC	43.5%	—
LIB	23.5%	—
NDP	24.3%	—
REFORM	6.3%	—
CHRISTIAN	1.4%	—
GREEN	0.4%	—
LIBERTARIAN	0.2%	—
NO AFFILIATION	0.2%	—
COMMUNIST	0.2%	—
TOTAL	60,531	—
SURREY-WHITE ROCK-NORTH DELTA	**1988**	**1984**
PC	—	53.6%
LIB	—	14.6%
NDP	—	30.6%
RHINO	—	0.7%
GREEN	—	0.4%
COMMUNIST	—	0.2%
TOTAL	—	73,797
VANCOUVER CENTRE	**1988**	**1984**
PC	37.2%	43.2%
LIB	22.8%	21.2%
NDP	36.8%	32.4%
REFORM	1.4%	—
GREEN	0.8%	1.1%
RHINO	0.4%	1.0%
LIBERTARIAN	0.2%	0.6%
INDEPENDENT	0.2%	—
NO AFFILIATION	0.1%	—
COMMUNIST	—	0.3%
CONFED RWP	—	0.2%
TOTAL	63,409	50,210

CONSTITUENCY RESULTS	1988	1984
VANCOUVER EAST	1988	1984
PC	15.6%	20.2%
LIB	29.8%	25.4%
NDP	51.1%	51.8%
GREEN	1.4%	—
LIBERTARIAN	0.7%	0.9%
RHINO	0.7%	1.0%
COMMUNIST	0.5%	0.7%
NO AFFILIATION	0.2%	—
TOTAL	39,201	35,649
VANCOUVER KINGSWAY	1988	1984
PC	—	18.1%
LIB	—	29.5%
NDP	—	51.1%
GREEN	—	0.8%
COMMUNIST	—	0.5%
TOTAL	—	39,490
VANCOUVER QUADRA	1988	1984
PC	30.5%	37.5%
LIB	44.0%	43.9%
NDP	21.4%	16.8%
REFORM	2.0%	—
RHINO	1.4%	0.4%
LIBERTARIAN	0.2%	0.2%
COMMUNIST	0.1%	0.0%
INDEPENDENT	0.1%	0.2%
NO AFFILIATION	0.1%	0.1%
CONFED RWP	0.1%	—
COMMONWEALTH	0.0%	0.0%
NO AFFILIATION	0.0%	—
GREEN	—	0.8%
INDEPENDENT	—	0.0%
INDEPENDENT	—	0.0%
TOTAL	54,654	49,604
VANCOUVER SOUTH	1988	1984
PC	42.2%	54.9%
LIB	28.8%	20.5%
NDP	23.7%	23.5%
REFORM	2.1%	—
LIBERTARIAN	1.9%	—
GREEN	0.7%	1.1%
RHINO	0.3%	—
NO AFFILIATION	0.1%	—
COMMUNIST	0.1%	—
TOTAL	50,294	46,414
VICTORIA	1988	1984
PC	29.9%	46.3%
LIB	21.4%	12.6%
NDP	38.0%	38.6%
REFORM	8.4%	—
GREEN	1.8%	1.1%
RHINO	0.4%	0.5%
INDEPENDENT	0.2%	0.2%
LIBERTARIAN	—	0.4%
CONFED RWP	—	0.3%
TOTAL	58,999	53,060

CONSTITUENCY RESULTS	1988	1984
PRINCE EDWARD ISLAND CARDIGAN	1988	1984
PC	43.9%	53.4%
LIB	51.6%	42.1%
NDP	4.5%	4.5%
TOTAL	18,066	19,801
EGMONT	1988	1984
PC	39.4%	44.6%
LIB	53.1%	49.8%
NDP	7.5%	5.6%
TOTAL	19,134	17,630
HILLSBOROUGH	1988	1984
PC	42.4%	53.2%
LIB	43.7%	39.3%
NDP	9.7%	4.9%
INDEPENDENT	2.8%	0.5%
CHRISTIAN	1.3%	—
NO AFFILIATION	—	1.9%
GREEN	—	0.2%
TOTAL	20,361	17,214
MALPEQUE	1988	1984
PC	40.2%	56.4%
LIB	51.9%	33.0%
NDP	7.9%	10.7%
TOTAL	18,075	18,769
SASKATCHEWAN ASSINIBOIA	1988	1984
PC	—	47.2%
LIB	—	19.1%
NDP	—	32.0%
CONFED RWP	—	1.8%
TOTAL	—	33,946
HUMBOLDT-LAKE CENTRE	1988	1984
PC	—	38.0%
LIB	—	17.3%
NDP	—	43.5%
CONFED RWP	—	1.2%
TOTAL	—	34,687
KINDERSLEY-LLOYDMINSTER	1988	1984
PC	45.0%	58.3%
LIB	15.0%	11.4%
NDP	33.4%	29.2%
REFORM	6.6%	—
CONFED RWP	—	1.2%
TOTAL	33,543	35,063
MACKENZIE	1988	1984
PC	36.9%	40.0%
LIB	14.6%	17.4%
NDP	46.5%	38.1%
REFORM	2.0%	—
CONFED RWP	—	4.5%
TOTAL	34,257	28,481

CONSTITUENCY RESULTS	1988	1984
MOOSE JAW	1988	1984
PC	—	46.0%
LIB	—	13.9%
NDP	—	38.8%
CONFED RWP	—	1.3%
TOTAL	—	34,349
MOOSE JAW-LAKE CENTRE	1988	1984
PC	41.1%	—
LIB	15.9%	—
NDP	42.2%	—
CONFED RWP	0.8%	—
TOTAL	37,691	—
PRINCE ALBERT	1988	1984
PC	—	34.8%
LIB	—	29.0%
NDP	—	35.6%
CONFED RWP	—	0.7%
TOTAL	—	37,569
PRINCE ALBERT-CHURCHILL RIVER	1988	1984
PC	25.9%	—
LIB	15.8%	—
NDP	56.4%	—
REFORM	1.6%	—
CONFED RWP	0.3%	—
TOTAL	31,755	—
QU'APPELLE-MOOSE MOUNTAIN	1988	1984
PC	—	49.8%
LIB	—	16.9%
NDP	—	29.0%
CONFED RWP	—	2.3%
INDEPENDENT	—	2.1%
TOTAL	—	29,039
REGINA EAST	1988	1984
PC	—	33.3%
LIB	—	20.9%
NDP	—	44.9%
CONFED RWP	—	0.9%
TOTAL	—	45,621
REGINA-LUMSDEN	1988	1984
PC	26.5%	—
LIB	15.6%	—
NDP	57.6%	—
NO AFFILIATION	0.4%	—
TOTAL	37,506	—
REGINA-QU'APPELLE	1988	1984
PC	31.5%	—
LIB	14.6%	—
NDP	54.0%	—
TOTAL	34,490	—

CONSTITUENCY RESULTS	1988	1984
REGINA-WASCANA	1988	1984
PC	34.0%	—
LIB	32.8%	—
NDP	32.9%	—
COMMUNIST	0.2%	—
LIBERTARIAN	0.1%	—
TOTAL	45,113	—
REGINA WEST	1988	1984
PC	—	31.5%
LIB	—	20.4%
NDP	—	46.8%
RHINO	—	0.6%
CONFED RWP	—	0.5%
COMMUNIST	—	0.2%
TOTAL	—	50,971
SASKATOON-CLARK'S CROSSING	1988	1984
PC	35.8%	—
NDP	47.9%	—
GREEN	0.5%	—
TOTAL	41,077	—
SASKATOON-DUNDURN	1988	1984
PC	31.8%	—
LIB	19.3%	—
NDP	47.9%	—
CONFED RWP	0.9%	—
COMMONWEALTH	0.1%	—
TOTAL	43,569	—
SASKATOON EAST	1988	1984
PC	—	36.9%
LIB	—	25.7%
NDP	—	36.0%
RHINO	—	0.7%
GREEN	—	0.4%
CONFED RWP	—	0.3%
TOTAL	—	46,284
SASKATOON-HUMBOLDT	1988	1984
PC	36.1%	—
LIB	20.6%	—
NDP	43.2%	—
TOTAL	40,938	—
SASKATOON WEST	1988	1984
PC	—	49.7%
LIB	—	12.1%
NDP	—	36.1%
RHINO	—	1.0%
CONFED RWP	—	0.6%
GREEN	—	0.3%
INDEPENDENT	—	0.2%
TOTAL	—	52,368

CONSTITUENCY RESULTS	1988	1984
SOURIS-MOOSE MOUNTAIN	**1988**	**1984**
PC	46.8%	—
LIB	19.0%	—
NDP	32.4%	—
CONFED RWP	1.7%	—
TOTAL	36,723	—
SWIFT CURRENT-MAPLE CREEK	**1988**	**1984**
PC	—	49.7%
LIB	—	20.3%
NDP	—	27.9%
CONFED RWP	—	2.0%
TOTAL	—	29,335
SWIFT CURRENT-MAPLE CREEK-ASSINIBOIA	**1988**	**1984**
PC	44.1%	—
LIB	22.0%	—
NDP	32.7%	—
CONFED RWP	1.3%	—
TOTAL	36,221	—
THE BATTLEFORDS-MEADOW LAKE	**1988**	**1984**
PC	40.4%	43.3%
LIB	15.1%	13.4%
NDP	42.5%	42.2%
REFORM	1.4%	—
CONFED RWP	0.6%	1.1%
TOTAL	34,130	29,775
YORKTON-MELVILLE	**1988**	**1984**
PC	34.6%	33.4%
LIB	14.2%	14.2%
NDP	51.1%	51.3%
CONFED RWP	—	1.1%
TOTAL	36,215	35,312

ALBERTA		
ATHABASKA	**1988**	**1984**
PC	52.8%	68.3%
LIB	12.3%	12.0%
NDP	27.3%	17.1%
REFORM	5.5%	—
CHRISTIAN	1.8%	—
COMMUNIST	0.3%	—
CONFED RWP	—	1.7%
SC	—	1.0%
TOTAL	32,660	35,130
BEAVER RIVER	**1988**	**1984**
PC	44.3%	—
LIB	21.0%	—
NDP	20.9%	—
REFORM	13.4%	—
CONFED RWP	0.4%	—
TOTAL	31,077	—

CONSTITUENCY RESULTS	1988	1984
BOW RIVER	**1988**	**1984**
PC	—	76.2%
LIB	—	7.2%
NDP	—	9.3%
RHINO	—	4.2%
CONFED RWP	—	2.6%
SC	—	0.6%
TOTAL	—	56,475
CALGARY CENTRE	**1988**	**1984**
PC	53.7%	66.4%
LIB	11.7%	15.9%
NDP	20.0%	13.7%
REFORM	12.4%	—
GREEN	1.3%	2.0%
LIBERTARIAN	0.7%	0.5%
NO AFFILIATION	0.2%	—
CONFED RWP	—	1.6%
TOTAL	53,601	37,562
CALGARY EAST	**1988**	**1984**
PC	—	58.9%
LIB	—	23.6%
NDP	—	13.7%
INDEPENDENT	—	1.6%
CONFED RWP	—	1.1%
SC	—	0.6%
LIBERTARIAN	—	0.5%
COMMUNIST	—	0.2%
TOTAL	—	62,572
CALGARY NORTH	**1988**	**1984**
PC	57.7%	72.8%
LIB	13.0%	12.7%
NDP	12.5%	13.1%
REFORM	16.2%	—
LIBERTARIAN	0.4%	—
CONFED RWP	0.2%	—
INDEPENDENT	—	1.4%
TOTAL	60,984	53,863
CALGARY NORTHEAST	**1988**	**1984**
PC	54.7%	—
LIB	16.2%	—
NDP	15.5%	—
REFORM	13.0%	—
INDEPENDENT	0.6%	—
TOTAL	47,323	—
CALGARY SOUTH	**1988**	**1984**
PC	—	77.9%
LIB	—	11.0%
NDP	—	8.6%
CONFED RWP	—	1.2%
INDEPENDENT	—	1.1%
COMMONWEALTH	—	0.2%
TOTAL	—	71,354

CONSTITUENCY RESULTS	1988	1984
CALGARY SOUTHEAST	1988	1984
PC	62.7%	—
LIB	10.2%	—
NDP	13.2%	—
REFORM	12.8%	—
RHINO	0.6%	—
NO AFFILIATION	0.2%	—
NO AFFILIATION	0.1%	—
CONFED RWP	0.1%	—
COMMONWEALTH	0.1%	—
TOTAL	51,825	—

CALGARY SOUTHWEST	1988	1984
PC	65.2%	—
LIB	11.5%	—
NDP	8.1%	—
REFORM	13.4%	—
INDEPENDENT	1.1%	—
RHINO	0.6%	—
CONFED RWP	0.1%	—
TOTAL	61,993	—

CALGARY WEST	1988	1984
PC	58.5%	74.7%
LIB	12.6%	11.4%
NDP	11.6%	10.8%
REFORM	16.6%	—
LIBERTARIAN	0.4%	0.5%
CONFED RWP	0.3%	1.0%
GREEN	—	1.2%
SC	—	0.4%
TOTAL	54,729	50,285

CROWFOOT	1988	1984
PC	53.7%	77.8%
LIB	6.6%	7.4%
NDP	7.7%	9.3%
REFORM	32.1%	—
CONFED RWP	—	4.6%
SC	—	0.9%
TOTAL	35,540	33,780

EDMONTON EAST	1988	1984
PC	36.5%	48.5%
LIB	18.2%	18.1%
NDP	38.2%	23.1%
REFORM	4.4%	—
CHRISTIAN	2.0%	—
COMMUNIST	0.3%	0.4%
NO AFFILIATION	0.2%	—
CONFED RWP	0.1%	0.7%
INDEPENDENT	—	8.6%
GREEN	—	0.7%
TOTAL	39,403	33,248

CONSTITUENCY RESULTS	1988	1984
EDMONTON NORTH	1988	1984
PC	39.9%	57.3%
LIB	19.5%	16.4%
NDP	32.9%	24.3%
REFORM	5.5%	—
CHRISTIAN	1.5%	—
NO AFFILIATION	0.3%	—
COMMUNIST	0.1%	0.4%
COMMONWEALTH	0.1%	—
CONFED RWP	0.1%	1.0%
SC	—	0.7%
TOTAL	45,257	50,749

EDMONTON NORTHWEST	1988	1984
PC	40.1%	—
LIB	17.3%	—
NDP	34.0%	—
REFORM	7.6%	—
NO AFFILIATION	0.5%	—
CONFED RWP	0.3%	—
COMMONWEALTH	0.2%	—
TOTAL	38,827	—

EDMONTON SOUTH	1988	1984
PC	—	62.5%
LIB	—	15.9%
NDP	—	18.1%
CONFED RWP	—	1.1%
GREEN	—	1.0%
RHINO	—	1.0%
INDEPENDENT	—	0.5%
TOTAL	—	52,046

EDMONTON SOUTHEAST	1988	1984
PC	48.7%	—
LIB	20.8%	—
NDP	18.9%	—
REFORM	10.7%	—
GREEN	0.4%	—
CONFED RWP	0.2%	—
COMMONWEALTH	0.2%	—
NO AFFILIATION	0.1%	—
TOTAL	48,481	—

EDMONTON-SOUTHWEST	1988	1984
PC	53.6%	—
LIB	19.2%	—
NDP	15.9%	—
REFORM	10.5%	—
LIBERTARIAN	0.7%	—
CONFED RWP	0.2%	—
TOTAL	53,987	—

CONSTITUENCY RESULTS	1988	1984
EDMONTON-STRATHCONA	1988	1984
PC	33.5%	61.4%
LIB	17.9%	15.5%
NDP	25.3%	20.2%
REFORM	22.2%	—
RHINO	0.4%	—
GREEN	0.3%	0.9%
INDEPENDENT	0.2%	—
NO AFFILIATION	0.1%	—
NO AFFILIATION	0.1%	—
CONFED RWP	0.1%	1.4%
SC	—	0.4%
COMMUNIST	—	0.3%
TOTAL	54,054	54,877
EDMONTON WEST	1988	1984
PC	—	58.8%
LIB	—	22.1%
NDP	—	16.8%
CONFED RWP	—	1.6%
GREEN	—	0.7%
TOTAL	—	43,799
ELK ISLAND	1988	1984
PC	48.2%	—
LIB	9.0%	—
NDP	22.4%	—
REFORM	20.1%	—
CONFED RWP	0.3%	—
TOTAL	40,360	—
LETHBRIDGE	1988	1984
PC	58.4%	—
LIB	18.6%	—
NDP	9.8%	—
REFORM	6.8%	—
CHRISTIAN	6.4%	—
TOTAL	45,790	—
LETHBRIDGE-FOOTHILLS	1988	1984
PC	—	67.4%
LIB	—	11.4%
NDP	—	14.7%
NO AFFILIATION	—	4.6%
SC	—	1.0%
CONFED RWP	—	0.9%
TOTAL	—	46,480
MACLEOD	1988	1984
PC	50.5%	—
LIB	9.4%	—
NDP	8.8%	—
REFORM	31.2%	—
COMMONWEALTH	0.2%	—
TOTAL	33,630	—

CONSTITUENCY RESULTS	1988	1984
MEDICINE HAT	1988	1984
PC	59.2%	75.8%
LIB	12.1%	9.0%
NDP	15.2%	10.4%
REFORM	10.8%	—
CHRISTIAN	2.7%	—
CONFED RWP	—	3.2%
SC	—	1.7%
TOTAL	42,520	44,854
PEACE RIVER	1988	1984
PC	54.3%	62.2%
LIB	13.4%	13.2%
NDP	17.2%	15.4%
REFORM	15.2%	—
CONFED RWP	—	7.0%
GREEN	—	1.4%
SC	—	0.9%
TOTAL	43,035	41,209
PEMBINA	1988	1984
PC	—	70.6%
LIB	—	11.6%
NDP	—	15.7%
CONFED RWP	—	2.0%
COMMUNIST	—	0.2%
TOTAL	—	62,388
RED DEER	1988	1984
PC	52.7%	75.4%
LIB	10.4%	9.4%
NDP	12.6%	9.4%
REFORM	20.8%	—
CHRISTIAN	2.9%	—
CONFED RWP	0.6%	4.5%
SC	—	1.3%
TOTAL	45,440	55,276
ST. ALBERT	1988	1984
PC	46.7%	—
LIB	16.7%	—
NDP	19.6%	—
REFORM	13.9%	—
CHRISTIAN	2.1%	—
RHINO	0.5%	—
NO AFFILIATION	0.3%	—
CONFED RWP	0.1%	—
TOTAL	42,695	—
VEGREVILLE	1988	1984
PC	65.3%	80.2%
LIB	7.8%	6.9%
NDP	16.1%	9.4%
REFORM	9.9%	—
NO AFFILIATION	0.5%	—
INDEPENDENT	0.4%	—
CONFED RWP	0.1%	1.3%
SC	—	0.9%
RHINO	—	0.9%
COMMUNIST	—	0.5%
TOTAL	37,596	40,498

CONSTITUENCY RESULTS	1988	1984
WETASKIWIN	1988	1984
PC	50.2%	70.9%
LIB	8.4%	7.6%
NDP	14.3%	13.2%
REFORM	18.5%	—
CHRISTIAN	7.7%	—
CONFED RWP	0.6%	7.2%
NO AFFILIATION	0.3%	—
SC	—	1.1%
TOTAL	40,022	42,474
WILD ROSE	1988	1984
PC	48.2%	—
LIB	10.1%	—
NDP	7.8%	—
REFORM	33.4%	—
CONFED RWP	0.5%	—
TOTAL	41,621	—
YELLOWHEAD	1988	1984
PC	44.6%	74.0%
LIB	10.0%	8.1%
NDP	15.4%	13.6%
REFORM	27.8%	—
CHRISTIAN	1.8%	—
CONFED RWP	0.2%	1.6%
NO AFFILIATION	0.2%	—
RHINO	—	1.5%
SC	—	1.1%
TOTAL	40,034	50,620

NEWFOUNDLAND BONAVISTA-TRINITY-CONCEPTION	1988	1984
PC	42.9%	55.0%
LIB	51.3%	40.8%
NDP	5.7%	4.1%
TOTAL	41,471	34,550
BURIN-ST. GEORGE'S	1988	1984
PC	45.6%	47.4%
LIB	48.4%	46.3%
NDP	6.0%	6.4%
TOTAL	38,314	27,836
GANDER-GRAND FALLS	1988	1984
PC	31.5%	—
LIB	55.8%	—
NDP	12.7%	—
TOTAL	36,410	—
GANDER-TWILLINGATE	1988	1984
PC	—	43.1%
LIB	—	53.1%
NDP	—	3.8%
TOTAL	—	30,314

CONSTITUENCY RESULTS	1988	1984
GRAND FALLS-WHITE BAY-LABRADOR	1988	1984
PC	—	42.3%
LIB	—	45.1%
NDP	—	12.6%
TOTAL	—	28,668
HUMBER-PORT AU PORT-ST. BARBE	1988	1984
PC	—	46.9%
LIB	—	48.3%
NDP	—	4.2%
INDEPENDENT	—	0.5%
TOTAL	—	36,051
HUMBER-ST. BARBE-BAIE VERTE	1988	1984
PC	29.4%	—
LIB	66.9%	—
NDP	3.7%	—
TOTAL	39,392	—
LABRADOR	1988	1984
PC	33.0%	—
LIB	53.5%	—
NDP	11.3%	—
INDEPENDENT	2.1%	—
TOTAL	13,320	—
ST. JOHN'S EAST	1988	1984
PC	44.1%	78.3%
LIB	19.1%	14.3%
NDP	35.3%	6.6%
CHRISTIAN	1.6%	—
LIBERTARIAN	—	0.8%
TOTAL	48,725	39,419
ST. JOHN'S WEST	1988	1984
PC	61.5%	76.0%
LIB	32.5%	19.6%
NDP	6.0%	4.4%
TOTAL	39,314	44,321

YUKON TERRITORY YUKON	1988	1984
PC	35.3%	56.8%
LIB	11.3%	21.7%
NDP	51.4%	16.1%
CHRISTIAN	2.0%	—
LIBERTARIAN	—	4.4%
RHINO	—	1.1%
TOTAL	12,823	11,704

CONSTITUENCY RESULTS	1988	1984	CONSTITUENCY RESULTS	1988	1984
NORTHWEST			WESTERN ARCTIC	1988	1984
TERRITORIES			PC	28.6%	46.1%
NUNATSIAQ	1988	1984	LIB	42.4%	25.9%
PC	22.9%	32.5%	NDP	25.1%	28.0%
LIB	39.9%	28.9%	INDEPENDENT	2.6%	—
NDP	33.2%	28.7%	INDEPENDENT	1.3%	—
INDEPENDENT	4.0%	10.0%	TOTAL	12,779	12,624
TOTAL	8,403	6,886			

*Denotes constituency winner
**1988 results from Preliminary Report of the Chief Electoral Officer. 1984 Results from Report of the Chief Electoral Officer.

Note: Numbers may not add to 100.0 percent due to rounding.

By Proportional Representation

TABLE A5
Results Under Proportional Representation

	1984	1988
Conservatives		
Vote	50%	43%
Actual Seats	211	169
Seats Under PR	142	127
Liberals		
Vote	28%	32%
Actual Seats	40	83
Seats Under PR	79	94
NDP		
Vote	18%	20%
Actual Seats	30	43
Seats Under PR	53	59
Others		
Vote	3%	5%
Actual Seats	1	0
Seats Under PR	8	15

The Contributors

STEPHEN CLARKSON is professor of Political Science at the University of Toronto, the author of *Canada and the Reagan Challenge*, and a student of federal politics.

ROBERT KRAUSE is associate professor of Political Science at the University of Windsor, and the author of several articles on Canadian politics.

LAWRENCE LEDUC is professor of Political Science at the University of Toronto, co-author of *Political Choice in Canada* and *Absent Mandate*, and author of numerous articles on elections and voting.

PETER MASER is Quebec correspondent for Southam News. He was a member of the Parliamentary Press Gallery from 1981 to 1988, reporting for *The Ottawa Citizen* and *Southam News*.

ALAN WHITEHORN is professor of Political Science at the Royal Military College, Kingston. He has written extensively on the New Democratic Party, and is currently finishing a book on the party.